Mastering and Using

Microsoft®
Excel

VERSION 5.0

Mastering and Using

Microsoft® Excel

VERSION 5.0

H. Albert Napier
Rice University and
Napier & Judd, Inc.

Philip J. Judd
Napier & Judd, Inc.

A DIVISION OF COURSE TECHNOLOGY
ONE MAIN STREET, CAMBRIDGE, MA 02142

an International Thomson Publishing company I(T)P

Cambridge • Albany • Bonn • Boston • Cincinnati • London • Madrid • Melbourne • Mexico City
New York • Paris • San Francisco • Singapore • Tokyo • Toronto • Washington

Mastering and Using Microsoft Excel Version 5.0 is published by CTI.

Acquisitions Editor	Anne E. Hamilton
Production Editor	Barbara Worth
Cover Design	Hannus Design
Manufacturing Coordinator	Tracy Megison
Marketing Manager	Daphne Snow

© 1995 by CTI.
A Division of Course Technology – I(T)P

For more information contact:

Course Technology
One Main Street
Cambridge, MA 02142

International Thomson Publishing Europe
Berkshire House 168-173
High Holborn
London WCIV 7AA
England

Thomas Nelson Australia
102 Dodds Street
South Melbourne, 3205
Victoria, Australia

Nelson Canada
1120 Birchmount Road
Scarborough, Ontario
Canada M1K 5G4

International Thomson Editores
Campos Eliseos 385, Piso 7
Col. Polanco
11560 Mexico D.F. Mexico

International Thomson Publishing GmbH
Kônigswinterer Strasse 418
53227 Bonn
Germany

International Thomson Publishing Asia
211 Henderson Road
#05-10 Henderson Building
Singapore 0315

International Thomson Publishing Japan
Hirakawacho Kyowa Building, 3F
2-2-1 Hirakawacho
Chiyoda-ku, Tokyo 102
Japan

ISBN 0-87709-308-3

Printed in the United States of America

10 9 8 7 6 5 4 3

Dedication

This book is dedicated to our families for their loving support and patience.
Liz, J.B. and Lanham

Valerie, Michelle, Jacob and Heather

BRIEF CONTENTS

CONTENTS

Chapter Three
Organizing Workbooks and Designing Worksheets Properly

Chapter Four
Creating and Printing Worksheets in a Workbook

Chapter Five
Improving the Appearance of a Worksheet

Chapter Six
Useful Excel Commands

Chapter Ten
Creating and Using a Template Workbook

Chapter Eleven
Creating and Using Multiple Worksheets and Files

Chapter Twelve
Consolidating Worksheets and Linking Workbook Files

Chapter Thirteen
Introduction to Lists, Databases, Sorting, and Filtering

Chapter Fourteen
Advanced Database Capabilities

Chapter Fifteen
Worksheet Functions in Microsoft Excel

Chapter Sixteen
Introduction to Macros

PREFACE

■ INTRODUCTION

Today, there are literally millions of people using personal computers. One of the most popular uses for personal computers is creating spreadsheets. Prior to the use of computers, spreadsheets were typically completed on what are called "columnar pad" sheets of paper. Spreadsheets are used extensively in accounting, financial analysis, and many other business planning and analysis situations. The words spreadsheets and worksheets are often used interchangeably.

■ OBJECTIVES OF THIS BOOK

This book was developed specifically for an introductory course on personal computers or worksheet analysis that utilizes IBM PCs or compatible hardware on which Microsoft Excel can be used. The objectives of this book are as follows:

- To acquaint the user with the process of using personal computers to solve worksheet analysis type problems.
- To provide a working knowledge of the basic and advanced capabilities of Excel.
- To encourage the use of good problem-solving techniques for situations in which worksheet solutions are appropriate.
- To permit learning through examples using an exercise-oriented approach.
- To provide the user with an excellent reference source to advance their knowledge of Excel.

■ LEVEL OF INSTRUCTION

This book is designed to introduce the beginning, intermediate, and advanced capabilities available in Microsoft Excel. It is pedagogically designed. First, the basic skills needed to create a worksheet are discussed. Subsequent chapters build on previously presented concepts and developed skills. A variety of practical examples provide an understanding of how Microsoft Excel can be used. The book assumes the user has little or no personal computer experience. However, individuals with some previous experience can also advance their knowledge of Excel. The book is characterized by its continuity, simplicity, and practicality. This book does not replace the Microsoft Excel User's Guide that accompanies the software package. Used in conjunction with the User's Guide and the Microsoft Help feature, this book will provide the user with a complete understanding of the capabilities of Microsoft Excel.

■ AUTHORS' EXPERIENCE

The authors have worked with personal computers since they were introduced. More than 40,000 people have participated in personal computer seminars for which the authors have been responsible for providing instruction. Insights from this experience are implicit throughout the book. In addition, the authors have more than 44 years of combined experience in teaching and consulting in the field of information systems.

■ MICROSOFT SOLUTION PROVIDER

The authors' consulting company, Napier & Judd, Inc., is a Microsoft Solution Provider Company. The company's training materials, instructors, and facilities have been approved by Microsoft Corporation. This book is based on materials that have been used in the company's training activities in which more than 15,000 participants have been trained on Excel and other spreadsheet software packages.

■ DISTINGUISHING FEATURES

The distinguishing features of this book include the following:

Research-Based Material

The design of the book is based on how experienced users actually utilize spreadsheet software. Napier, Batsell, Lane, and Guadagno at Rice University completed a study of 40 experienced spreadsheet users from eight large organizations and determined the set of commands used most often by the individuals. The users studied had an average of 2.5 years experience and worked in a variety of corporations and governmental agencies.

The research indicates that 27 commands accounted for 85 percent of the commands issued by the experienced individuals. The materials in this book have been carefully planned to provide extensive coverage of these 27 most frequently used commands.

Learning Through Examples

The book is designed for learning through examples rather than learning a series of commands. The materials are built around a series of example problems. Commands are learned for one example, then reinforced. New commands are learned on subsequent examples. The example problems are logically related and integrated throughout the book.

Step-by-Step Instructions and Screen Illustrations

All examples include step-by-step instructions. Screen illustrations are used extensively to assist the user while learning Microsoft Excel.

Extensive Exercises

At the end of each chapter, there are exercises providing comprehensive coverage of the topics introduced in the chapter.

Emphasis on Business and Organizational Problem Solving

The book includes many example problems that may be encountered in a business or other type of organization.

Workbooks with Multiple Worksheets

Extensive coverage of the use of multiple worksheets within a workbook file is presented. The process for linking worksheets between workbook files is illustrated.

What You Should Know Concept Lists

Each chapter includes a list of key concepts emphasizing what should be learned in the chapter.

Emphasis on Proper Worksheet Design

Proper design of a worksheet can make its use more effective. Such design can also reduce the probability of errors in a worksheet. A chapter is included on worksheet design.

Comprehensive Coverage

Major topics represented are: creating and printing worksheets and charts; templates; using multiple worksheets in a workbook file; combining and consolidating worksheets; database management; functions; and macros.

Charts

One of the most powerful options available in Excel is charts. Charts can be useful in business analysis and presentations. The user learns how to create and print column, line, bar, combination, stacked column, pie, XY (Scatter), area, doughnut, radar, and open-high-low-close charts.

Templates

Most experienced users of Excel make extensive use of template worksheets. This book covers the process of building and using template worksheets.

Combining Information Between Worksheets

Many worksheet applications require movement of data from one worksheet to another or the combining of data from several worksheets into one worksheet. The process of using templates to create such "detail" worksheets and then combining information into a "summary" worksheet is covered. A method for linking worksheets in different files through the use of formulas is also presented.

Database Capabilities

While Excel is not a database management system, it does have many database-like commands that can be applied to data in a worksheet. For example, we discuss how to create a list, how to sort data in a list, filter data in a list, fill cells with sequences of data, create data tables for decision-making purposes, and create subtotals.

Macros

With experience in using Excel, the use of macros increases. Much of the power of Excel is really available to users of macros. This book introduces the process for creating and using macros. A method for automatically recording macro instructions is included.

Proven Materials

This book is based on proven materials that have been used in college and university classes as well as training seminars. More than 15,000 individuals have learned to use Excel and other spreadsheet software utilizing materials on which this book is based. For example, the authors have been responsible for training more than 6,000 members of the Texas Society of CPAs employing materials from this book.

■ ORGANIZATION/FLEXIBILITY

The book is organized in a manner that takes the user through the fundamentals of Microsoft Excel and then builds on the solid foundation to cover more advanced subjects. The book is useful for college courses, training classes, individual learning, and as a reference manual.

In Chapter 1, the Microsoft Excel package is described and explained. Typical applications are presented. The process for starting the software package is explained. The various parts of the Excel Window are detailed along with methods to move around the worksheet. The method for exiting Excel is specified.

Chapter 2 provides a "quick start" for using Excel. The processes for creating, editing, and printing a worksheet are illustrated. The methods for saving a worksheet in a workbook file, and opening and closing workbook files are explained.

When you create worksheets, it is important to use good design principles. Chapter 3 explains how to organize a workbook and design a worksheet properly.

Chapter 4 contains a step-by-step process for creating, building, and printing a worksheet. Operations included are: entering worksheet titles, column titles, and row titles; widening columns; entering assumptions; entering numbers and formulas and copying information; selecting a format for the data; inserting rows; entering underlines and double underlines; saving and replacing a worksheet; correcting rounding errors; and preparing the printer, previewing, and printing a worksheet. A method for completing "What-if" analysis is illustrated.

Chapter 5 discusses how to improve the appearance of a worksheet. Some of the topics covered are boldfacing text, changing the font size of text, shading cells, adding a border to a range of cells, creating and using styles, changing the appearance of a worksheet using automatic formats, and removing gridlines.

A variety of useful Excel commands are presented in Chapter 6. Some of the topics include: keeping a cell reference constant in a formula; correcting cell entries; using the Undo feature; formatting numbers; filling a cell with a set of characters; moving cell contents; using the Drag and Drop feature to move and copy data; inserting and deleting cells; setting row and column print titles; printing headers and footers; excluding gridlines on printouts; inserting page breaks; printing cell formulas of a worksheet in tabular form; magnifying or shrinking the worksheet; controlling the recalculation of a worksheet; suppressing zeros; protecting data; hiding portions of a worksheet; creating and deleting range names; finding and replacing data; splitting windows; viewing more than one window; sizing a window; moving a window; customizing the toolbar; performing worksheet documentation; using the Goal Seek and Solver features, and using Scenarios.

Numerous types of charts can be prepared using Excel. In Chapter 7, some charting capabilities are covered, including column chart, line chart, bar chart, combination chart, stacked column chart, pie chart, XY (Scatter) chart, area chart, doughnut chart, and radar chart. Other topics discussed are printing a chart, embedding a chart in a worksheet, printing an embedded chart, printing an embedded chart and a worksheet, and deleting an embedded chart from a worksheet.

In Chapter 8, additional charting capabilities are discussed. Included topics are creating 3D charts, creating an open-high-low-close chart, and adding and deleting data in a chart.

Chapter 9 discusses how to enhance the appearance of a chart. Topics include changing the location of a legend, removing and changing axes scales, changing the fonts of chart text, changing colors and hatch patterns, inserting gridlines, adding unattached text and graphic objects to a chart, and sizing and moving an embedded chart.

In Chapter 10, the process for creating and using template worksheets is discussed. A template is a worksheet that is constructed and saved as a "shell" for the creation of worksheets at a later time containing the same formulas and/or text.

Sometimes it is useful to utilize more than one worksheet in a file. Chapter 11 includes a discussion of the use of multiple worksheets in a workbook file. Topics incorporated are: creating the initial worksheet, copying information between worksheets, entering data and formulas in multiple worksheets, formatting multiple worksheets, printing multiple worksheet data, and using multiple workbook files.

Many practical applications of worksheets require that information be combined from one or more worksheets into one or more other worksheets. The process for consolidating information from one or several worksheets into a summary worksheet is illustrated in Chapter 12. Methods for linking workbook files are also covered.

While Excel does not provide all the capabilities of a database management system, many database-like operations can be applied to data in a worksheet. Chapter 13 includes a discussion of creating a list, entering data for a list, sorting data in a list, and using a filter to complete a query. Chapter 14 contains the following topics: filling cells with data, creating and using data tables for what-if analysis, and creating subtotals in a list.

There are many preprogrammed functions available in Excel. In Chapter 15, many of the functions available in Excel such as the functions for statistical, financial, date and time, logical, database, math and trig, functions for special analyses such as lookup and reference and text functions are discussed and illustrated.

In many situations, the same steps are applied to the development of a worksheet each time it is used. For example, an organization may summarize the budget expenditures of three departments into one worksheet. In Excel, a macro can be developed that instructs the computer to repeat the steps automatically rather than have the user enter the set of steps each time the worksheets are summarized. An introduction to the process of creating and using macros appears in Chapter 16. A method for recording a macro is discussed and illustrated. The concept of using the Personal Macro Workbook for storing macros that are used in many types of applications is presented.

■ ACKNOWLEDGEMENTS

We would like to thank and express our appreciation to the many fine and talented individuals who have contributed to the completion of this book. Special thanks go to: Cristal Ewald, Iowa State University and Carmen Wheatcroft for their editorial review of the materials.

No book is possible without the motivation and support of an editorial staff. Therefore, we wish to acknowledge with great appreciation the following people at boyd & fraser: Tom Walker, president and publisher, for the opportunity to write this book and for his constant encouragement; Jim Edwards, Anne Hamilton, and Barbara Worth, for their keen assistance in the editing process; and the production staff for support in completing the book.

We are very appreciative of the personnel at Napier & Judd, Inc. who helped prepare this book. We acknowledge, with great appreciation the assistance provided by Nancy Onarheim and Ollie Rivers in preparing and checking the many drafts of this book.

H. Albert Napier
Philip J. Judd
Houston, Texas

CHAPTER ONE

GETTING STARTED WITH MICROSOFT EXCEL

OBJECTIVES

In this chapter, you will learn to:
- Define the Microsoft Excel software package
- Start the Microsoft Excel software package
- Identify the basic features of the Microsoft Excel window
- Move around the workbook window
- Use the Help feature
- Exit Microsoft Excel

CHAPTER OVERVIEW

This book assumes that you have little or no knowledge of Microsoft Excel. Chapter One introduces you to the capabilities of Microsoft Excel and typical applications of the software. The chapter explains the **hardware** and **software requirements** for using Microsoft Excel and the process for starting the software package. The basic items that appear in the Microsoft Excel window are explained. Various methods of moving around the Microsoft document window are covered. The chapter also presents the Microsoft Excel Help feature. Finally, the chapter specifies the process for exiting the software package.

DEFINING THE MICROSOFT EXCEL SOFTWARE PACKAGE

Microsoft Excel can be used for creating spreadsheets (interchangeably referred to as worksheets), preparing charts, executing some database management operations, creating high-quality presentation documents, and automating frequently performed tasks using macros.

Figure 1-1 shows an example of a worksheet. The next chapter shows you how to create, print, save, and edit a simple worksheet.

Figure 1-1

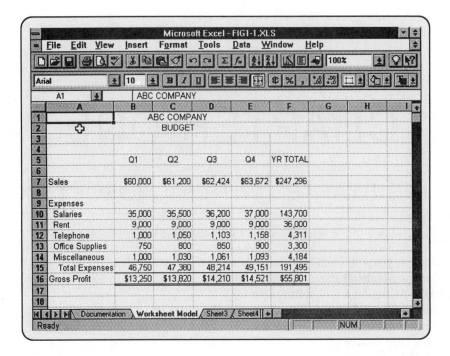

Figure 1-2 is a chart that includes information from the worksheet in Figure 1-1.

Figure 1-2

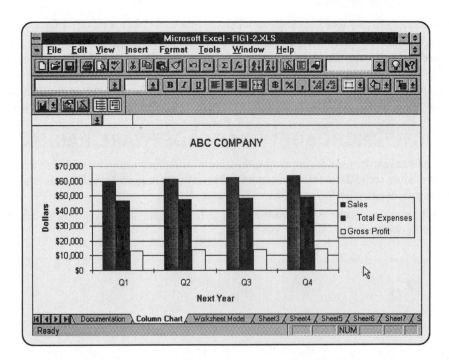

> *In This Book*
>
> The **file names** appearing on the title bar for most figures in this book usually refer to the figure number. In most cases, your file name will be different.

Microsoft Excel can perform some database management operations on a worksheet. For example, information on a worksheet can be sorted. Figure 1-3 is a worksheet that has salary information for a group of individuals.

Figure 1-3

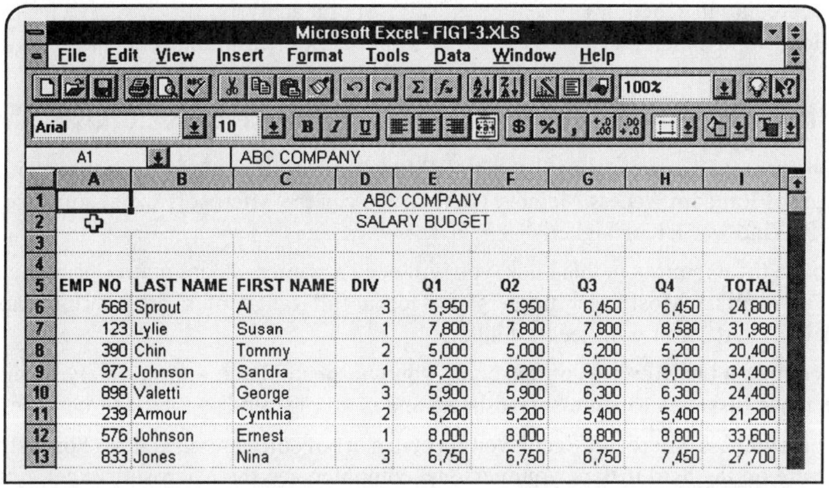

	A	B	C	D	E	F	G	H	I
1					ABC COMPANY				
2					SALARY BUDGET				
3									
4									
5	EMP NO	LAST NAME	FIRST NAME	DIV	Q1	Q2	Q3	Q4	TOTAL
6	568	Sprout	Al	3	5,950	5,950	6,450	6,450	24,800
7	123	Lylie	Susan	1	7,800	7,800	7,800	8,580	31,980
8	390	Chin	Tommy	2	5,000	5,000	5,200	5,200	20,400
9	972	Johnson	Sandra	1	8,200	8,200	9,000	9,000	34,400
10	898	Valetti	George	3	5,900	5,900	6,300	6,300	24,400
11	239	Armour	Cynthia	2	5,200	5,200	5,400	5,400	21,200
12	576	Johnson	Ernest	1	8,000	8,000	8,800	8,800	33,600
13	833	Jones	Nina	3	6,750	6,750	6,750	7,450	27,700

Suppose you needed to sort the information in Figure 1-3 by division number. Figure 1-4 shows the data from Figure 1-3 sorted in ascending order by division number.

Figure 1-4

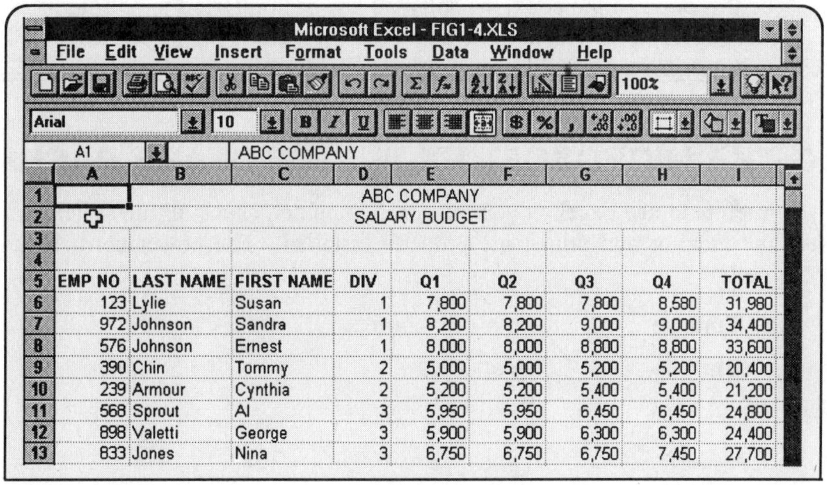

	A	B	C	D	E	F	G	H	I
1					ABC COMPANY				
2					SALARY BUDGET				
3									
4									
5	EMP NO	LAST NAME	FIRST NAME	DIV	Q1	Q2	Q3	Q4	TOTAL
6	123	Lylie	Susan	1	7,800	7,800	7,800	8,580	31,980
7	972	Johnson	Sandra	1	8,200	8,200	9,000	9,000	34,400
8	576	Johnson	Ernest	1	8,000	8,000	8,800	8,800	33,600
9	390	Chin	Tommy	2	5,000	5,000	5,200	5,200	20,400
10	239	Armour	Cynthia	2	5,200	5,200	5,400	5,400	21,200
11	568	Sprout	Al	3	5,950	5,950	6,450	6,450	24,800
12	898	Valetti	George	3	5,900	5,900	6,300	6,300	24,400
13	833	Jones	Nina	3	6,750	6,750	6,750	7,450	27,700

Typical Applications

Microsoft Excel is used in thousands of business organizations as well as for personal use. Some examples of Microsoft Excel applications include:

Advertising expense forecasts	Income statement forecasts
Balance sheet forecasts	Income tax projections
Budgets	Income tax records
Cash flow analysis	Inventory forecasting
Checkbook balancing	Job bids and costing
Depreciation schedules	Sports analysis
Household expenses	Stock portfolio analysis and records

■ DETERMINING HARDWARE AND SOFTWARE REQUIREMENTS

To use Microsoft Excel, you must have an IBM or compatible personal computer with a minimum of four megabytes of Random Access Memory (RAM). To run the Microsoft Excel software, you must also have Microsoft Windows 3.1 or higher.

To complete the exercises in this book, you will need a printer. A dot matrix printer can print spreadsheets as well as charts. Most laser printers provide a full range of chart-printing capabilities. For very high-quality charts, you will need a plotter.

As you complete the exercises in this book, you will need blank, appropriately formatted diskettes. You will use these diskettes to store spreadsheets and charts in files so they can be used at a later time.

When you purchase Microsoft Excel, you receive a set of software diskettes. For instructions on installing the software on the hard disk of your personal computer, see the Microsoft Excel *User's Guide* that came with your software.

In This Book

To this point in the book, the software has been referred to as Microsoft Excel. In most cases for the rest of this book, the software is simply called Excel.

■ STARTING THE MICROSOFT EXCEL SOFTWARE PACKAGE

Before you attempt to use Excel on your personal computer, check all the system's hardware connections. Make sure the monitor and printer are properly installed. The power cord should be connected to an appropriate outlet.

Turn on	the computer
Start	Windows

In This Book

You can use either a mouse or the keyboard with Excel. The use of the mouse and the keyboard are shown in two columns. The directions in the left, or first, column are for the mouse method, and they appear in normal type. The instructions for using the keyboard appear in the second column in *italics*. In most cases, you can mix the use of the mouse and the keyboard methods.

When referring to a mouse operation, **click** means to press a mouse button and then release it. **Drag** means to press and hold the mouse button down and then move the mouse. **Double-click** means to press a mouse button twice very rapidly.

When the instructions for using a mouse tell you to click the mouse button, they assume the left mouse button. The alternate mouse button refers to the right mouse button. If you switch the mouse buttons in the Install process, press the right mouse button when the instructions refer to the mouse button and press the left mouse button when they refer to the alternate mouse button.

Locate the Microsoft Excel group icon and then:

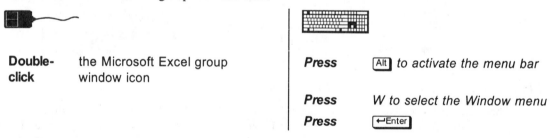

Double-click	the Microsoft Excel group window icon	*Press*	Alt *to activate the menu bar*
		Press	*W to select the Window menu*
		Press	←Enter

The Microsoft Excel icons now appear on your screen. To start Microsoft Excel:

Double-click	the Microsoft Excel icon	*Press*	*the pointer-movement keys* ←, →, ↓, *or* ↑ *to select the Microsoft Excel icon*
		Press	←Enter

The program title appears on your screen. In a few seconds, the **Microsoft Excel window** will be displayed on your screen, and it should look similar to Figure 1-5.

Figure 1-5

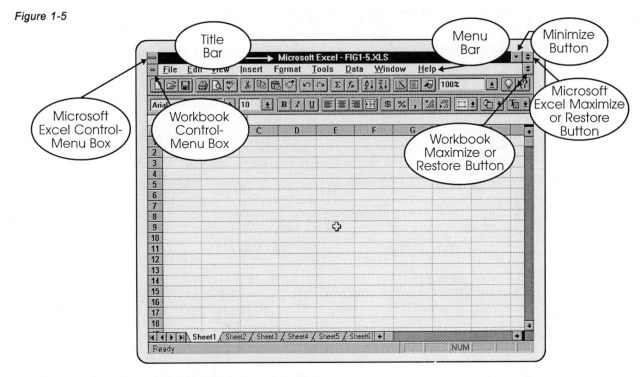

■ THE MICROSOFT EXCEL WINDOW

The Microsoft Excel window is displayed on your screen. Each file you use is called a workbook. A **workbook** can include many sheets. For example, a workbook may contain worksheets and chart sheets. The sheet names appear on the tabs at the bottom of the workbook. A **window** is a rectangular area on your screen in which you can view a software application such as Excel or an application document.

Figure 1-6 is the standard form of the Microsoft Excel window.

Figure 1-6

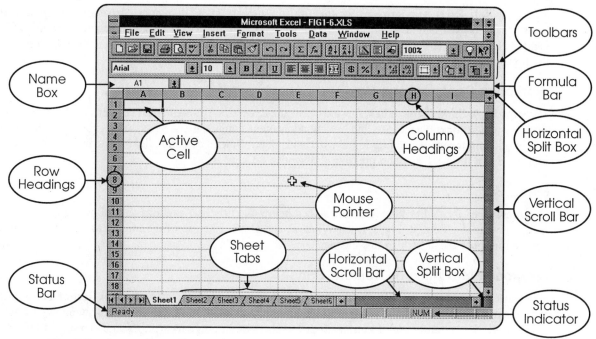

The following sections discuss the components identified in Figures 1-5 and 1-6.

Microsoft Excel Control-Menu Box

The **Microsoft Excel Control-menu box** is used to display the Control menu. Every window has a Control menu. The Control menu typically contains commands such as: Restore, Move, Size, Minimize, Maximize, Close, and Switch To. In some Control menus, all of the commands may not be available and will be shown in a lighter color than other commands. You can access the Control-menu box by moving the mouse pointer to the Control-menu box and clicking the mouse button or by holding down the ALT key and then pressing the SPACE BAR key.

Title Bar

The **title bar** appears at the top of the Microsoft Excel window. It includes the Microsoft Excel Control-menu box, the software product name, the workbook number, the Minimize button, and the Maximize or Restore button.

Minimize Button

The **Minimize button** appears in the top-right corner of the window and resembles an upside-down triangle. Use this button to reduce the Excel window to an icon. When you move the mouse pointer to the Minimize button and click the mouse button, the Excel window changes to an icon.

Microsoft Excel Maximize or Restore Button

The **Microsoft Excel Maximize** or **Restore button** appears in the top-right corner of the window and resembles a double triangle. It is used to maximize the size of the window on your screen. If your window is already maximized, use the button to restore the window to its previous size. To use the button, move the mouse pointer to the button and click the mouse button.

Workbook Control-Menu Box

The **workbook Control-menu box**, located below the Excel Control-menu box, contains the Restore, Move, Size, Minimize, Maximize, Close, and Next window menu commands. Access the workbook Control-menu box by moving the mouse pointer to the workbook Control-menu box and clicking the mouse button or by holding down the ALT key and pressing the hyphen (-) key.

Menu Bar

The **menu bar**, located at the top of the screen below the title bar, contains the following menus: File, Edit, View, Insert, Format, Tools, Data, Window, and Help. The use of the menu bar and menus will be covered in more detail later in this chapter.

Workbook Maximize or Restore Button

The **workbook Maximize** or **Restore button** is located below the Excel Maximize or Restore button. Use it to maximize the size of the workbook window on your screen. If the workbook window is already maximized, the button is used to restore the worksheet to its previous size. You can use this button by moving the mouse pointer to the maximize or restore button and clicking the mouse button.

Toolbars

The **toolbars**, located below the menu bar, contain a set of icons called buttons. Excel initially displays the Standard toolbar and the Formatting toolbar. These buttons represent commonly used Excel commands. The buttons allow you to quickly perform tasks by clicking on the button. There are several additional toolbars available for use in Excel.

Name Box

The **name box** is located below the Formatting toolbar on the left side of the window. This area displays the location of the active cell or name of a group of cells. If a range of cells is selected, the name box includes the initial cell in the range.

Formula Bar

The **formula bar** is also located below the Formatting toolbar and includes the name box. This bar displays characters and formulas that are entered into a cell.

Mouse Pointer

Use the **mouse pointer** to select different parts of your screen to be affected by your next action. The shape of the mouse pointer changes depending on the area of the screen where it is located and the action being performed. For example, when the mouse pointer is in the worksheet, it appears as a thick cross symbol and can be used to select any cell in a worksheet.

Window Border

The **window border** is the solid line that borders the entire worksheet. When the window is in the Restore view, you can use this border to change the size of the window. All windows have a border; however, when a window is maximized, the border is not visible.

Column Headings

Across the top border of the worksheet on your screen is a set of letters called **column headings**. These headings identify columns with the letters A through Z, AA through AZ, BA through BZ, and so forth, until the letter IV is reached for a total of 256 column headings in a worksheet.

Row Headings

Along the left border of a worksheet is a set of numbers called **row headings**. There are a total of 16,384 rows available in a worksheet.

Cell

A **cell** is the area on a worksheet at the intersection of a column and a row. Data are stored in a cell. The cell reference, A1, refers to the cell at the intersection of column A and row 1.

Active Cell

The **active cell** is distinguished by a thick, heavy border. The next data entry or operation affects this cell. The contents of the active cell are displayed in the formula bar. The name box contains the location of the active cell. To make a cell active, move the mouse pointer to the cell and click the mouse button. Alternatively, you can use the pointer-movement keys on the keyboard to make a cell active.

Sheet Tabs

The **sheet tabs** appear just below the bottom row visible in a workbook window. When you click the mouse button with the mouse pointer on a particular sheet tab, that sheet becomes the active worksheet. You can use the **tab scrolling** buttons to move between various worksheets.

Horizontal and Vertical Scroll Bars

The **horizontal scroll bar** appears just below the bottom row visible in a workbook window and to the right of the sheet tabs. This scroll bar includes **scroll arrows** as well as a **scroll box**. The scroll bars are used to view different parts of a worksheet. The **vertical scroll bar** appears on the right side of the workbook window and also contains a scroll box and scroll arrows.

Horizontal and Vertical Split Boxes

The **vertical split box** appears to the right of the horizontal scroll bar as a thick, black line. It is used to split the worksheet window into two vertical panes. The **horizontal split box** located above the vertical scroll bar is also a thick, black line. This split box is used to split the worksheet window into two horizontal panes.

Status Bar

The **status bar**, located at the bottom of the Microsoft Excel window, includes the name of the currently selected command or current activity. **Status indicators** are activated only when certain conditions are present: for example, when the Caps Lock is on, the CAPS indicator is activated.

In This Book

For the remainder of this book, the workbook document window is referred to as the workbook window.

■ MOVING AROUND THE WORKBOOK WINDOW

As mentioned earlier, the active cell is highlighted by a thick, heavy border. Using the mouse pointer and the pointer-movement keys to move around the worksheet window, you can make any cell the active cell.

In This Book

When you use Excel features with the keyboard method, you will often be asked to press one key, and while still holding the key down, to press another key. For example, you may be asked to hold down the ALT key and then press the letter N. This type of instruction appears in the text as:

Press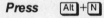

Selecting the Active Cell

The **mouse** and the **arrow keys** are used to make a cell the active cell. On some keyboards, the arrow keys are placed on the numeric keypad (sometimes called "the ten key"). On newer keyboards, they may also be in a separate location, as Figure 1-7 depicts.

Figure 1-7

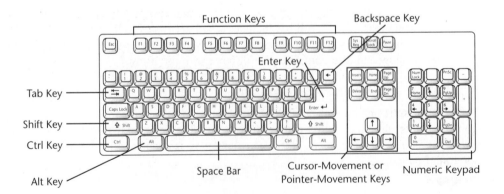

To illustrate the process for making a cell the active cell:

| **Move** | the mouse pointer to cell H1 | ***Locate*** | *the arrow keys* |
| **Click** | the mouse button | ***Press*** | → *seven times* |

As Figure 1-8 shows, the active cell is now cell H1. Note that H1 appears in the name box.

Figure 1-8

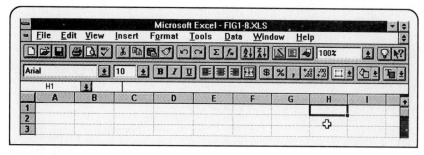

To make cell J1 the active cell:

Move	the mouse pointer to the → scroll arrow on the horizontal scroll bar	***Press***	→ *two times*
Click	the mouse button		
Move	the mouse pointer to cell J1		
Click	the mouse button		

Your screen should look like Figure 1-9.

Figure 1-9

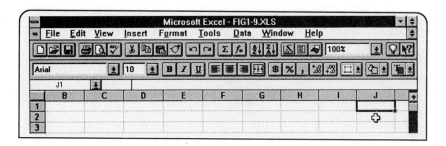

As Figure 1-9 illustrates, the active cell has been moved to column J and column A has disappeared from your screen.

To make cell A1 the active cell:

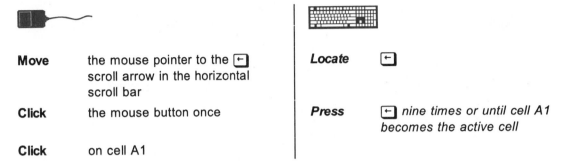

Move	the mouse pointer to the [←] scroll arrow in the horizontal scroll bar	*Locate*	[←]
Click	the mouse button once	*Press*	[←] *nine times or until cell A1 becomes the active cell*
Click	on cell A1		

Using the PAGE UP and PAGE DOWN Keys to Move the Active Cell

You can move the active cell up and down a worksheet in a workbook using the PAGE UP and PAGE DOWN keys.

To move the active cell down a number of rows:

Locate	[Page Down]
Press	[Page Down]

The number of rows the active cell moves down is equal to the number of rows appearing in the workbook window. In this case, the active cell is cell A19. Your screen should look like Figure 1-10.

Figure 1-10

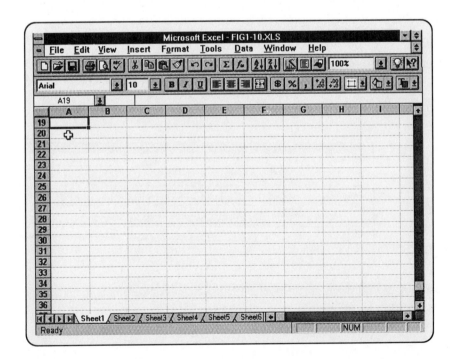

To move up a number of rows:

Locate   Page Up

Press   Page Up

The active cell is now cell A1.

Using the Go To Key (the F5 Function Key) to Move the Active Cell

Sometimes you need to make a particular cell in a worksheet within the workbook window the active cell. For example, to make cell IV16384 the active cell:

Locate   *the* F5 *function key*

Press   F5

As Figure 1-11 displays, the Go To dialog box appears on your screen. The F5 key performs the same command as selecting the Go To command on the Edit menu. You are now ready to enter the desired cell reference in the Reference text box. Dialog boxes and their contents are discussed in more detail as you encounter them.

Figure 1-11

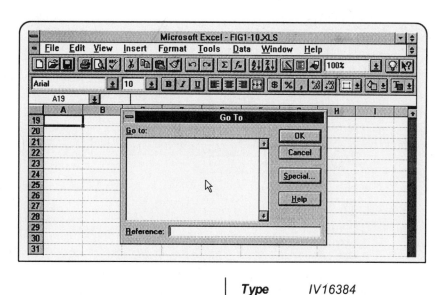

Type   *IV16384*

Figure 1-12 depicts the entering of the cell reference IV16384.

Figure 1-12

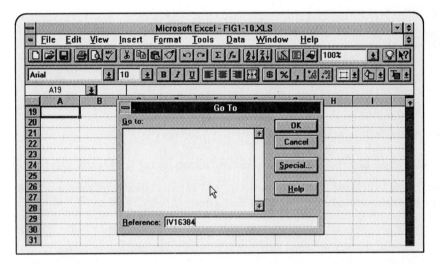

Note that you can use either lowercase or uppercase letters when you type the cell reference.

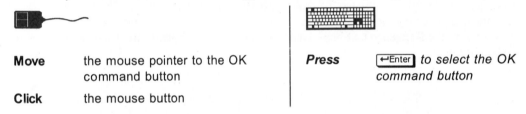

Move	the mouse pointer to the OK command button	***Press***	*⏎Enter to select the OK command button*
Click	the mouse button		

As Figure 1-13 illustrates, the active cell is now cell IV16384.

Figure 1-13

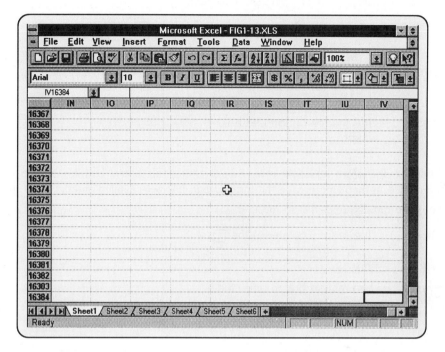

Cell IV16384 is the cell in the bottom-right corner of a worksheet in the workbook window. In other words, column IV is the last column in the worksheet and row 16,384 is the last row in the worksheet.

Using the CTRL+HOME Keys to Move the Active Cell

You can move the active cell to cell A1 quickly by pressing the CTRL+HOME keys. To demonstrate this operation:

Locate   *the* Ctrl *and* Home *keys*

Press   Ctrl + Home

Cell A1 is now the active cell.

Viewing Different Parts of a Worksheet Window Using the Scroll Bars

You can use the vertical and horizontal scroll bars to quickly view a different area of a worksheet in a workbook.

To view a different part of a worksheet vertically:

Move	the mouse pointer to the ⬇ scroll arrow on the vertical scroll bar
Press	the mouse button and hold it down

After moving down 20 or 30 rows, stop pressing the mouse button. Notice that the active cell, A1, referenced in the name box on the formula bar, has not changed and does not appear on your screen.

To move rapidly up in a worksheet:

Move	the mouse pointer to the ⬆ scroll arrow on the vertical scroll bar
Press	the mouse button and hold it down until row one can be seen

Notice that you can see the active cell, A1, again.

An alternative method for moving vertically in a worksheet is to click above or below the scroll box in the vertical scroll bar.

To move down a number of rows:

Move	the mouse pointer below the scroll box in the vertical scroll bar
Click	the mouse button

Now your screen should look like Figure 1-14.

Figure 1-14

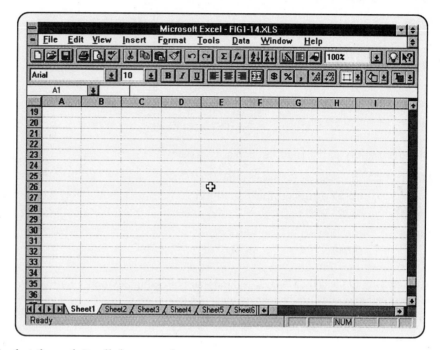

Notice again that the active cell does not change.

To move up a number of rows:

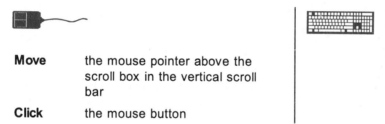

Move   the mouse pointer above the scroll box in the vertical scroll bar

Click   the mouse button

Notice that the active cell, A1, is now on your screen.

A final method for moving vertically through a worksheet is to drag the scroll box up and down the vertical scroll bar.

To move down several rows:

Move   the mouse pointer to the scroll box in the vertical scroll bar

Drag   the scroll box down a couple of inches

To move up several rows:

Move   the mouse pointer to the scroll
              box in the vertical scroll bar

Drag   the scroll box up a couple of
              inches

To move rapidly to the right through a worksheet:

Move   the mouse pointer to the →
              scroll arrow on the horizontal
              scroll bar

Press   the mouse button and hold it
              down

After moving to the right 10 or 20 columns, stop pressing the mouse button. Notice that the active cell has not changed and does not appear on your screen.

To move rapidly to the left in a worksheet:

Move   the mouse pointer to the ←
              scroll arrow on the horizontal
              scroll bar

Press   the mouse button and hold it
              down until column A can be seen

Notice that you can now see the active cell, A1, again.

An alternative method for moving horizontally in a worksheet is to click to the left or to the right of the scroll box in the horizontal scroll bar.

To move to the right a number of columns:

Move   the mouse pointer to the right of
              the scroll box in the horizontal
              scroll bar

Click   the mouse button

Your screen now should look like Figure 1-15.

Figure 1-15

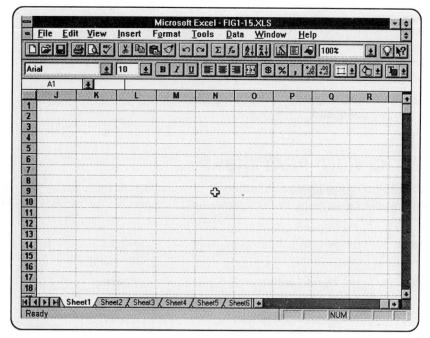

Notice that the active cell does not change.

To move to the left a number of columns:

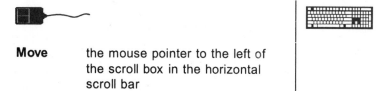

Move   the mouse pointer to the left of the scroll box in the horizontal scroll bar

Click   the mouse button

Notice that the active cell, A1, now appears on your screen.

A final method for moving horizontally through a worksheet is to drag the scroll box to the right or to the left in the horizontal scroll bar.

To move to the right several columns:

Move   the mouse pointer to the scroll box in the horizontal scroll bar

Drag   the scroll box to the right a couple of inches

To move to the left several columns:

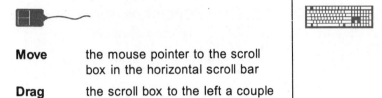

Move the mouse pointer to the scroll box in the horizontal scroll bar

Drag the scroll box to the left a couple of inches

■ USING THE HELP FEATURE

The HELP feature allows you to access an on-line reference for Excel on your screen. The HELP feature is accessible by choosing the Help menu from the menu bar or pressing the F1 key. To use the Help feature:

Move the mouse pointer to the Help menu name

Press `Alt`

Click the mouse button

Press `→` *until the Help menu name is selected*

Move the mouse pointer to the Contents command

Press `←Enter` *to select the Help menu*

Click the mouse button

Press `←Enter` *to select the Contents command*

The Help window appears, and your screen should look similar to Figure 1-16.

Figure 1-16

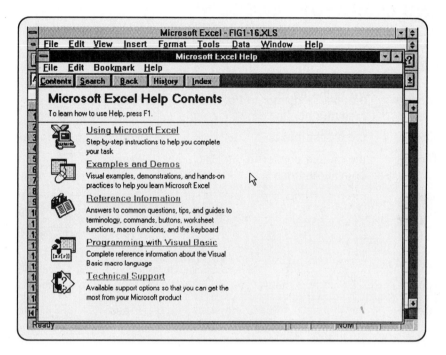

You can then move the mouse pointer to the desired Help topic and click the mouse button to select it. Note that the mouse pointer becomes a pointing hand when you move it to the list of Help topics. Note also that you cannot use the arrow keys to select Help topics.

To close the Help window:

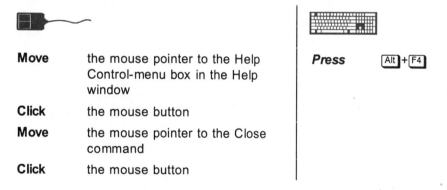

Move	the mouse pointer to the Help Control-menu box in the Help window	***Press***	Alt + F4
Click	the mouse button		
Move	the mouse pointer to the Close command		
Click	the mouse button		

Excel uses several other function keys beside the Help F1 key and the Go To F5 key. Later chapters demonstrate the uses of other function keys.

■ EXITING MICROSOFT EXCEL

When you are ready to exit Microsoft Excel:

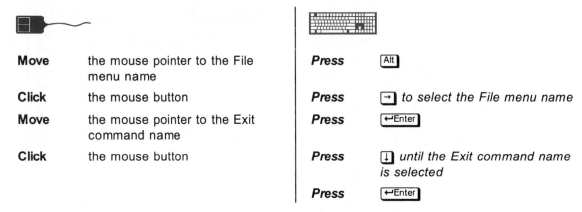

Move	the mouse pointer to the File menu name	*Press*	[Alt]
Click	the mouse button	*Press*	[→] *to select the File menu name*
Move	the mouse pointer to the Exit command name	*Press*	[↵Enter]
Click	the mouse button	*Press*	[↓] *until the Exit command name is selected*
		Press	[↵Enter]

If you have not saved changes to a workbook that you have made, a beep will sound and a dialog box appears for each workbook not saved. When you want to save the workbook to a file before exiting:

Move	the mouse pointer to the Yes command button	*Press*	[↵Enter] *to select the Yes command button*
Click	the mouse button		

You can then enter a file name and save the workbook using the file name. Creating file names and saving workbooks are discussed more thoroughly in the next chapter. To complete the process for exiting:

Move	the mouse pointer to the Yes command button	*Press*	[↵Enter] *to select the Yes command button*
Click	the mouse button		

If you do not want to save the workbook:

Move	the mouse pointer to the No command button	*Press*	[Tab⇄] *to select the No command button*
Click	the mouse button	*Press*	[↵Enter]

When you want to cancel the Exit command and not leave Excel:

Move	the mouse pointer to the Cancel command button	*Press*	[Esc]
Click	the mouse button		

SUMMARY

This chapter provides an overview of the Microsoft Excel software. Excel is often used for business, government, and personal applications. Personal computer hardware is required to use Excel. The software can be executed on IBM-compatible PCs. The important items on the Microsoft Excel window are the Microsoft Excel Control-menu box, the title bar, the Minimize button, the Microsoft Excel Maximize or Restore button, the workbook Control-menu box, the menu bar, the workbook Maximize or Restore button, the Standard and Formatting toolbars, the name box, the formula bar, the mouse pointer, the window border, the column headings, the row headings, the active cell, the sheet tabs, the horizontal and vertical scroll bars, the horizontal and vertical split boxes, and the status bar. You can move through the worksheet window by using a mouse, the arrow keys, the PAGE DOWN and PAGE UP keys, the F5 function key, and the CTRL+HOME keys.

KEY CONCEPTS

Active cell
Arrow keys
Cell
Click
Column headings
Ctrl+Home keys
Dialog box
Double-click
Drag
Esc key
File names
Formula bar
Go To F5 key
Hardware requirements
Help F1 key
Home key
Horizontal scroll bar
Horizontal split box
Menu bar
Microsoft Excel Control-menu box
Microsoft Excel Maximize or Restore button
Minimize button

Mouse
Mouse pointer
Name box
Page Down key
Page Up key
Row headings
Scroll box
Scroll arrows
Sheet tabs
Software requirements
Status indicators
Status bar
Tab scrolling buttons
Title bar
Toolbars
Vertical scroll bar
Vertical split box
Window
Window border
Workbook
Workbook Control-menu box
Workbook Maximize or Restore button

EXERCISE 1

INSTRUCTIONS: Answer the following questions in the space provided.

1. Define the following terms:

    a. Row Headings _____

    _____

    b. Column Headings _____

    _____

    c. Cell _____

    _____

    d. Active Cell _____

    _____

    e. Click _____

    _____

    f. Name Box _____

    _____

    g. Status Bar _____

    _____

    h. Formula Bar _____

    _____

    i. Workbook _____

    _____

    j. Window _____

    _____

    k. Workbook Maximize or Restore Button _____

    _____

l.   Minimize Button _____

_____

m. Menu Bar _____

_____

n.   Mouse Pointer _____

_____

o.   Sheet Tabs _____

_____

p.   Toolbars _____

_____

q.   Horizontal and Vertical Scroll Bars _____

_____

r.   Scroll Box _____

_____

s.   Horizontal and Vertical Split Boxes _____

_____

2. Describe the process for using the Excel menu bar with a mouse.

_____

_____

_____

3. Describe the process for using the Excel menu bar with the keyboard.

_____

_____

_____

4. Describe the purpose of the function keys.

_____

_____

_____

EXERCISE 2

INSTRUCTIONS: Identify the circled and enclosed items on the Excel window in Figure 1-17.

Figure 1-17

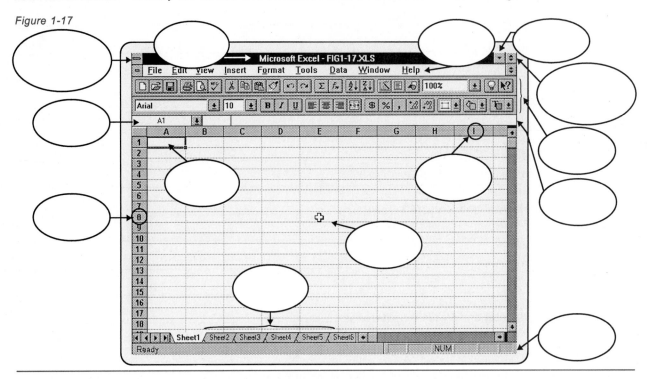

EXERCISE 3

INSTRUCTIONS: Initiate the use of Excel.

Exit from Excel using the mouse method.

EXERCISE 4

INSTRUCTIONS: Initiate the use of Excel.

Exit from Excel using the keyboard method.

CHAPTER TWO

QUICK START FOR MICROSOFT EXCEL

OBJECTIVES

In this chapter, you will learn to:

- Create a worksheet
- Edit a worksheet
- Use the Microsoft Excel menus
- Print a worksheet
- Save a workbook to a file
- Close a workbook
- Open a new workbook document
- Open an existing workbook file
- Exit Microsoft Excel

■ CHAPTER OVERVIEW

When you create a worksheet in a workbook using Excel, you usually go through the following steps:

1. Access the Excel software.
2. Create a worksheet by keying in the text and data.
3. Make changes to the worksheet.
4. Print the worksheet.
5. Save the workbook document in a file on a disk.

In other situations, you may open an existing workbook file from a disk and make changes to a worksheet in the workbook. After completing the changes, you save the workbook document again. You may also print the worksheet. When you are finished using a worksheet, you usually close the workbook document so you can create or use another workbook. Finally, you exit the software when you are finished.

This chapter gives you a quick overview of the processes of creating, editing, printing, and saving a worksheet in a workbook. It also introduces the process of closing the workbook document on your screen. You will open a workbook from a file on a disk, make some changes to a worksheet in the workbook, and save the workbook document again. You also will complete the procedure for exiting Excel.

■ CREATING A WORKSHEET

Access the Excel software on your personal computer (PC). If you are unfamiliar with this task, refer to Chapter 1. In this exercise, you will create the worksheet shown in Figure 2-1.

Figure 2-1

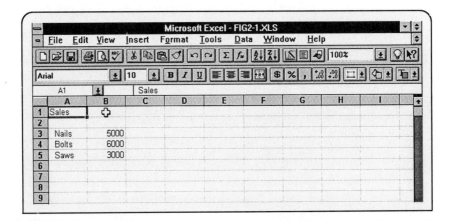

> *In This Book*
>
> To save space, the symbols representing the mouse and keyboard are omitted in the remainder of the book. The directions in the left-hand column are for using a mouse. They appear in normal type. The directions in the right-hand column are for using the keyboard. They appear in *italic* type.

To specify the information to enter in cell A1:

| **Type**   Sales | **Type**   *Sales* |

See Figure 2-2. The word Sales appears in the formula bar. Notice that when you type the first character, the word Enter appears in the status bar indicating that something is being entered. The enter and cancel boxes also appear to the left of the formula bar.

Figure 2-2

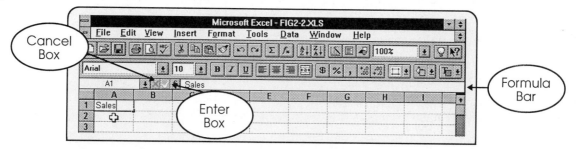

To place the information in cell A1:

Move	the mouse pointer to the enter box ☑	***Press***	⟵Enter
Click	the mouse button		

The word Sales appears in cell A1 and will remain there until you delete it. Sales also appears in the formula bar if you click the enter box. When you press the ENTER key to place text in a cell, the cell immediately below becomes the active cell. Assuming you clicked the enter box, your screen should look like Figure 2-3.

Figure 2-3

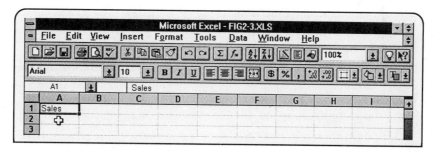

Note that the text is **left-aligned** in cell A1. Left-aligned means that the characters begin at the leftmost position of the cell. When a number is entered, it is **right-aligned**. That is, the number appears in the rightmost part of the cell.

To place the text "Nails" and "Bolts" in cells A3 and A4:

Move	the mouse pointer to cell A3	***Press***	⬇ *until cell A3 is the active cell*
Click	the mouse button		

To indent the product names two spaces and enter them:

Press	the space bar twice	***Press***	*the space bar twice*
Type	Nails	***Type***	*Nails*

Move	the mouse pointer to the enter box ☑		*Press*	⏎Enter
Click	the mouse button		*Press*	*the space bar twice*
Move	the mouse pointer to cell A4		*Type*	*Bolts*
Click	the mouse button		*Press*	⏎Enter
Press	the space bar twice			
Type	Bolts			
Move	the mouse pointer to the enter box ☑			
Click	the mouse button			

In This Book

To make a cell active using the mouse, you have been instructed to move the mouse to a cell and then click the mouse button. For the remainder of the book, these two steps are combined by asking you to click on the cell.

To make a cell active using the keyboard, you have been asked to press an arrow key. In the rest of the book you are instructed to activate the cell.

When entering information using the mouse, you have been directed to move the mouse pointer to the enter box ☑ and click the mouse button. From this point forward, you are asked to click the enter box ☑.

To enter the sales amount for Nails:

Click	on cell B3		*Activate*	*cell B3*
Type	4000		*Type*	*4000*
Click	the enter box ☑		*Press*	⏎Enter

To input the sales value for Bolts:

Click	on cell B4		*Activate*	*cell B4*
Type	6000		*Type*	*6000*
Click	the enter box ☑		*Press*	⏎Enter

Assuming you clicked the enter box, your screen should now look like Figure 2-4.

Figure 2-4

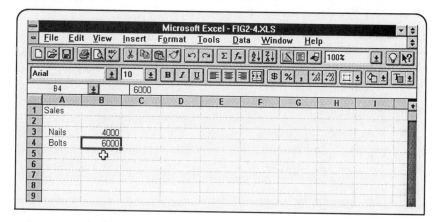

■ EDITING A WORKSHEET

Suppose the sales value for Nails should have been 5000. To change the number:

Click	on cell B3	*Activate*	*cell B3*
Type	5000	*Type*	*5000*
Click	the enter box ☑	*Press*	⏎Enter

The sales value for Nails is changed. Assuming you clicked the enter box, your screen should look like Figure 2-5.

Figure 2-5

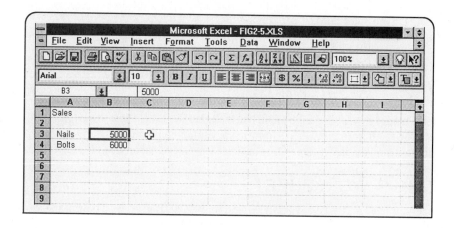

User Tip

Use the F2 function key to edit information in a cell. When you press the F2 key, an insertion point appears at the end of the entry in the cell. You can use the left and right arrow keys, as well as the HOME and END keys, to move the insertion point to various characters in an entry. To delete a character, move the insertion point to the left of the character you wish to delete and then press the DELETE key. You can also delete a character by placing the insertion point to the right of the character you wish to delete and then pressing the BACKSPACE key. To insert a character, move the insertion point to the place you want the new character(s) to appear and then type the text. After you edit the contents of a cell, click the enter box or press the ENTER key.

Additional editing methods are presented in Chapter 6.

■ USING THE EXCEL MENUS

Chapter 1 briefly mentioned Excel menus. You will use the Excel menus in the next section to print the worksheet you have created.

The Excel menu bar always appears on your screen. See Figure 2-6.

Figure 2-6

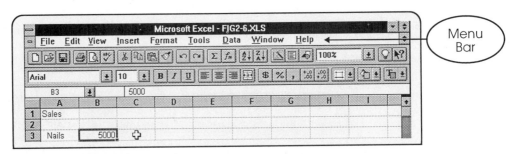

The menu bar appears immediately below the Microsoft Excel title bar.

Menu names available on the menu bar include File, Edit, View, Insert, Format, Tools, Data, Window, and Help. Use these menus to perform a variety of commands on a worksheet. Many of the menus and commands available in Excel are illustrated in later chapters.

■ PRINTING A WORKSHEET

Once you have prepared a worksheet, you may want to print it. To print the worksheet you created earlier in this chapter, use the Print command on the File menu.

To begin printing the worksheet:

Move	the mouse pointer to the File menu name	*Press*	Alt
Click	the mouse button	*Press*	→ *to select the File menu name*
		Press	←Enter

Notice that a pull-down menu containing the available File commands appears on the screen. Your screen should look similar to Figure 2-7.

Figure 2-7

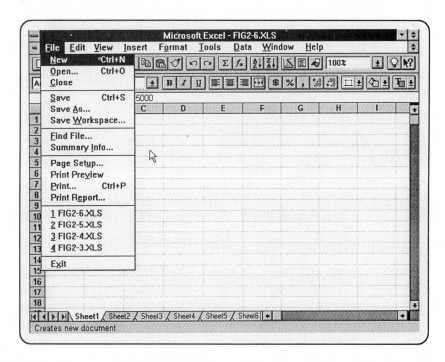

An ellipsis (...) beside a command indicates that a dialog box appears if the command is selected. Commands shown in a lighter color are not available at this time.

Move	the mouse pointer to the Print command	*Press*	↓ *until the Print command is selected*
Click	the mouse button	*Press*	←Enter

Notice that the Print dialog box appears on your screen. Your screen should look like Figure 2-8.

Figure 2-8

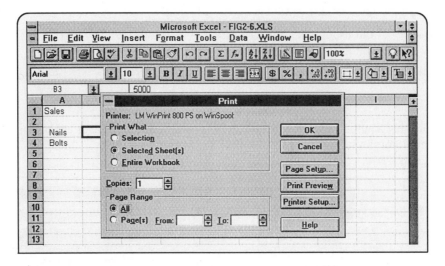

To print the worksheet document:

Move	the mouse pointer to the OK command button	**Press**	⌐Enter
Click	the mouse button		

The printer should print your worksheet. Additional printing options will be discussed in later chapters.

■ SAVING A WORKBOOK TO A FILE

Any changes you make while creating or editing a worksheet in a workbook are stored in your computer's memory. If the power to the computer fails or you turn off the computer, your work will be lost. You can prevent such a loss by using the Save or Save As commands on the File menu.

You can save the workbook to a file without losing your place on the worksheet and then continue creating or editing the worksheet. As you work, it is a good idea to save the worksheet every 10 to 15 minutes.

Making cell A1 the active cell prior to saving a workbook is an optional step. If you make cell A1 the active cell before saving, the workbook is saved with A1 as the active cell. When the workbook file is opened, A1 is the active cell.

To make cell A1 the active cell:

Click	on cell A1	**Press**	Ctrl + Home

The first time you save a workbook to a file, you should use the Save As command on the File menu to give the workbook a file name. After the workbook is saved to a file, you can use the Save command on the File menu to resave the workbook to the same file name.

To save the workbook to a file:

Move	the mouse pointer to the File menu name	*Press*	`Alt`
Click	the mouse button	*Press*	`→` *to select the File menu name*
Move	the mouse pointer to the Save As command	*Press*	`←Enter`
Click	the mouse button	*Press*	`↓` *until the Save As command is selected*
		Press	`←Enter`

The Save As dialog box appears on your screen. To save the worksheet to the file named EXAMPLE:

Type	EXAMPLE	*Type*	*EXAMPLE*
Move	the mouse pointer to the OK command button	*Press*	`←Enter`
Click	the mouse button		

User Tip

Another method for saving a workbook to a file is to click the Save 🖫 button on the Standard toolbar. If the workbook has never been saved, the Save As dialog box appears on the screen. If you have previously named the workbook, use the Save 🖫 button to save the workbook file; no dialog box appears.

File names for workbooks can contain a maximum of eight characters. Any character except a period and a space is acceptable as a part of a workbook file name. The EXAMPLE workbook file contains the information you have entered into your worksheet in the EXAMPLE workbook.

In This Book

Note that you may set up Excel to save files on a different disk or directory other than the one in which Excel is installed. In this book, it is assumed that you have specified an appropriate directory to save your workbook files. As you use this book, save a workbook to a file only when you are instructed to do so.

A Summary Info dialog box appears on your screen. The Summary Info feature allows you to classify documents with a title, subject, author, keywords, and comments. Use these categories to find files.

To enter a title for the workbook:

Type	My first workbook		*Type*	*My first workbook*
Move	the mouse pointer to the OK command button		*Press*	⊣Enter
Click	the mouse button			

Notice that the name of the workbook file (EXAMPLE) and its extension (XLS) now appear on the title bar.

User Tip

An alternative method for selecting menu names and commands using the keyboard is to press the letter corresponding to the underlined character for the menu name or command. This approach saves time in creating and editing worksheets. Initially, it may be useful to select the appropriate item with the arrow keys and then press the ENTER key. Once you are comfortable with how menus are structured, you can use the underlined characters for selecting menu names and commands. After working with Excel for a short while, most individuals use the underlined character when they use the keyboard method.

■ CLOSING A WORKSHEET

Before starting to work on a worksheet in another workbook, you usually close the current workbook document and open a new workbook.

In This Book

When using a mouse, so far you have been choosing a menu name or command by moving the mouse pointer to the desired option and clicking the mouse button. For the remainder of this book, you are instructed to simply **choose** a command rather than being told to move the mouse pointer to the menu name or command and click the mouse button.

In selecting items from the menus using the keyboard, you may either use the arrow keys to select a menu option or command and press the ENTER key, or you many press the letter for the underlined character in the menu name or command. For the remainder of this book, you are instructed to **select** the menu name or command rather than being told to use either the arrow keys or the underlined letter for selecting commands.

To close the current workbook document:

Choose	File		***Press***	*Alt*
Choose	Close		***Select***	*File*
			Select	*Close*

The **Null menu bar** is displayed on your screen. Your screen should look like Figure 2-9.

Figure 2-9

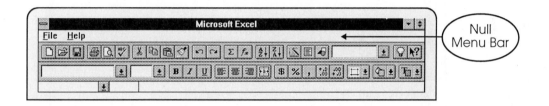

This menu bar appears when all workbook documents are closed.

■ OPENING A NEW WORKBOOK DOCUMENT

To open a new worksheet document:

Choose	File		***Press***	*Alt*
Choose	New		***Select***	*File*
			Select	*New*

A new worksheet document similar to the one in Figure 2-10 appears on your screen.

Figure 2-10

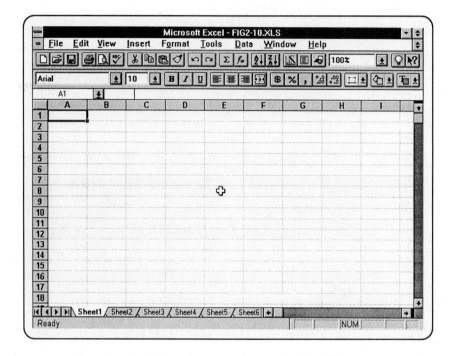

User Tip

Another method for opening a new worksheet document is to click the New Workbook ▢ button on the Standard toolbar.

Before proceeding to the next section, you need to close the current worksheet.

Choose	File		***Press***	Alt
Choose	Close		***Select***	*File*
			Select	*Close*

The Null menu bar appears again.

■ OPENING AN EXISTING WORKBOOK FILE

The EXAMPLE workbook is stored in the EXAMPLE file you saved earlier in this chapter. To open the EXAMPLE workbook file:

Choose	File		***Press***	Alt
Choose	Open		***Select***	*File*

Click	on EXAMPLE in the File Name list box	*Select*	*Open*
Click	the OK command button	*Press*	Tab↹ *to select the File Name list box*
		Press	↓ *until the EXAMPLE file name is selected*
		Press	↵Enter

User Tip

Another method for opening an existing workbook file is to move the mouse pointer to the Open ⬦ button on the Standard toolbar and click the mouse button. Then click on the file name you desire and click the OK command button.

When you select the File menu, you may notice the name of your file at the bottom of the File menu. If this occurs, you can type the number beside the file name or move the mouse pointer to the file name and click the mouse button. In either case, the file is opened and the workbook document appears on your screen.

The EXAMPLE workbook should appear. Your screen should look like Figure 2-11.

Figure 2-11

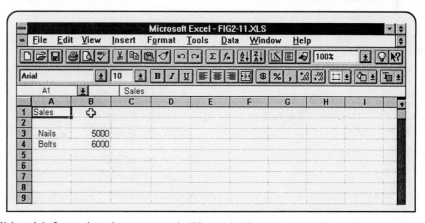

Enter the additional information that appears in Figure 2-12 on your worksheet.

Figure 2-12

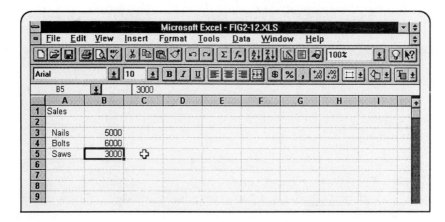

Click	on cell A5	*Activate*	*cell A5*
Press	the space bar twice	*Press*	*the space bar twice*
Type	Saws	*Type*	*Saws*
Click	the enter box ☑	*Press*	⏎Enter
Click	on cell B5	*Activate*	*cell B5*
Type	3000	*Type*	*3000*
Click	the enter box ☑	*Press*	⏎Enter

After modifying a worksheet in a workbook, you usually save the workbook again using the same file name.

To save the workbook that contains your worksheet with the same file name:

Click	on cell A1	*Activate*	*cell A1*
Click	the Save 🖫 button	*Press*	Alt
		Select	*File*
		Select	*Save*

Notice that you used the File Save command instead of the File Save As command because you had already saved the workbook file.

■ EXITING MICROSOFT EXCEL

When you finish using Microsoft Excel, you will need to exit from the software.

To exit Microsoft Excel:

Choose	File	*Press*	Alt
Choose	Exit	*Select*	*File*
		Select	*Exit*

SUMMARY

This chapter presented an overview of the processes for creating a worksheet, editing a worksheet, saving a workbook, printing a worksheet, closing a workbook document, and opening a workbook document. The process for exiting Microsoft Excel was also illustrated.

KEY CONCEPTS

Enter box ☑   Left-aligned
File Close   Menu
File Exit   New Workbook ▯ button
File New   Null menu bar
File Open   Open ☞ button
File Print   Right-aligned
File Save   Save 💾 button
File Save As

EXERCISE 1

INSTRUCTIONS: Circle T if the statement is true and F if the statement is false.

T   F   1.   The only way to edit an entry in a worksheet is to type the entry again and press the ENTER key.

T   F   2.   A workbook containing worksheets can be saved to a file on a diskette but not on a hard disk.

T   F   3.   The maximum number of characters that can appear in a workbook file name is eight.

T   F   4.   A period can be used in a workbook file name.

T   F   5.   A workbook can be saved to a file only one time.

T   F   6.   It is a good idea to save a workbook to a file about every 10 to 15 minutes.

T   F   7.   To print a worksheet in a workbook, you need to specify a range of cells to print.

T   F   8.   The File menu is used to access the Exit command.

T   F   9.   The File Save command is used to open a workbook document.

T   F   10. The File Save As command should be used the first time a workbook document is saved.

EXERCISE 2

INSTRUCTIONS: Describe a typical situation that uses the following commands from the File menu:

Problem 1:   Save As

Problem 2:   Print

Problem 3:   Open

Problem 4:   Save

Problem 5:   Close

Problem 6:   Exit

Problem 7:   New

EXERCISE 3

INSTRUCTIONS: Create the worksheet shown in Figure 2-13.

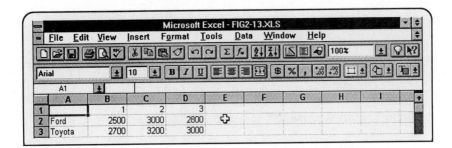

1. Print the worksheet.
2. Save the workbook to a file using the name CARS.
3. Close the workbook document.

EXERCISE 4

INSTRUCTIONS: Create the worksheet shown in Figure 2-14.

Figure 2-14

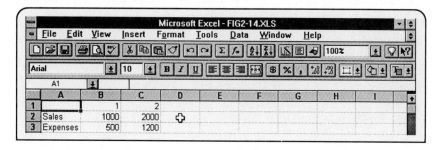

1. Print the worksheet.
2. Save the workbook to a file using the name INCOME.
3. Close the workbook document.

EXERCISE 5

INSTRUCTIONS: Open the CARS workbook file created in Exercise 3.

1. Change the values for Ford sales to 4000, 4200, and 4800 in periods 1, 2, and 3, respectively.
2. Save the workbook to a file using the name CARS1.
3. Print the worksheet.
4. Close the workbook document.

EXERCISE 6

INSTRUCTIONS: Open the INCOME workbook file created in Exercise 4.

1. Change the values for Expenses to 300 and 900 in periods 1 and 2, respectively.
2. Save the workbook to a file using the name INCOME1.
3. Print the worksheet.
4. Close the workbook document.

CHAPTER THREE

ORGANIZING WORKBOOKS AND DESIGNING WORKSHEETS PROPERLY

OBJECTIVES

In this chapter, you will learn to:
- Design worksheets within a workbook
- Layout a workbook
- Name a sheet tab
- Save a workbook

■ CHAPTER OVERVIEW

When you create workbooks consisting of worksheets, remember to use good design principles. Properly laid-out workbooks and properly designed worksheets are easier for individuals to modify at a later date. Furthermore, if a workbook is organized effectively and worksheets are designed appropriately, it takes less effort for someone to understand how a worksheet prepared by someone else actually operates.

■ DESIGNING WORKSHEETS WITHIN A WORKBOOK

Excel is a tool that enhances productivity. Worksheets within a workbook should be designed so they are useful for the individuals who create them as well as for other people who may use them. A worksheet should be designed so that it is easy for the developer or anyone else to modify in the future.

In designing a worksheet, Thommes (1992) has suggested several criteria to consider, including (1) accuracy, (2) clarity, (3) flexibility, (4) efficiency, and (5) auditability.

The first criterion is accuracy. That is, if a worksheet does not give its user correct results, it is worthless. As you will see later in this book, there are many situations in which you may enter the wrong formula or value that lead to incorrect answers. The formulas and functions used in Excel are not immediately visible to a worksheet user. Proper design and documentation can improve the worksheet so that people are less likely to use the worksheet improperly.

Clarity is the second design criterion. The creator and designer of a worksheet must understand how the worksheet works. Proper layout and documentation improve the clarity for everyone who uses a workbook and its worksheet.

The next criterion is flexibility. When designing and developing a worksheet, you should consider possible future modifications.

Efficiency, the fourth criterion, has three aspects. First, you should consider the amount of computer memory required to process the worksheet. Second, think of the time the computer requires to process the worksheet. Third, the user should be able to easily find the important sections of the worksheet.

The final criterion is auditability. In many situations, worksheets may require auditing for accuracy. An individual should be able to determine what items are used to calculate the value in a cell. Proper layout and documentation can ease the effective checking of worksheets.

■ WORKBOOK AND WORKSHEET LAYOUT

Thommes (1992) and Ronen, Palley, and Lucas (1989) discuss some formats to use in designing the worksheet layout. The layout suggested by Ronen, Palley, and Lucas, and discussed in the work by Thommes, has been adopted and slightly adapted for use in this book. Figure 3-1 shows the suggested layout.

Figure 3-1

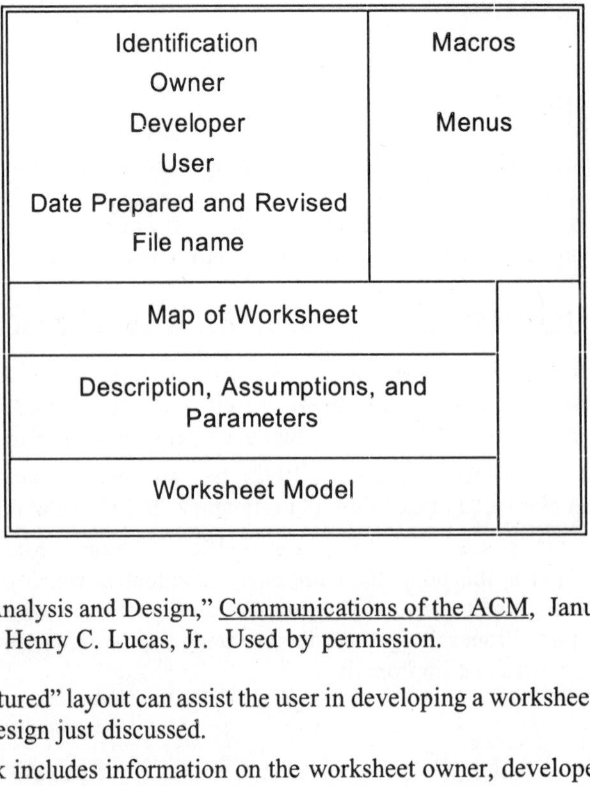

Source. "Spreadsheet Analysis and Design," <u>Communications of the ACM</u>, January 1989 by Boaz Ronen, Michael A. Palley, and Henry C. Lucas, Jr. Used by permission.

Use of this "block-structured" layout can assist the user in developing a worksheet to satisfy the five criteria for proper worksheet design just discussed.

The identification block includes information on the worksheet owner, developer, and user. The date the worksheet was created and last revised are also specified in the identification block. The identification block also provides the file name for the workbook.

The macros and menus block is to the right of the identification block. Macros are used to improve the efficiency of processing a worksheet and are discussed more thoroughly in Chapter 16. In Excel, macros and menus are placed in a separate workbook, in the Personal Macro Workbook, or in the same workbook in which it will be used. Menus improve the clarity of worksheets for users and allow worksheet developers to customize worksheet applications. The macros/menu block is placed in a separate file to prevent cells from being erased or blank cells from being introduced into the worksheet. If either error occurs, the macros and menus may not work correctly.

A map of the worksheet appears below the identification block. This block shows the order of the various areas in the worksheet. For example, the macros and menus block appears to the right of the identification block.

The next block includes additional documentation about the worksheet. This block includes a general description of the worksheet and provides the parameters and assumptions used in the worksheet. For example, it might show growth rates and interest rates.

The final block contains the worksheet model. In this block, the actual rows and columns of the worksheet appear. Formulas are included to calculate values based on the parameters and assumptions specified for the worksheet.

In this book, the various blocks are placed on separate worksheets in a workbook.

The identification; map of workbook; and description, assumptions, and parameters blocks are placed on one worksheet. The worksheet model block is entered on a separate worksheet. Macros and menus related to macros are also placed on separate worksheets. Notice that the name of the map of worksheet block has been changed to map of workbook.

Example Problem

Suppose you are asked to create a worksheet for ABC Company that projects various budget items for the last three quarters of a year based on data from the first quarter. The information from the first quarter and the projections are as follows:

	1st Quarter	Projected Increases per Quarter
Sales	$60,000	2%
Salaries	35,000	(given below)
Rent	9,000	(constant for all periods)
Telephone	1,000	5%
Office Supplies	750	$50
Miscellaneous	1,000	3%

The salary amounts for each quarter are: $35,000; $35,500; $36,200; and $37,000.

You will create and print the worksheet model in the next chapter. In the rest of this chapter, you will create (1) the identification block, (2) a map of the workbook block, and (3) the description, assumptions, and parameters block. You place this information on the first worksheet of a workbook.

Prior to entering the data for the identification block, it is a good idea to place the name of the company at the beginning of the worksheet. Make sure you have a blank workbook on your screen. If not, close the current workbook and open a new workbook.

Click	on cell A1		***Activate***	*cell A1*
Type	ABC COMPANY		***Type***	*ABC COMPANY*
Click	the enter box ☑		***Press***	⏎Enter

In the identification block, you include the following items:

1. The name of the workbook owner.
2. The name of the person who developed the workbook.
3. The workbook user(s).
4. The date the workbook was completed.
5. The date the workbook was last revised.

To enter the data for the identification block:

Click	on cell A3		***Activate***	*cell A3*
Type	Identification:		***Type***	*Identification:*
Click	the enter box ☑		***Press***	⏎Enter
Click	on cell A4		***Press***	*the space bar twice*
Press	the space bar twice		***Type***	*Owner: Financial Planning Department*
Type	Owner: Financial Planning Department		***Press***	⏎Enter
Click	the enter box ☑		***Press***	*the space bar twice*
Click	on cell A5		***Type***	*Developer: Your name*
Press	the space bar twice		***Press***	⏎Enter
Type	Developer: Your name		***Press***	*the space bar twice*
Click	the enter box ☑		***Type***	*User: Marsha Thompson*
Click	on cell A6		***Press***	⏎Enter
Press	the space bar twice		***Press***	*the space bar twice*
Type	User: Marsha Thompson		***Type***	*Date: 9/14/94*
Click	the enter box ☑		***Press***	*the space bar 10 times*
Click	on cell A7		***Type***	*Revised: 4/3/95*
Press	the space bar twice		***Press***	⏎Enter *twice*
Type	Date: 9/14/94			

Press	the space bar 10 times
Type	Revised: 4/3/95
Click	the enter box ☑
Click	on cell A9

Cell A9 is the active cell. To enter the file name where the workbook will be stored:

Type	Workbook File: BUDGET	*Type*	*Workbook File: BUDGET*
Click	on cell A11	*Press*	⎗Enter *twice*

Cell A11 is the active cell. Your screen should look like Figure 3-2.

Figure 3-2

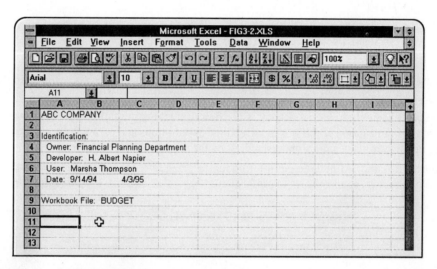

Now enter the information for the map of the workbook. This block shows the order of the various parts of the worksheet.

Use the information shown in Figure 3-3 to enter the data for the map of the workbook block. You will use cells A11 through A16.

Figure 3-3

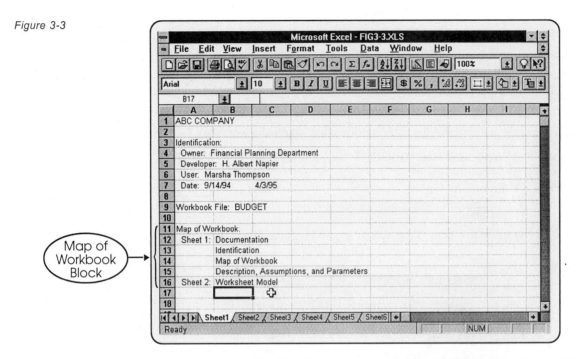

The next segment of the workbook is the description, assumptions, and parameters block. The inclusion of a brief description of the workbook and the assumptions and parameters used in the workbook simplifies the developer's and user's understanding of the workbook.

Figures 3-4 and 3-5 include the information to place on your worksheet for the description, assumptions, and parameters block. Enter the information shown in Figures 3-4 and 3-5.

Figure 3-4

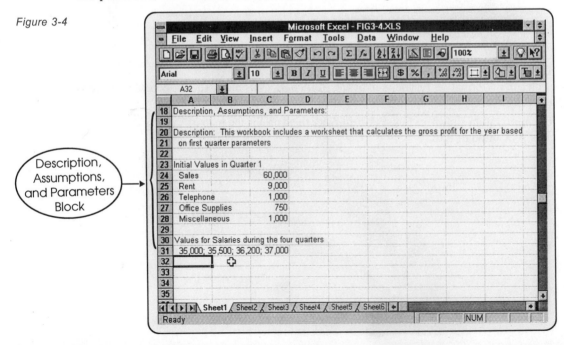

Figure 3-5

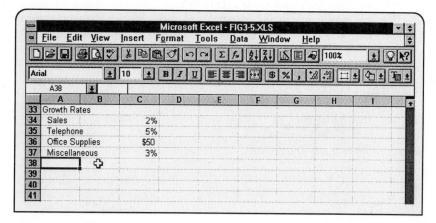

■ NAMING A SHEET TAB

Since various information is placed on different worksheets, it is a good idea to name the various sheets using the sheet tabs. To name the first sheet tab:

Double-click   the Sheet1 tab

The Rename Sheet dialog box appears. Your screen should look like Figure 3-6.

Figure 3-6

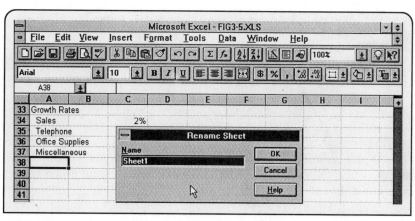

To name the Sheet1 tab:

Type	Documentation
Click	the OK command button

Type	*Documentation*
Press	⏎Enter

The last block is the worksheet model. This block includes the actual worksheet on which calculations are made. Various data and formulas are contained in this block. The worksheet model will be placed on the second worksheet in the workbook. You will create the worksheet model in the next chapter.

■ SAVING A WORKBOOK

To save a workbook:

Click	on cell A1		***Press***	Ctrl + Home
Click	the Save 🖫 button		***Press***	Alt
			Select	*File*
			Select	*Save*

When prompted for the file name:

Type	BUDGET		***Type***	*BUDGET*
Click	the OK command button		***Press***	↵Enter
Type	Budget Forecast Workbook in the Title text box		***Type***	*Budget Forecast Workbook in the Title text box*
Click	the OK command button		***Press***	↵Enter

SUMMARY

This chapter has described the basics of organizing workbooks and designing worksheets in a workbook. The five criteria for good worksheet design are accuracy, clarity, flexibility, efficiency, and auditability. The "block-structured" layout is a popular worksheet design. The primary blocks in the block-structured layout are the identification; macros and menus; map of the worksheet; description, assumptions, and parameters; and the worksheet model. For more detailed information on designing worksheets, see the references at the end of this chapter.

KEY CONCEPTS

Block-structured layout
Design criteria
Workbook layout
Worksheet design

EXERCISE 1

INSTRUCTIONS: Answer the following questions in the space provided:

1.   Briefly describe the following criteria for good worksheet design:

    a.   Accuracy _____

    _____

    b.   Clarity _____

    _____

    c.   Flexibility _____

    _____

    d.   Efficiency_____

    _____

    e.   Auditability_____

    _____

2.   Briefly describe the following blocks of a "block-structured" worksheet:

    a.   Identification block _____

    _____

    b.   Macros and menus block _____

    _____

    c.   Map of worksheet _____

    _____

    d.   Description, assumptions, and parameters _____

    _____

    e.   Worksheet model _____

    _____

EXERCISE 2

INSTRUCTIONS: Circle T if the statement is true and F if the statement is false.

T   F   1.   It is important to properly organize a workbook and design worksheets.

T   F   2.   Documenting the parameters and assumptions in a worksheet is important.

T   F   3.   You should not specify the name of the workbook developer.

T   F   4.   You should note the last date a workbook was changed on the second worksheet in a workbook.

T   F   5.   You cannot change sheet tab names.

References

Ronen, B., Palley, M. A., Lucas, Jr., H. C., "Spreadsheet Analysis and Design," Communications of the ACM, Volume 32, No. 1 (January 1989), pp. 84–93.

Thommes, M.C., Proper Spreadsheet Design, boyd & fraser publishing company, Danvers, MA, 1992.

CHAPTER FOUR

CREATING AND PRINTING WORKSHEETS IN A WORKBOOK

OBJECTIVES

In this chapter, you will learn to:

- Open a workbook file
- Enter worksheet titles, column titles, and row titles
- Expand the width of a column
- Enter assumptions
- Enter numbers, formulas, and copy information in a worksheet
- Select a numeric format for the data
- Insert blank rows in a worksheet
- Enter underlines and double underlines
- Correct rounding errors
- Prepare the printer, use print preview, and print a worksheet
- Use various numeric formats for a worksheet
- Change the assumptions to complete a "what-if" analysis
- Use formulas in Excel

■ CHAPTER OVERVIEW

One of the difficulties facing you as a beginning Excel user in learning to create a worksheet within a workbook is how to begin! Chapter 4 cites an example problem and provides step-by-step instructions for solving the problem with a properly designed Excel worksheet. While guiding you through the process for building the worksheet, the instructions detail Excel's capabilities as you need them.

The instructions address typical problems you may have as a beginning user, such as how to solve rounding problems and how to change the numeric display of a worksheet.

■ EXAMPLE PROBLEM

In Chapter 3, you entered some information about the worksheet model you will create in this chapter. The description of the problem is included here again for clarity.

Suppose you are asked to create a worksheet for ABC Company that projects various budget items for the last three quarters of a year based on data from the first quarter. The information from the first quarter and the projections are provided in the following table:

	1st Quarter	Projected Increases per Quarter
Sales	$60,000	2%
Salaries	35,000	(given below)
Rent	9,000	(constant for all periods)
Telephone	1,000	5%
Office Supplies	750	$50
Miscellaneous	1,000	3%

The salary amounts for each quarter are: $35,000; $35,500; $36,200; and $37,000.

Some common procedures for creating a worksheet using Excel are shown below:

> Entering worksheet titles for the worksheet
>
> Entering column titles for the worksheet
>
> Entering row titles for the worksheet
>
> Expanding the width of a column
>
> Entering assumptions
>
> Entering numbers, formulas, and copying information in a worksheet
>
> Selecting a format for the data
>
> Inserting blank rows in a worksheet
>
> Entering underlines and double underlines

In this chapter, you will create the worksheet model to complete the workbook you started in Chapter 3. Figures 4-1 and 4-2 display the completed worksheet model.

Figure 4-1

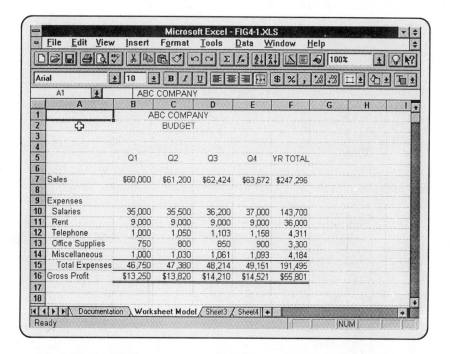

Figure 4-2

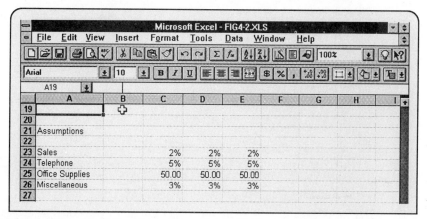

In This Book

The first three chapters of this book provided instructions for using a mouse and the keyboard for selecting commands from menus and other options. To save space, in the remainder of this book, it is assumed that you will use the mouse or keyboard, but only the instructions for using a mouse are provided.

■ OPENING A WORKBOOK FILE

To open the BUDGET workbook file:

Click   the Open ⬚ button on the Standard toolbar

The Open dialog box appears. To specify the file to open:

Click   the BUDGET file name in the File Name list
                             box

Click   the OK command button

Your screen should look like Figure 4-3.

Figure 4-3

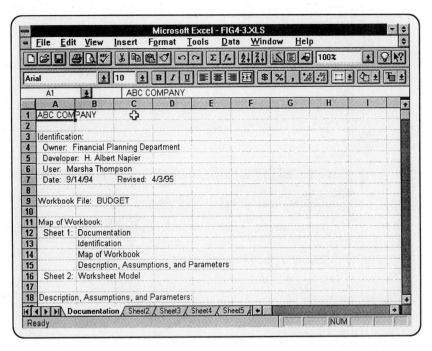

The BUDGET workbook is visible on your screen. Now, you can make changes or print the entire workbook or a selected worksheet. Any changes you make only affect the document on the screen, not the file on the disk. To save any changes to the BUDGET file, choose the Save command on the File menu. To save your changes to a separate file, choose the Save As command on the File menu.

To place the worksheet model on the second worksheet:

Click   the Sheet2 tab

Note that the second worksheet is now the current worksheet. The Sheet2 tab name is also bold.

To name the Sheet2 tab:

Double-click	the Sheet2 tab
Type	Worksheet Model
Click	the OK command button

Your screen should look like Figure 4-4.

Figure 4-4

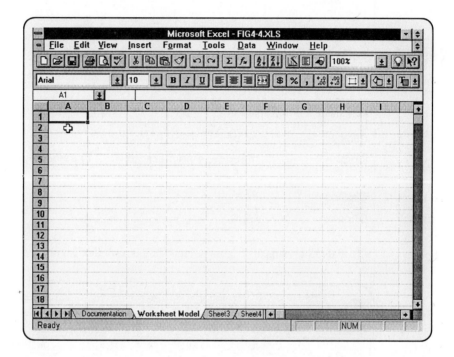

■ ENTERING WORKSHEET TITLES, COLUMN TITLES, AND ROW TITLES

Entering Worksheet Titles

Beginning in cell A1, you will enter the title of the worksheet. Make sure cell A1 is the active cell.
To enter the title:

Type	ABC COMPANY
Click	on cell A2
Type	BUDGET
Click	the enter box ☑

The worksheet title information appears in cells A1 and A2. Your screen should look like Figure 4-5.

Figure 4-5

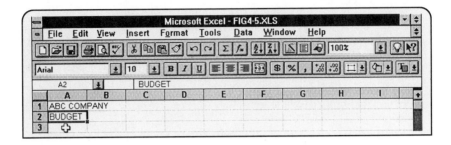

Centering Worksheet Titles

Now that you have entered the worksheet titles, you need to center them across the columns in the worksheet.

To center the worksheet title information:

Click	on cell A1
Drag	the mouse pointer to cell F2 to select cells A1:F2
Choose	Format
Choose	Cells

The Format Cells dialog box appears. Your screen should look like Figure 4-6.

Figure 4-6

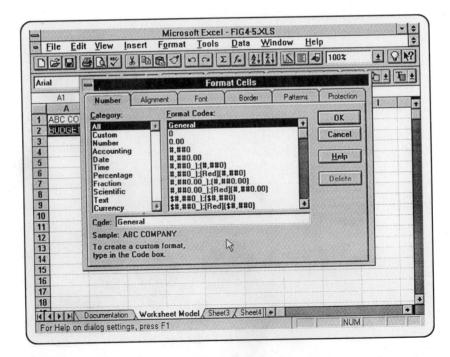

Click	the Alignment tab
Click	the Center across selection option button in the Horizontal group box
Click	the OK command button

The worksheet title information is now centered across the columns. After making cell A1 the active cell, your screen should look like Figure 4-7.

Figure 4-7

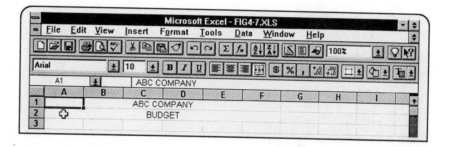

User Tip

Another method for centering text across a range of columns is to first select the range of cells. Then click the Center Across Columns 🔲 button on the Formatting toolbar.

Entering Column Titles

Before entering information in Excel, you can select a range of cells. When you type the text or data for a cell and click the enter box ✓ or press the ENTER key, Excel enters the text or data and moves the active cell to the next cell in the selected range.

User Tip

A **range** of cells is any block of adjoining cells. A range may consist of cells within several columns or rows, single columns or rows, or even a single cell.

You can select a range in one of two ways: by using the mouse to drag across the desired cells or by holding down the SHIFT key and selecting the cells with the arrow keys.

A range address consists of the cell addresses of two opposite corners of the range separated by a colon (:). Normally, the upper-left and lower-right cell addresses are used. For example, the address B2:C10 indicates a range of cells extending from row 2 through row 10 in columns B and C. If you think of the colon for the word "through," you would call the range of cells "B2 through C10." The address B1:B1 denotes a range consisting of the single cell B1.

Rather than use the specific cell addresses each time you refer to a range, you can create a range name. For example, you could create the range name, TEXT, for the range B2:C10. Then you can use the range name when referring to the range of cells B2:C10.

To select the cells for entering the column titles:

Move	the mouse pointer to cell B5
Drag	the mouse pointer to cell F5

To enter the column titles:

Type	Q1
Click	the enter box ☑
Type	Q2
Click	the enter box ☑
Type	Q3
Click	the enter box ☑
Type	Q4
Click	the enter box ☑
Type	YR TOTAL
Click	the enter box ☑

To deselect the cells at any time, you can click on a specific cell or press any arrow key.

Centering Column Titles

The column titles are left-aligned. To center the titles in the cells:

Select	cells B5:F5 (if necessary)
Choose	Format
Choose	Cells
Click	the Alignment tab (if necessary)
Click	the Center option button in the Horizontal group box
Click	the OK command button

After making cell A5 the active cell, your screen should look like Figure 4-8.

Figure 4-8

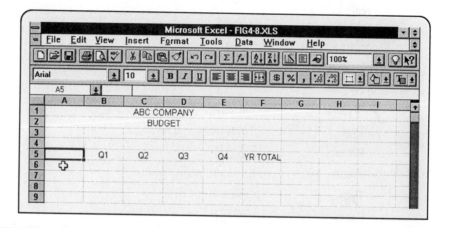

User Tip

An alternative method for centering text within cell(s) is to select the cell(s) and then click the Center ≣ button on the Formatting toolbar.

Entering Row Titles

In cells A7 through A15, enter the row titles that describe the contents of the rows. To select the cells to enter the row titles:

Move	the mouse pointer to cell A7
Drag	the mouse pointer to cell A15

User Tip
If you are using the mouse method, rather than clicking the enter box ☑, you can press the ENTER key.

To enter the row titles into cells A7 to A15:

Type	Sales
Press	⏎Enter
Type	Expenses
Press	⏎Enter
Press	the space bar twice
Type	Salaries
Press	⏎Enter
Press	the space bar twice
Type	Rent
Press	⏎Enter
Press	the space bar twice
Type	Telephone
Press	⏎Enter
Press	the space bar twice
Type	Office Supplies
Press	⏎Enter
Press	the space bar twice
Type	Miscellaneous
Press	⏎Enter
Press	the space bar four times
Type	Total Expenses
Press	⏎Enter
Type	Gross Profit
Press	⏎Enter

After making cell A6 the active cell, your worksheet should look like Figure 4-9.

Figure 4-9

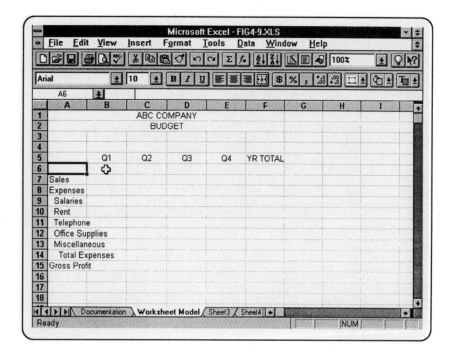

■ EXPANDING THE WIDTH OF A COLUMN

Notice that several row titles extend into column B. You must widen column A so that you can see all the row and column titles. To increase the width of column A:

Click   on the cell containing the longest row title in
                         column A

In this example, cell A14, Total Expenses, should be your active cell.

To expand the width of the column:

Choose   Format

Choose   Column

Choose   Width

The Column Width dialog box appears. Your screen should look like Figure 4-10.

Figure 4-10

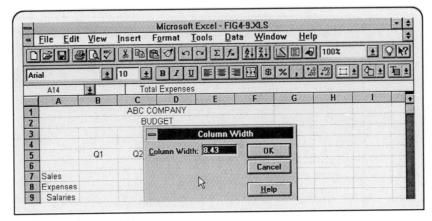

To specify the current column width:

Type 15

Click the OK command button

Because column A now occupies more space, column B has shifted to the right and part of column I no longer appears on the screen. Your screen should look like Figure 4-11.

Figure 4-11

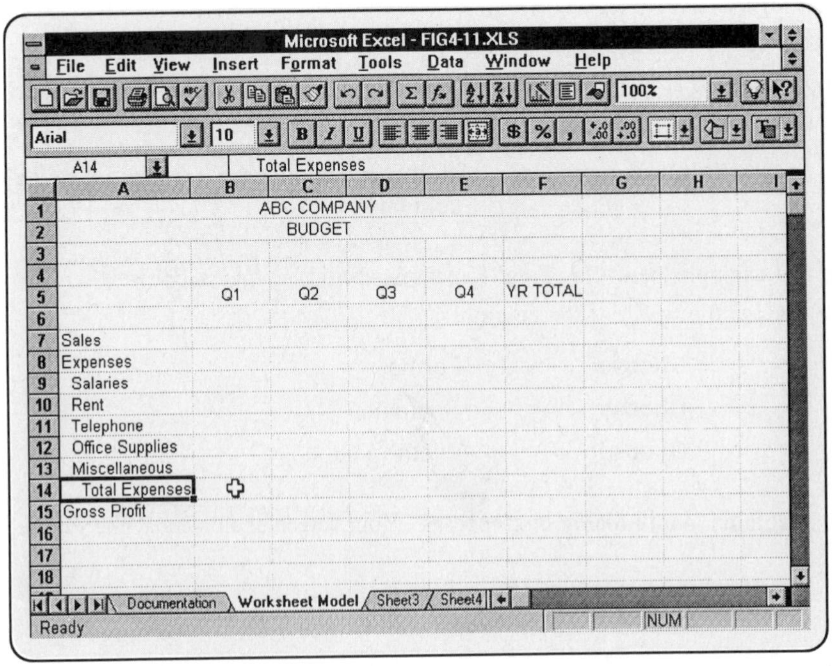

User Tip

An alternative method for expanding the width of a column is to move the mouse pointer to the boundary line between two column headings. A two-headed horizontal arrow appears. Press and hold the mouse button down.

Drag the two-headed arrow to the right of the longest data entry in the column. Notice as you drag the mouse that the column width in the reference area changes. When you release the mouse button, the column width has been changed.

In This Book

To choose a range of cells, you can move the mouse pointer to the first cell and then drag the mouse pointer to the last cell you wish to include in the range. Another method of selecting a range of cells is to make the first cell of the desired range the active cell. Then hold down a SHIFT key and press the appropriate arrow keys until the range is selected.

In the remainder of the book, you are asked to **select** a range of cells. You may use either method for specifying the range of cells.

User Tip

In Excel, dialog boxes are used to assist you in completing commands. Please choose the Print command on the File menu so the Print dialog box appears on your screen. There are several elements in this dialog box that are common to many Excel dialog boxes.

In the Print What group box, there are three **option buttons** to the left of the "Selection," "Selected Sheet(s)," and "Entire Workbook" options. Whenever these buttons appear, only one can be active in the box. In this example, the "Selected Sheet(s)" option button is selected.

You can choose the appropriate option button by clicking on the desired option button or by typing the underlined letter for the desired option. If you want to select an option button that is in a different box, you may need to hold down the ALT key and then press the underlined letter.

Two **text boxes** appear if you choose the "Page(s)" option button in the Page Range group box. These text boxes are used to indicate the first and last page to print.

Command buttons are rectangular buttons. In this dialog box, there are six command buttons: OK, Cancel, Page Setup, Print Preview, Printer Setup, and Help. Note than an ellipsis (...) appears at the end of the Page Setup command button. The ellipses indicate that another dialog box appears if that command button is chosen. To remove or clear a dialog box from your screen, you can click the Cancel command button or press the ESC key.

An alternative for moving between the various items in a dialog box is to press the TAB key.

■ ENTERING ASSUMPTIONS

Design Tip

Whenever you create a worksheet, you should include the assumptions you use in a separate part of the worksheet. If someone else looks at the worksheet, it is much easier for the person to determine how the values appearing in the worksheet are computed. "What-if" analysis is also easier when the assumptions for the worksheet are in a separate location. In this example, you will place the assumptions below the worksheet.

To enter the row titles for the assumptions:

Click	on cell A18
Type	Assumptions
Click	on cell A20

Cell A20 is the active cell. To enter the appropriate row titles in cells A20 through A23:

Select	cells A20:A23
Type	Sales
Press	[↵Enter]
Type	Telephone
Press	[↵Enter]
Type	Office Supplies
Press	[↵Enter]
Type	Miscellaneous
Press	[↵Enter]

After making cell A19 the active cell, your screen should look like Figure 4-12.

Figure 4-12

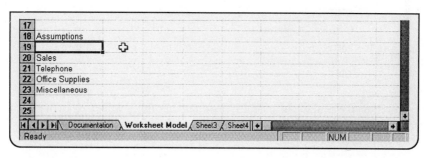

To input the assumed Sales growth rate for Quarters 2, 3, and 4 in columns C, D, and E:

Select	cells C20:E20
Type	.02
Press	[↵Enter]

Cell D20 is the active cell.

Type	.02
Press	[↵Enter]

When cell E20 is the active cell:

Type   .02
Click   the enter box ☑

The Sales growth rate is not placed in column B because the rate is not needed for the first quarter.

In This Book

To enter text or a number, you have been instructed to type the information and then click the enter box ☑ or press the ENTER key. For the remainder of the book, you are asked to enter the information. You may use either method of entering the text or number.

To input the Telephone, Office Supplies, and Miscellaneous expense rates for Q2:

Select   cells C21:C23
Enter   .05

The growth rate for Telephone expenses appears in cell C21. Cell C22 is the active cell.
To place the rate for Office Supplies in cell C22:

Enter   50

Cell C23 is the active cell. To input the Miscellaneous growth rate in cell C23:

Enter   .03

You will enter the remaining quarterly assumptions for Telephone, Office Supplies, and Miscellaneous expenses using a more efficient process in the next section. After making cell B21 the active cell, your screen should look like Figure 4-13.

Figure 4-13

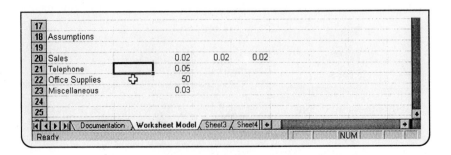

■ ENTERING NUMBERS, FORMULAS, AND COPYING INFORMATION IN A WORKSHEET[1]

To enter the Sales amount for the first quarter:

Click	on cell B7
Enter	60000

A formula is an effective way to compute values in Excel. Formulas may include cell addresses, range names, numbers, arithmetic operators, and parentheses.

These parts are included in a formula to define the calculations necessary to compute the value for a specific cell in a worksheet.

To enter the sales amount for the second quarter, you need to show a 2% increase over the value for Sales in the second quarter. The formula for Sales in the second quarter multiplies the Sales amount in the first quarter by 1.02 to show the 2% projected increase.

To make sure the active cell is the cell where the formula will be entered:

Click	on cell C7

Begin entering the formula:

Type	=

An equal sign (=) indicates that a formula is being created.

Click	on cell B7

Note that a moving border appears around the referenced cell B7.

Type	*

The asterisk (*) is the symbol for multiplication.

Type	(1+
Click	on cell C20
Type	)
Click	the enter box ☑

The number 61200 should now appear in cell C7. With cell C7 as the active cell, look at the formula bar. The formula =B7*(1+C20) is displayed as the formula used to calculate the number 61200 (refer to Figure 4-14).

---

[1]See the section at the end of this chapter for additional information on using formulas in Excel.

Figure 4-14

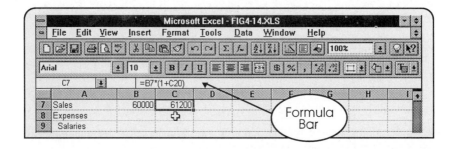

Design Tip

You can type a formula directly into a cell. For example, by typing =B7*(1+C20) in cell C7 and clicking the enter box ☑ or pressing the ENTER key you will obtain the same result. It is *best* to point to the cells when creating a formula because you tend to make fewer errors in specifying the formula.

The formulas in Excel are based on **relative cell location**. For example, the formula in cell C7, =B7*(1+C20), tells Excel to "multiply the contents of the cell immediately to the left of the formula location times the quantity 1 plus the number appearing 13 cells below the formula location." The Sales for Quarters 3 and 4 are also projected to increase from the previous quarter (the previous cell) by 2 percent. Therefore, the formula =B7*(1+C20) can be copied to cells D7 and E7 and adjusted to =C7*(1+D20) and =D7*(1+E20). The Copy and Paste commands on the Edit menu are used to copy the formulas.

Make sure cell C7 is the active cell.

| **Choose** | Edit |
| **Choose** | Copy |

Notice cell C7 is not only selected, but also has a moving border around it. Your screen should look like Figure 4-15.

Figure 4-15

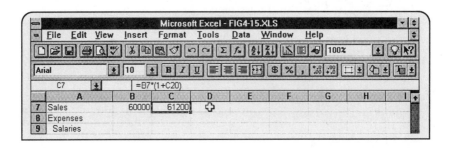

This command places the formula on the Windows "clipboard." To paste the formula from the clipboard to cells D7 and E7:

Select	cells D7:E7
Choose	Edit
Choose	Paste

The formula in cell C7 has been copied to cells D7 and E7 (Quarters 3 and 4).

After making cell F7 the active cell, your screen should look like Figure 4-16.

Figure 4-16

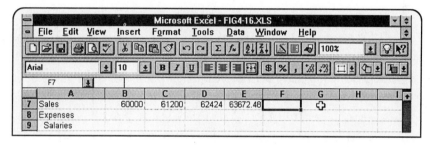

Notice the moving border around cell C7 did not disappear. To remove the moving border, press the ESC key.

User Tip

An alternative method for copying the contents of a cell or range of cells to another cell or range of cells is to use the Copy 🖺 and Paste 🖺 buttons on the Standard toolbar. This procedure is demonstrated when you copy the Telephone, Office Supplies, and Miscellaneous expense assumptions.

To copy the assumptions for Telephone, Office Supplies, and Miscellaneous expense categories from Quarter 2 to Quarters 3 and 4:

Select	cells C21:C23

To copy the cells to the clipboard:

Click	the Copy 🖺 button on the Standard toolbar

Your screen should look like Figure 4-17.

Figure 4-17

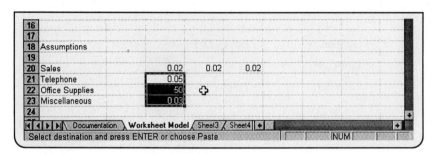

To paste the contents from the keyboard to the proper cells:

> **Select**   cells D21:E23
>
> **Choose**   the Paste 📋 button on the Standard toolbar

The expense assumptions have been copied. After you make cell F21 the active cell and press ESC to remove the moving border, your screen should look like Figure 4-18.

Figure 4-18

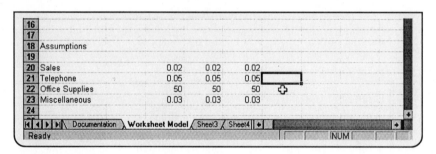

To input the data for Salaries:

> **Select**   cells B9:E9
>
> **Enter**   35000

Cell C9 is the active cell. To enter the salary amounts for Quarters 2, 3, and 4:

> **Enter**   35500
>
> **Enter**   36200
>
> **Enter**   37000

After making cell B8 the active cell, your screen should look like Figure 4-19.

Figure 4-19

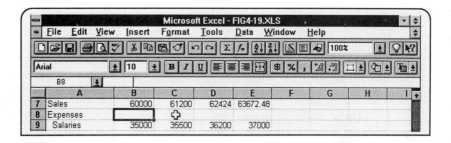

User Tip

An alternative method for copying the contents of a cell or range of cells to another location on a worksheet is to use AutoFill. This procedure is demonstrated when you enter the Rent data. AutoFill is not available with the keyboard.

To input the data for Rent:

Click	on cell B10
Enter	9000

To copy the contents of cell B10 to cells C10 through E10:

Move	the mouse pointer to the fill handle in the bottom right corner of cell B10. A "+" appears.
Drag	the fill handle to cell E10

The number 9000 should now be copied to cells C10 through E10. After making cell A10 the active cell, your screen should look like Figure 4-20.

Figure 4-20

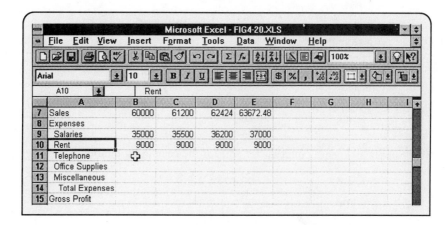

To input the Telephone expense data for the first quarter:

Click	on cell B11
Enter	1000

You can enter the following formula to indicate that Telephone expenses will increase by 5 percent for the second quarter:

Click	on cell C11
Type	=
Click	on cell B11 (Telephone expense for Quarter 1)
Type	*(1+
Click	on cell C21 (Telephone expense growth rate)
Type	)
Click	the enter box ☑

The number 1050 should appear in cell C11 and the formula =B11*(1+C21) should appear in the formula bar. Your screen should look like Figure 4-21. The formulas for Quarters 3 and 4 are completed later in this chapter.

Figure 4-21

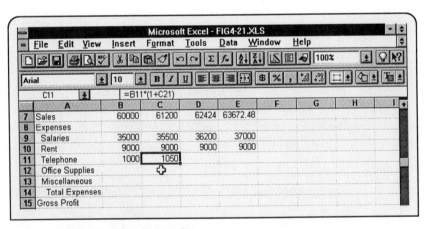

To input the data for Office Supplies for the first quarter:

Click	on cell B12
Enter	750

Office Supplies expenses increase by $50 for the remaining quarters. To enter the appropriate formula:

Click	on cell C12
Type	=

Click	on cell B12
Type	+
Click	on cell C22
Click	the enter box ✓

The number 800 appears in cell C12. The formula =B12+C22 is displayed in the formula bar. Your screen should look like Figure 4-22. The formulas for Quarters 3 and 4 are completed later in this section.

Figure 4-22

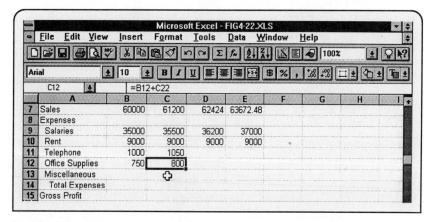

To input the data for Miscellaneous expenses in the first quarter:

| **Click** | on cell B13 |
| **Enter** | 1000 |

To enter the formula that indicates Miscellaneous expenses are to increase by 3 percent:

Click	on cell C13
Type	=
Click	on cell B13
Type	*(1+
Click	on cell C23
Type	)
Click	the enter box ✓

The number 1030 appears in cell C13. The formula =B13*(1+C23) is displayed in the formula bar. Your screen should look like Figure 4-23. The formulas for Quarters 3 and 4 are completed later in this section.

Figure 4-23

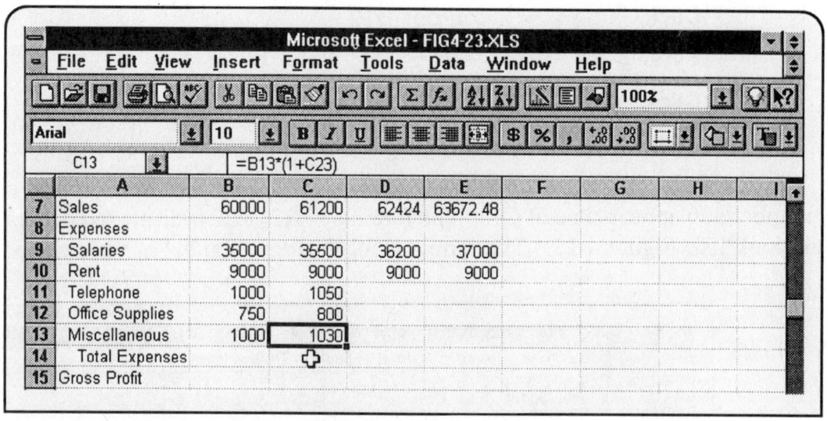

To copy the formulas for Telephone, Office Supplies, and Miscellaneous in Quarter 2 to Quarters 3 and 4:

Select   cells C11:C13

Move   the mouse pointer to the fill handle in the
              bottom right corner of cell C13

Drag   the mouse pointer to cell E13

The formulas in cells C11 through C13 that project Telephone, Office Supplies, and Miscellaneous expenses have been copied to cells D11 through E13. After making cell F11 the active cell, your screen should look like Figure 4-24.

Figure 4-24

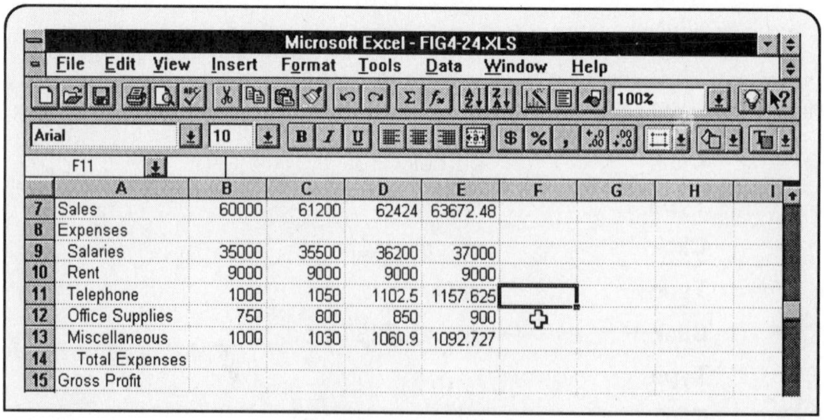

You now need to sum the quarterly values for the various items to obtain Total Expenses for the first quarter. Excel has a function that makes it easy to sum the expense values. The general format for the sum function is:

=SUM(first cell:last cell)

Note that a range of cells is specified within the set of parentheses. By placing the = character prior to the word SUM, you have indicated that you want to use the **SUM** function. Other functions available in Excel are discussed in Chapter 15.

To enter the SUM function for calculating Total Expenses in the first quarter:

Click	on cell B14
Type	=SUM(
Move	the mouse pointer to cell B9 (the first item in column B to include in the total)
Drag	the mouse pointer to cell B13
Type	)
Click	the enter box ☑

The number 46750 appears in cell B14. The formula =SUM(B9:B13) is displayed in the formula bar. Your screen should look like Figure 4-25.

Figure 4-25

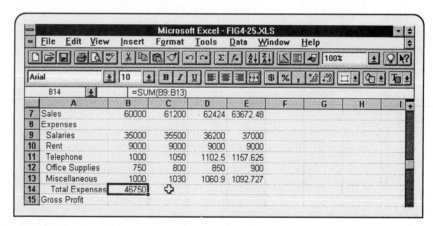

To compute Gross Profit, you must create a formula that subtracts Total Expenses from Sales.

Click	on cell B15
Type	=
Click	on cell B7 (Sales)
Type	-
Click	on cell B14 (Total Expenses)
Click	the enter box ☑

The number 13250 should appear in cell B15. The formula =B7-B14 is displayed in the formula bar.

To copy the formulas for Total Expenses and Gross Profit to the remaining quarters:

Select	cells B14:B15
Move	the mouse pointer to the fill handle box in cell B15
Drag	the fill handle box to cell E15

After making cell F14 the active cell, your screen should look like Figure 4-26.

Figure 4-26

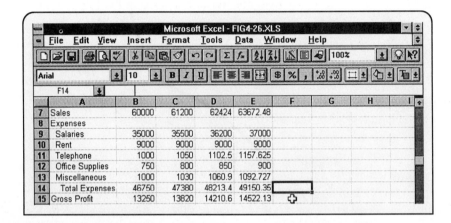

User Tip

An alternative method for summing the contents of adjoining cells is to use the AutoSum $\boxed{\Sigma}$ button. The process for using this button is illustrated when you calculate the total Sales for the year.

To compute the total Sales for the year:

Click	on cell F7
Click	the AutoSum $\boxed{\Sigma}$ button
Click	the enter box $\boxed{\checkmark}$

When you click the AutoSum $\boxed{\Sigma}$ button, a suggested range is displayed in the formula bar. You accept the suggested sum by clicking the enter box $\boxed{\checkmark}$.

The number 247296.5 appears in cell F7. The formula =SUM(B7:E7) appears in the formula bar.

User Tip

Another method for copying the contents of one or more cells to another cell or range of cells is to use the menu bar associated with the alternate mouse button. Select the cell or range of cells to be copied. Click the alternate mouse button and choose Copy. Then select the cell or cells to which the information is to be copied. Click the alternate mouse button and choose Paste.

To copy the SUM formula in cell F7 to the appropriate rows below the Sales row:

Click	on cell F7
Click	the alternate mouse button
Choose	Copy
Select	cells F9:F15
Click	the alternate mouse button
Choose	Paste

The formula =SUM(B7:E7) has been copied from cells F9 through F15. After making cell G9 the active cell, your screen should look like Figure 4-27.

Figure 4-27

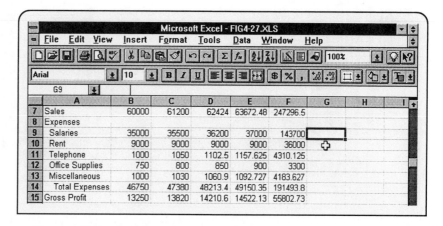

■ SELECTING A FORMAT FOR THE DATA

To format the entire worksheet, you must first select the entire worksheet. To select the entire worksheet:

Move	the mouse pointer to the Select All ▭ button (the button at the intersection of the column and row headings)
Click	the mouse button

> *User Tip*
>
> An alternative method for selecting the entire worksheet is to press CTRL+SHIFT+SPACE BAR.

To choose the appropriate format (insert commas and include no decimal places):

Choose	Format
Choose	Cells
Click	the Number tab

The Category and Format Codes list boxes appear on your screen, as Figure 4-28 shows.

Figure 4-28

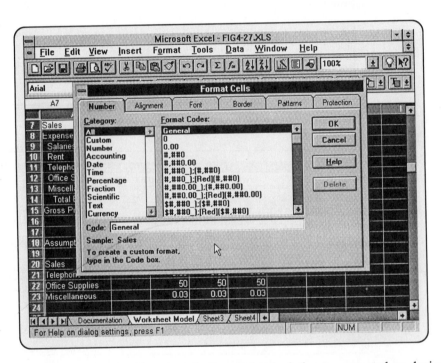

To change the format code from General to the format that includes commas and no decimal places:

Click	the Number choice in the Category list box
Click	the #,##0 code in the Format Codes list box
Click	the OK command button

After making cell A6 the active cell, your screen should look like Figure 4-29.

Figure 4-29

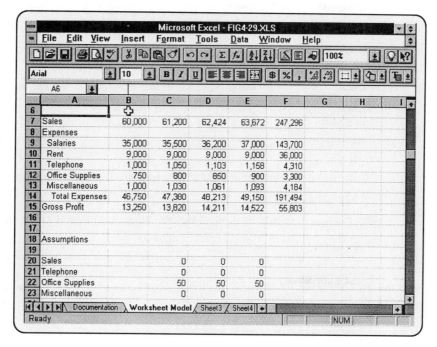

Notice that the various growth rates no longer have decimal places on the worksheet. This is because the previous command indicated that the format for all numbers does not include any characters to the right of the decimal point.

To have the proper format for the Sales and Telephone growth rate assumptions, you must format the range of cells from C20 through E21 again and include percent signs.

Select	cells C20:E21
Choose	Format
Choose	Cells
Click	the Number tab (if necessary)
Click	the Percentage choice in the Category list box
Click	the 0% code in the Format Codes list box (if necessary)
Click	the OK command button

To have the proper format for the Office Supplies growth rates, you must format the range of cells C22 through E22 again.

Select	cells C22:E22
Choose	Format

Choose	Cells
Click	the Number tab (if necessary)
Click	the Number choice in the Category list box (if necessary)
Click	the 0.00 code in the Format Codes list box
Click	the OK command button

> *User Tip*
>
> An alternative method for increasing the number of decimal places in a cell(s) is to select the cell(s) and then click the Increase Decimal button until the proper number of decimal places appears. To decrease the number of decimal places in a cell(s), select the cell(s) and then click the Decrease Decimal button until the appropriate number of decimal places appears.

To have the proper format for the Miscellaneous growth rate, you must format the range of cells C23 through E23 again.

Select	cells C23:E23
Choose	Format
Choose	Cells
Click	the Number tab (if necessary)
Click	the Percentage choice in the Category list box
Click	the 0% code in the Format Codes list box (if necessary)
Click	the OK command button

After making cell A19 the active cell, your screen should look like Figure 4-30.

Figure 4-30

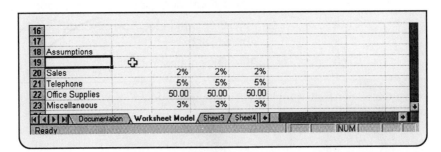

Before proceeding, make sure cell A1 on the Budget Worksheet Model is the active cell.

Notice that rounding errors occur (e.g., Sales of 247,296 minus Total Expenses of 191,494 should equal 55,802 rather than 55,803). The rounding error occurred because the numbers are *formatted* to *show* 0 decimal places on the worksheet, but the *values* in the cells are not truly *rounded* to 0 decimal places. Rounding errors are resolved later in this chapter.

■ INSERTING BLANK ROWS IN A WORKSHEET

To insert a blank row between Sales and Expenses:

Click	on cell A8
Choose	Insert
Choose	Rows

Note that the entire row does not have to be highlighted. Also notice that the active cell does not have to be in column A to insert rows; it can be in any column. Your screen should look like Figure 4-31.

Figure 4-31

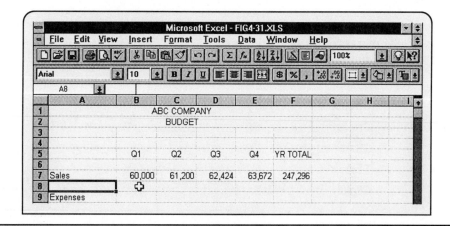

> *User Tip*
> An alternative method for inserting a row using the mouse is to click the row number where you want to insert a row to select an entire row. Then choose the Rows command on the Insert menu.

The worksheet formulas and values remain correct and are adjusted to the new location. For example, the formula for Quarter 2's Gross Profit in cell C16 has been changed from =B7-B14 to =B7-B15.

If you insert too many rows, you can delete a row or range of rows. You use the Delete command on the Edit menu to delete rows.

■ ENTERING UNDERLINES AND DOUBLE UNDERLINES

To underline the entries in the Miscellaneous and Total Expenses rows:

Select	cells B14:F15
Choose	Format
Choose	Cells
Click	the Border tab

The Border and Style group boxes appear. To place the underlines on the worksheet:

Click	the Bottom box in the Border group box until a line pattern appears
Click	the OK command button
Click	on cell A14

Note that the bottom border of cells B14 through F15 are darker than the other cell borders. Your screen should look like Figure 4-32.

Figure 4-32

11	Rent	9,000	9,000	9,000	9,000	36,000
12	Telephone	1,000	1,050	1,103	1,158	4,310
13	Office Supplies	750	800	850	900	3,300
14	Miscellaneous	1,000	1,030	1,061	1,093	4,184
15	Total Expenses	46,750	47,380	48,213	49,150	191,494
16	Gross Profit	13,250	13,820	14,211	14,522	55,803
17						
18						

Documentation \ **Worksheet Model** / Sheet3 / Sheet4
Ready   NUM

Now place double underlines below the Gross Profit cells.

To make the bottom border of cells B16 through F16 appear as double underlines:

Select	cells B16:F16
Choose	Format
Choose	Cells
Click	the Bottom box until a line pattern appears
Click	the double underline box in the Style group box
Click	the OK command button

After making cell A18 the active cell, your screen should like Figure 4-33.

Figure 4-33

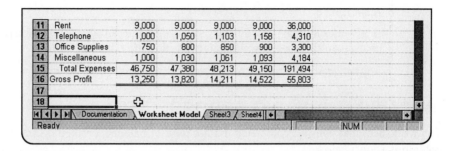

User Tip

Another method for adding a solid border along the bottom edge of a cell or range of cells is to first select the cell or range of cells. Then click the down arrow on the Borders ⊞▾ button on the Formatting toolbar and choose the desired border.

To place an additional two blank rows between the Assumptions and the Gross Profits:

Select	the row headings A19:A20
Choose	Insert
Choose	Rows

After making cell A27 the active cell, your screen should look like Figure 4-34.

Figure 4-34

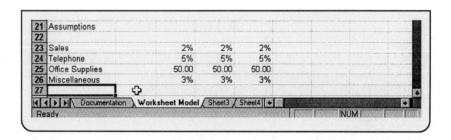

To save the completed worksheet:

Click	on cell A1
Choose	File
Choose	Save

Since the BUDGET file already exists on the disk, the file is replaced by the current workbook.

> *User Tip*
>
> If a workbook has already been saved to a file, an alternative method for saving changes to the current workbook is to click the Save 🖫 button.

■ CORRECTING ROUNDING ERRORS

The worksheet that you just completed did not **foot**, or balance, correctly. The result in the YR TOTAL column is shown below:

Sales	247,296	
Total Expenses	-191,494	
Gross Profit	55,803	(does not foot correctly)

When you use multiplication, division, or exponents in a formula, you can use the ROUND function to round a number to a specific number of decimal places. Otherwise, Excel uses the "hidden" decimal place in computation that results in rounding errors. The following steps can be used for rounding the appropriate formulas where necessary in this example.

Note that you should *immediately* use the ROUND function when creating formulas rather than editing them at a later time. This example was completed differently to show the results of *not* using the ROUND function.

The formulas for the Sales, Telephone, and Miscellaneous expenses use multiplication, so they need to be edited to use the ROUND function.

The format of the ROUND function is:

=ROUND(number or formula, number of digits to round to)

Both the number or formula and the number of digits to round to must be specified.

Sales will be the first formula edited. The formula for projecting Sales for the fourth quarter is =D7*(1+E23). The value of the computation is 63372.48.

See a summary of the differences below:

Formula	Value	Appearance Using #,##0 Format Code	Number Used in Computation
+D7*(1+E23)	63672.48	63,672	63672.48
=ROUND(D7*(1+E23),0)	63672	63,672	63,672

The ROUND function may not remove rounding errors properly for all situations. You may need to "plug" a number to obtain the desired results.

To round the Sales projections to 0 decimal places:

Click	on cell C7
Type	=ROUND(
Click	on cell B7
Type	*(1+
Click	on cell C23
Type	),

To indicate zero decimal places:

Type	0
Type	)
Click	the enter box ☑

The formula =ROUND(B7*(1+C23),0) appears in the formula bar for cell C7. The formula =B7*(1+C23) is rounded to 0 decimal places. Your screen should look like Figure 4-35.

Figure 4-35

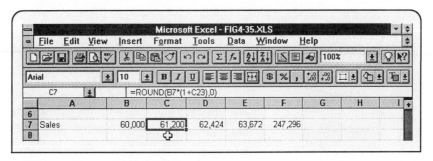

To copy the formula to the other Sales cells:

Move	the mouse pointer to the fill handle in cell C7
Drag	the fill handle to cell E7

The projections for Sales in Quarters 3 and 4 are now rounded to 0 decimal places.

The second set of formulas you need to round is for Telephone expenses. The formula for Telephone expenses in the second quarter is =B12*(1+C24). To round the Telephone expenses to 0 decimal places:

Click	on cell C12

Rather than typing the formula again, use a shortcut method to edit the current formula.

Move	the mouse pointer to the formula bar (it becomes an "I-beam") and move the I-beam to the right of the = sign
Click	the mouse button
Type	ROUND(
Move	the I-beam to the right of the)
Click	the mouse button
Type	,0)
Click	the enter box ☑

The formula =ROUND(B12*(1+C24),0) appears in the formula bar for cell C12.

To copy the formula to the other Telephone expenses cells:

Move	the mouse pointer to the fill handle in cell C12
Drag	the fill handle to cell E12

Telephone expenses are now rounded to 0 decimal places.

The final set of formulas is for Miscellaneous expenses. The formula for Miscellaneous expenses in the second quarter is =B14*(1+C26). To round the Miscellaneous expenses to 0 decimal places:

Click	on cell C14
Move	the mouse pointer to the formula bar until it is an "I-beam") and move to the right of the = sign
Click	the mouse button
Type	ROUND(
Move	the I-beam to the right of the)
Click	the mouse button
Type	,0)
Click	the enter box ☑

The formula =ROUND(B14*(1+C26),0) appears in the formula bar for cell C14.

To copy the formula to the remaining Miscellaneous expenses cells:

Move	the mouse pointer to the fill handle in cell C14
Drag	the fill handle to cell E14

The projections for Miscellaneous expenses are rounded to 0 decimal places. The rounding errors in the worksheet have been corrected. The corrected results in the YR TOTAL column are shown below:

Sales	247,296
Total Expenses	-191,495
Gross Profit	55,801

After making cell A1 active, your screen should look like Figure 4-36.

Figure 4-36

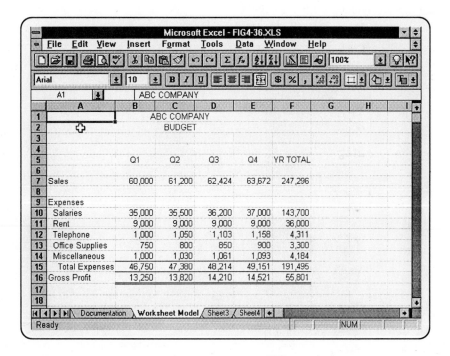

Save the workbook to the BUDGET file by clicking the Save 🖫 button or by selecting the Save command on the File menu.

■ PREPARING THE PRINTER, USING PRINT PREVIEW, AND PRINTING THE WORKSHEET

The following steps outline the process for printing the worksheet.

Preparing the Printer for Use

Make sure your printer is on and the paper is in the proper position.

Printing the Worksheet

You use the Print command on the File menu to print a worksheet. If you do not define the range of cells to print, Excel prints the selected worksheet. In this case, the Worksheet Model is selected.

To preview the information before printing it:

Choose	File
Choose	Print Preview

Your screen should look like Figure 4-37.

Figure 4-37

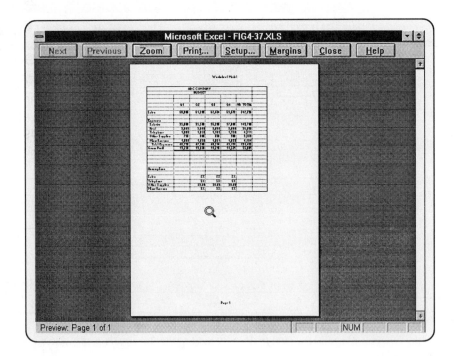

To close the preview screen:

Click	the Close command button

To print the Worksheet Model:

Choose	File
Choose	Print

The Print dialog box appears on your screen. To accept the default settings:

Click	the OK command button

Your printout should look like Figure 4-38.

Figure 4-38

ABC COMPANY					
BUDGET					
	Q1	Q2	Q3	Q4	YR TOTAL
Sales	60,000	61,200	62,424	63,672	247,296
Expenses					
Salaries	35,000	35,500	36,200	37,000	143,700
Rent	9,000	9,000	9,000	9,000	36,000
Telephone	1,000	1,050	1,103	1,158	4,311
Office Supplies	750	800	850	900	3,300
Miscellaneous	1,000	1,030	1,061	1,093	4,184
Total Expenses	46,750	47,380	48,214	49,151	191,495
Gross Profit	13,250	13,820	14,210	14,521	55,801
Assumptions					
Sales		2%	2%	2%	
Telephone		5%	5%	5%	
Office Supplies		50.00	50.00	50.00	
Miscellaneous		3%	3%	3%	

The worksheet tab name appears at the top of the page and the page number appears at the bottom. The worksheet is printed with gridlines. The Page Setup command on the File menu can be used to change the appearance of the worksheet when it is printed. This command is covered in more detail in Chapter 6.

To print the entire workbook:

Choose	File
Choose	Print
Click	the Entire Workbook option button in the Print What group box
Click	the OK command button

Note that each worksheet is printed on a separate page. The appropriate worksheet tab name appears at the top of each page. The pages are numbered consecutively beginning with the first page.

User Tip

An alternative method for previewing or printing the current worksheet is to select the appropriate worksheet and then click the Print Preview 🔍 button or the Print 🖨 button on the Standard toolbar.

In some situations, you may want to change the **font** of your text or **shade** some cells when a worksheet is printed. See Chapter 5 for instructions on improving the appearance of a worksheet.

■ USING VARIOUS NUMERIC FORMATS FOR THE WORKSHEET

In this section, you learn how to use some of the other available format specifications.

Formatting a Portion of the Worksheet with Dollar Signs

It is assumed that the Worksheet Model is displayed on your screen. If it is not, open the BUDGET workbook file and click the Worksheet Model sheet tab.

To change the format of some of the numbers in the worksheet so that dollar signs are added and two decimal places are shown:

Select	cells B7:F16
Choose	Format
Choose	Cells
Click	the Number tab
Click	the Currency choice in the Category list box
Click	the $#,##0.00_);($#,##0.00) code in the Format Codes list box
Click	the OK command button

After making cell B6 the active cell, your screen should look like Figure 4-39.

Figure 4-39

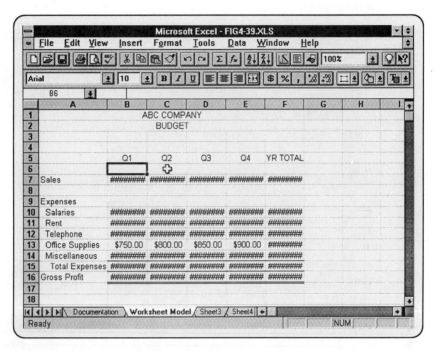

Notice that # signs fill some of the cells in the worksheet instead of numbers. Due to the addition of a dollar sign, a period, and two decimal places to each cell containing a number, some of the columns are not wide enough to display numbers. Sometimes, # signs may appear in only one or two cells in a column, rather than throughout the entire worksheet. The columns need to be widened for you to see the contents of the cell(s) containing # signs.

First, you must select the columns:

Move	the mouse pointer to the column B heading
Drag	the mouse pointer to column F

Then, you widen the columns:

Choose	Format
Choose	Column
Choose	Width
Type	12 in the Column Width text box
Click	the OK command button

The column width for columns B through F is now 12. After making cell A1 the active cell, your screen should look like Figure 4-40.

Figure 4-40

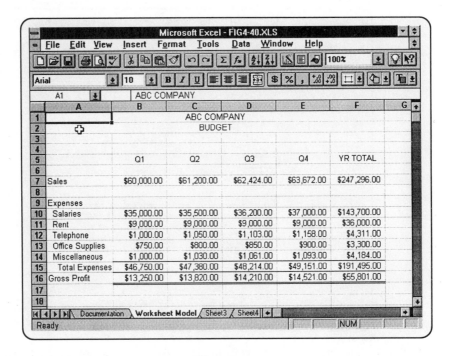

Close the workbook document. Do not save any changes.

Using More Than One Numeric Format in a Worksheet

In this exercise, you will alter the Worksheet Model so that only the Sales and Gross Profit rows of the worksheet display dollar signs.

Open the BUDGET workbook file and click the Worksheet Model sheet tab.

Before formatting the Sales and Gross Profit rows, you must select the appropriate cells:

Select	cells B7:F7
Move	the mouse pointer to cell B16
Hold down	the Ctrl key
Select	cells B16:F16

Note that two nonadjoining ranges have been selected.

To format the selected cells:

Choose	Format
Choose	Cells

Click	the Number tab (if necessary)
Click	the Currency choice in the Category list box
Click	the $#,##0_);$#,##0) code in the Format Codes list box (if necessary)
Click	the OK command button

Note that when you selected the $#,##0_);($#,##0) format code the "_" is for allowing a space to include a ")" to indicate a number is negative. Since the numbers in cells B7 through F7 and B16 through F16 are positive, a blank space appears to the right of the last digit in each number.

The numbers in cells B10 through F15 do not include a blank space to the right of the last digit. To place a blank space to the right of each number so the numbers align properly with the numbers in the Sales and Gross Profit rows, you must choose a new format code.

To format the numbers in cells B10 through F15 so that a blank will appear when a number is positive and a ")" will appear to the right of the last digit:

Select	cells B10:F15
Choose	Format
Choose	Cells
Click	the Number choice in the Category list box (if necessary)
Click	the #,##0_);(#,##0) choice in the Format Codes list box
Click	the OK command button

After making cell A1 the active cell, your screen should look like Figure 4-41.

Figure 4-41

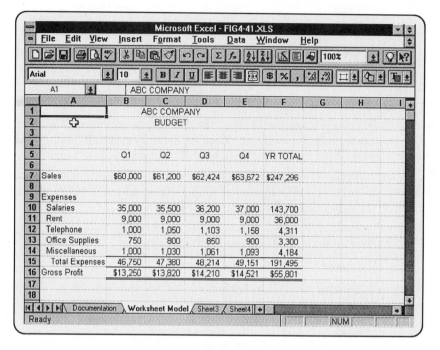

The dollar signs in the Currency format do not align with each other in a column; the dollars signs are placed flush to the formatted number. If the dollar signs must be aligned, you can select an appropriate format code from the Accounting category.

Save the workbook to the BUDGET file by clicking the Save button or by choosing the Save command on the File menu.

■ CHANGING THE ASSUMPTIONS TO COMPLETE A "WHAT-IF" ANALYSIS

One advantage of using Excel is the ability to change the assumptions and see the impact of the changes on other values in the worksheet. For example, suppose you show your supervisor the BUDGET worksheet results. Your supervisor may then ask some "what-if" questions and request that you complete some further analysis.

Suppose you are asked to determine the impact on Gross Profit if the growth rates for Sales are 5%, 9%, and 6% in Quarters 2 through 4, respectively.

To place the new growth rates on your worksheet:

Select	cells C23:E23
Enter	.05
Enter	.09
Enter	.06

Your worksheet is recalculated to reflect the new growth rates each time you change one of them. You can now see the new values for Gross Profit that were calculated using these new assumptions. If desired, you can change some of the other assumptions. After making cell A1 the active cell, your screen should look like Figure 4-42.

Figure 4-42

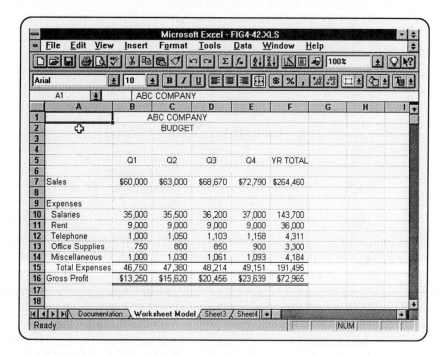

Close the workbook document. Do not save any changes.

■ USING FORMULAS IN EXCEL

Excel allows the use of formulas to perform operations such as addition and subtraction. This section discusses the types of formulas and the order in which operations occur in formulas.

Types of Formulas

The three types of formulas that can be entered into a cell in Excel are arithmetic, text, and comparison.

Arithmetic Formulas

Arithmetic formulas are used to calculate numeric values using arithmetic operators such as + and -. For example, if the formula =A3-10 appears in cell B5, then the number 10 is subtracted from the number appearing in cell A3.

Text Formulas

Text formulas are used to calculate labels using the text operator (&). For example, if the text formula =C5&"Expenses" appears in cell K7, the resulting text appearing in cell K7 will combine the data appearing in cell C5 with the text Expenses.

Comparison Formulas

Comparison formulas are used to compare values in two or more cells using comparison operators such as < and >. Depending on the result of a comparison formula, a "TRUE" or "FALSE" appears in the cell in which the comparison is made. For example, if the formula =C3<=25000 appears in cell D3, the text "TRUE" will appear in cell D3 whenever the value in cell C3 is less than or equal to 25000. Otherwise, the text "FALSE" is placed in cell D3.

Operators and Order of Precedence

Excel uses various operators in formulas to indicate arithmetic operations. Listed below are the mathematical operators allowed in Excel. The operators are listed in the order that operations are completed.

Operator(s)	Definition(s)
- +	Negative, Positive
^	Exponentiation
* /	Multiplication, Division
+ -	Addition, Subtraction

The operations higher on the list are performed before the operations lower on the list. For example, if the arithmetic formula =10+5^2 is used in cell A5, the result that appears in cell A5 is 35 (10 + 25 (5 squared)), not 225 (15 raised to the power of two).

Excel can tell the difference between a + or - sign that means a positive or negative number as opposed to the + or - sign meaning addition or subtraction. For example, if the formula =10/-5+10 appears in cell B8, the result that appears in the cell is 8 (-2+10), not 2 (10/5).

Multiplication and division operations are performed before addition and subtraction. For example, if cell C8 contains the formula =7-3/2, the value in cell C8 is 5.5 (7-(3/2)), not 2 ((7-3)/2).

You can change the order in which operations are completed by using sets of parentheses. If more than one set of parentheses is included in a formula, Excel begins with the innermost set of parentheses and proceeds to the outermost set of parentheses. For example, suppose the formula =(10/(2+3))*4 is used for cell E1; the result in cell E1 is 8.

The AND, OR, and NOT operators take precedence to all other operators. These operators are discussed in Chapter 13.

SUMMARY

Creating worksheets is faster and more effective using a software package like Excel than preparing a worksheet by hand. You can create formulas and include values that can be copied. Inserting and deleting rows and columns with Excel commands is easy. A saved worksheet is simple to edit later. These are just a few of the advantages of the Excel software package.

KEY CONCEPTS

Aligning information
Assumptions
AutoFill
AutoSum Σ button
Cancel box
Center ≡ button
Center Across Columns 🔳 button
Clipboard
Command buttons
Copy 📑 button
Edit Copy
Edit Delete
Edit Paste
Enter box ✔
File Close
File Open
File Print
File Print Preview
File Save
File Save As
Format Cells Alignment
Format Cells Border

Format Cells Number
Format Cells Number Currency
Format Cells Number Percentage
Format Column Width
Formula
Insert Rows
Open 📂 button
Option buttons
Paste 📋 button
Print 🖨 button
Print Preview 📖 button
Range
Relative cell location
Replacing a workbook file
ROUND function
Save 💾 button
Saving a workbook
Select All ▦ button
SUM function
Text boxes

EXERCISE 1

INSTRUCTIONS: Circle T if the statement is true and F if the statement is false.

T F 1. One way to correct data is to make the cell containing the incorrect data the active cell. Then retype the data correctly and click the enter box ✔ or press the ENTER key to enter the correction.

T F 2. The formula SUM(A1:A7) will add the data in cells A1 through A7.

T F 3. To round a number to two decimal places, you can use the Cells command on the Format menu.

T F 4. The Close command on the File menu erases the workbook currently in use from the main memory of your computer.

T F 5. You must specify a print range before you can print a worksheet.

T F 6. The = sign must precede functions such as the SUM and ROUND functions.

T   F   7.   Excel automatically saves changes that are made to a worksheet in the workbook document on a disk.

T   F   8.   Use the Open command on the File menu to look at a previously saved file.

T   F   9.   "BUDGET 1" is an acceptable file name.

T   F   10.   The letter "X" is the symbol for multiplication in Excel.

EXERCISE 2

INSTRUCTIONS: Explain a typical situation when the following items are used in Excel:

Problem 1:   File Save

Problem 2:   Insert Rows

Problem 3:   =B1*1.09

Problem 4:   Format Column Width

Problem 5:   File Close

Problem 6:   File Open

Problem 7:   File Print

Problem 8:   Alt

Problem 9:   =B7-B6

Problem 10:   File Print Preview

Problem 11:   Format Cells Alignment

Problem 12:   =ROUND(B7*B8,0)

Problem 13:   =SUM(B1:B25)

Problem 14:   Format Cells Number Currency

Problem 15:   Format Cells Number Percentage

Problem 16:   Edit Copy

Problem 17:   File Save As

Problem 18:   Edit Paste

Problem 19:   Format Cells Border

EXERCISE 3 -- Correcting a Worksheet

INSTRUCTIONS: The following example illustrates a common error. Follow the instructions below to create the error and answer the questions.

Clear the screen (choose the Close command on the File menu).

Open a new workbook (choose the New command on the File menu).

In cell A1, enter 52.

In cell A2, enter 30.

In cell A3, enter A1-A2.

Your screen should look like Figure 4-43.

Figure 4-43

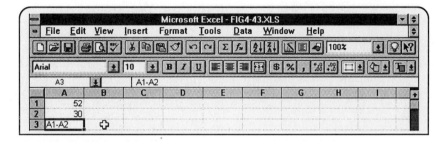

1.   What caused the error in cell A3?
2.   How can you correct the error?
3.   Close the workbook document. Do not save any changes.

EXERCISE 4 -- Correcting a Worksheet

INSTRUCTIONS: The following example illustrates a common error. Use the instructions below to create the error and answer the questions:

   Clear the screen (choose the Close command on the File menu).

   Open a new workbook (choose the New command on the File menu).

   In cell A1, enter 52.

   In cell A2, enter 30.

   In cell A3, enter =A1. Then enter =-A2 in cell A3.

   Your screen should look like Figure 4-44.

Figure 4-44

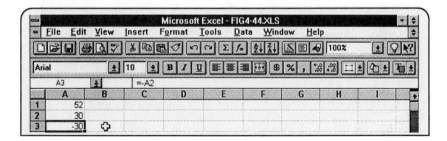

1.   What caused the error in computing A1-A2?
2.   How can you correct the error?
3.   Close the workbook document. Do not save any changes.

EXERCISE 5 -- Correcting a Worksheet

INSTRUCTIONS: Create the worksheet displayed in Figure 4-45. Place appropriate information on the Documentation worksheet, and put the worksheet itself on the Worksheet Model worksheet. Use the SUM function to calculate the quarterly totals and the monthly totals. The worksheet column titles are centered. Column A has a width of 18. Save the workbook to a file using the name JACKSON. Print the entire workbook.

Figure 4-45

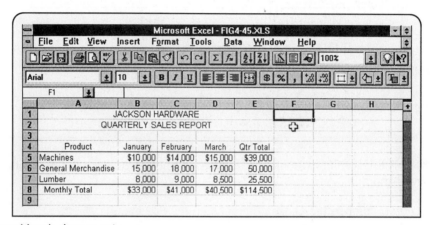

Close the workbook document.

EXERCISE 6 -- Correcting a Worksheet

INSTRUCTIONS: Create the worksheet displayed in Figure 4-46. Place appropriate information on the Documentation worksheet, and put the worksheet itself on the Worksheet Model worksheet. Use the SUM function to calculate the district totals and the expense category totals. The worksheet headings for columns B through E have a column width of 14 and are right-aligned. Save the workbook to a file using the name MOUNTAIN. Print the entire workbook.

Figure 4-46

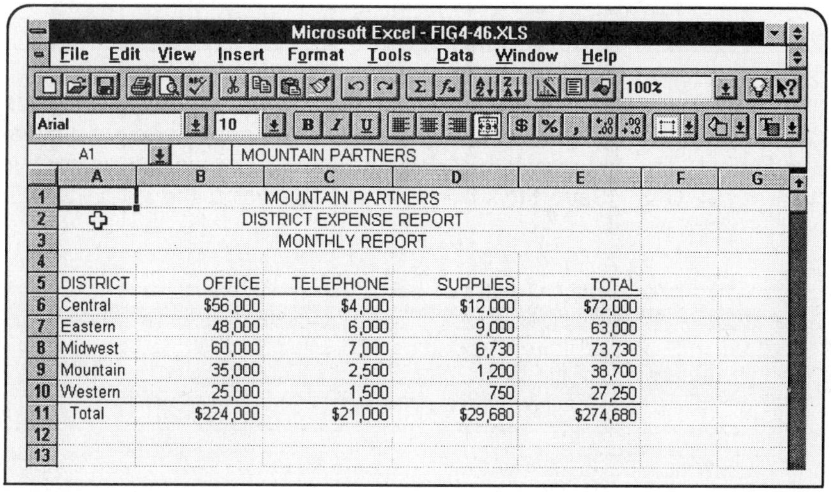

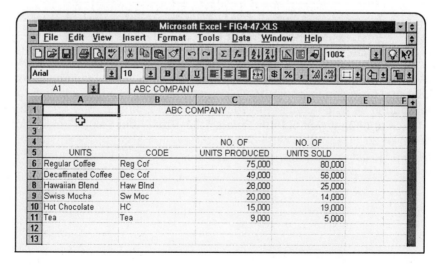

Microsoft Excel - FIG4-46.XLS

A1 MOUNTAIN PARTNERS

MOUNTAIN PARTNERS
DISTRICT EXPENSE REPORT
MONTHLY REPORT

DISTRICT	OFFICE	TELEPHONE	SUPPLIES	TOTAL
Central	$56,000	$4,000	$12,000	$72,000
Eastern	48,000	6,000	9,000	63,000
Midwest	60,000	7,000	6,730	73,730
Mountain	35,000	2,500	1,200	38,700
Western	25,000	1,500	750	27,250
Total	$224,000	$21,000	$29,680	$274,680

Close the workbook document.

EXERCISE 7 -- Creating a Worksheet

INSTRUCTIONS: Create the worksheet displayed in Figure 4-47. It will be used for exercises in other chapters. Place appropriate information on the Documentation worksheet, and put the worksheet itself on the Worksheet Model worksheet. The column width for columns A through D is 17 and the column titles are centered. The worksheet contains data only (no formulas). Save the workbook to a file using the name UNITPROD (for Unit Production). Print the entire workbook.

Figure 4-47

Microsoft Excel - FIG4-47.XLS

A1 ABC COMPANY

ABC COMPANY

UNITS	CODE	NO. OF UNITS PRODUCED	NO. OF UNITS SOLD
Regular Coffee	Reg Cof	75,000	80,000
Decaffinated Coffee	Dec Cof	49,000	56,000
Hawaiian Blend	Haw Blnd	28,000	25,000
Swiss Mocha	Sw Moc	20,000	14,000
Hot Chocolate	HC	15,000	19,000
Tea	Tea	9,000	5,000

Close the workbook document.

EXERCISE 8 -- Creating a Worksheet

INSTRUCTIONS: Create the worksheet displayed in Figure 4-48. It will be used for exercises in other chapters. Place appropriate information on the Documentation worksheet, and put the worksheet itself on the Worksheet Model worksheet. The column width of column B is 18. The worksheet contains data only, except for the SUM function in cell C13. Save the workbook to a file using the name SALES. Print the entire workbook.

Figure 4-48

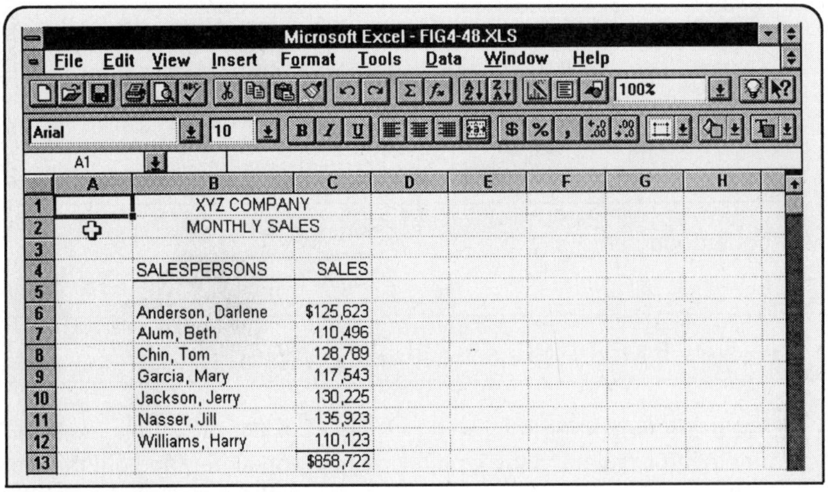

Microsoft Excel - FIG4-48.XLS

	A	B	C
1		XYZ COMPANY	
2		MONTHLY SALES	
3			
4		SALESPERSONS	SALES
5			
6		Anderson, Darlene	$125,623
7		Alum, Beth	110,496
8		Chin, Tom	128,789
9		Garcia, Mary	117,543
10		Jackson, Jerry	130,225
11		Nasser, Jill	135,923
12		Williams, Harry	110,123
13			$858,722

Close the workbook document.

EXERCISE 9 -- Creating a Worksheet

INSTRUCTIONS: Create and print the worksheet displayed in Figure 4-49. Place appropriate information on the Documentation worksheet, and put the worksheet itself on the Worksheet Model worksheet. Revenue is $22,500 in YEAR 1 and projected to increase by 6 percent for YEARS 2 through 5. Expenses are $13,500 in YEAR 1 and projected to be 60 percent of Revenue in YEARS 2 through 5. Profit Before Tax is Revenue minus Expenses. Taxes are 40 percent of Profit Before Tax. Profit After Tax is Profit Before Tax less Taxes. Column A has a width of 20. Use formulas to place the Revenue and Expenses value in cells B7 and B8. Save the workbook to a file using the name PRACTICE. This file will be used in subsequent chapters. Print the entire workbook.

Figure 4-49

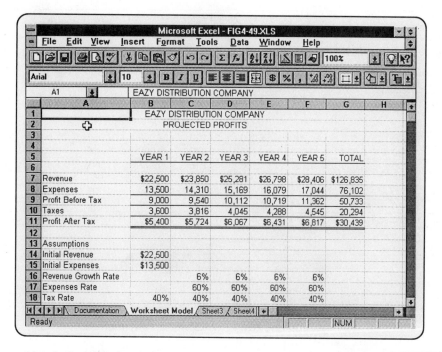

Close the workbook document.

EXERCISE 10 -- Editing a Worksheet

INSTRUCTIONS: Open the BUDGET workbook file. Edit the Worksheet Model using the instructions below. Use Figure 4-50 as a guide. Note that the new workbook file created will be named BUDGET2 and will be needed for exercises in later chapters.

1.   Expand the worksheet model to include projections through YEAR 10. Insert six columns (F-K) between QTR4 and YR TOTAL using the Edit Insert command sequence. Rename the headings through YEAR 10. Change the YR TOTAL column title to TOTAL. Copy the growth rate information to YEAR 5 through YEAR 10. Copy the formulas, values, subtotal lines, and total lines from YEAR 4 (E7:E16) to YEAR 5 through YEAR 10 (F7:K16).

2.   Change the sums under TOTAL to reflect the additional years. Change the formula in cell L7 from =SUM(B7:E7) to =SUM(B7:K7). Copy the formula in cell L7 to cells L10:L16.

3.   Save the workbook to a file using the name BUDGET2. BUDGET and BUDGET2 are two separate workbook files on the disk. The final result should look like Figure 4-50 (the entire worksheet will not be visible on the screen at one time).

Figure 4-50

	YEAR 1	YEAR 2	YEAR 3	YEAR 4	YEAR 5	YEAR 6	YEAR 7	YEAR 8	YEAR 9	YEAR 10	TOTAL
ABC COMPANY											
BUDGET											
Sales	$60,000	$61,200	$62,424	$63,672	$64,945	$66,244	$67,569	$68,920	$70,298	$71,704	$656,976
Expenses											
Salaries	35,000	35,500	36,200	37,000	37,000	37,000	37,000	37,000	37,000	37,000	365,700
Rent	9,000	9,000	9,000	9,000	9,000	9,000	9,000	9,000	9,000	9,000	90,000
Telephone	1,000	1,050	1,103	1,158	1,216	1,277	1,341	1,408	1,478	1,552	12,583
Office Supplies	750	800	850	900	950	1,000	1,050	1,100	1,150	1,200	9,750
Miscellaneous	1,000	1,030	1,061	1,093	1,126	1,160	1,195	1,231	1,268	1,306	11,470
Total Expenses	46,750	47,380	48,214	49,151	49,292	49,437	49,586	49,739	49,896	50,058	489,503
Gross Profit	$13,250	$13,820	$14,210	$14,521	$15,653	$16,807	$17,983	$19,181	$20,402	$21,646	$167,473
Assumptions											
Sales		2%	2%	2%	2%	2%	2%	2%	2%	2%	
Telephone		5%	5%	5%	5%	5%	5%	5%	5%	5%	
Office Supplies		50.00	50.00	50.00	50.00	50.00	50.00	50.00	50.00	50.00	
Miscellaneous		3%	3%	3%	3%	3%	3%	3%	3%	3%	

Close the workbook document.

EXERCISE 11 -- Order of Precedence

INSTRUCTIONS: Work the following set of problems using the information provided to make sure you understand the order of precedence in the calculation of formulas. Assume that cell A1=6, cell B2=5, and cell C4=3.

	Formula	Order of Precedence	Answer
a.	=C4-B2*2	3-(5*2)	_____
b.	=B2-A1-C4/B2	5-6-(3/5)	_____
c.	=B2-(A1-C4)/B2	5-((6-3)/5)	_____
d.	=A1/-3+3	(6/-3)+3	_____
e.	=A1-4*C4/B2^2	6-((4*3)/5^2)	_____
f.	=(A1-4)*C4/B2^2	(6-4)*(3/5^2)	_____
g.	=A1*B2/C4-10/2	((6*5)/3-(10/2))	_____

CHAPTER FIVE

IMPROVING THE APPEARANCE
OF A WORKSHEET

OBJECTIVES

In this chapter, you will learn to:
- Understand basic terms related to creating presentation-quality documents
- Improve the appearance of a worksheet
- Create and use styles

■ CHAPTER OVERVIEW

In the previous chapters, you have used the standard printing capabilities of Excel. You can also use Excel to create presentation-quality materials.

Introduction

By using various features available in Excel, you can:

Include several fonts on any printed document
Boldface text and numbers
Add degrees of shading to areas on a worksheet
Add a horizontal or vertical border to a cell or a range of cells
Place a box around one cell or outline a range of cells
Print color documents when a color printer is available

With these capabilities, you can enhance your reports and presentations with improved quality documents.

By using styles, you can change the format of a cell dramatically. A **style** is a set of format options. Some format options available include changing the font, boldfacing characters, specifying colors for numbers and text, placing solid lines on the edges of a cell, and creating various degrees of shading.

Fonts are sets of printed characters with the same size and appearance. A font can be described in four ways: typeface, weight, style, and point size. Some typefaces include:

Courier   Times New Roman

Mural Script   Arial

Typeface refers to the design and appearance of the characters on a printed document. **Weight** refers to bold, medium, or light print density. Normal print is in medium weight. **Font style** refers to upright or italic print. **Point size** refers to the height of the printed characters.

■ IMPROVING THE APPEARANCE OF A WORKSHEET

To illustrate the process for improving the appearance of a worksheet, open the BUDGET workbook file and click the Worksheet Model sheet tab.

Suppose you want to change the appearance of the worksheet as follows:

> Change the font of the worksheet titles
> Boldface the worksheet titles, column titles, and row titles
> Add shading to the column titles
> Place an outline around the cells containing the assumptions

To change the font of the worksheet titles to Times New Roman 14 point bold:

Select	cells A1:A2
Choose	Format
Choose	Cells
Click	the Font tab

The Format Cells dialog box appears with the Font tab selected. To indicate the appropriate font, font style, and point size:

Click	the Times New Roman choice in the Font list box (you may have to scroll down through the font choices)
Click	the Bold choice in the Font Style list box
Click	the 14 choice in the Size box
Click	the OK command button

Notice that the row height for rows 1 and 2 automatically increased when the point size changed.

User Tip

An alternative method for changing the font of a cell or range of cells is to first select the cell or range of cells. Then click the down arrow on the Font [Arial] [↕] button on the Formatting toolbar and choose the desired font. To change the font size of a cell or range of cells, click the down arrow on the Font Size [10] [↕] button on the Formatting toolbar and choose the appropriate size.

To boldface the column titles:

Select	cells B5:F5
Choose	Format
Choose	Cells
Click	the Font tab (if necessary)
Click	the Bold choice in the Font Style list box
Click	the OK command button

The column titles are now bold.

User Tip

An alternative method for boldfacing the contents of a cell or range of cells is to first select the cell or range of cells. Then click the Bold [**B**] button on the Formatting toolbar.

To boldface the row titles in cells A7 through A26:

Select	cells A7:A26
Click	the Bold [**B**] button

After making cell A1 the active cell, your screen should look like Figure 5-1.

Figure 5-1

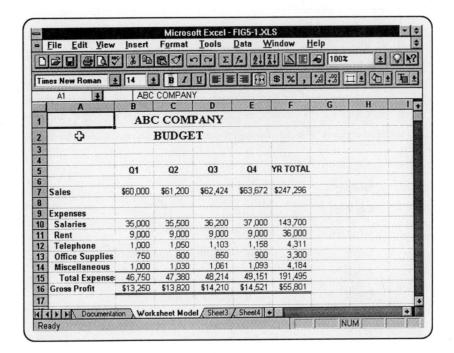

Notice that column A is not wide enough to display the row titles. Widen column A to 18 so the row titles can be seen.

To place a light shading in the cells containing the column titles:

Select	cells B5:F5
Choose	Format
Choose	Cells
Click	the Patterns tab
Click	the light gray color on the color grid in the Cell Shading group box. The color is the seventh color from the left on the second row.
Click	the OK command button

After making cell A1 the active cell, your screen should look like Figure 5-2.

Figure 5-2

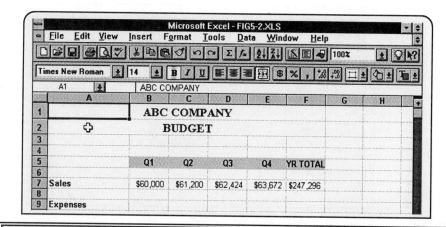

The Pattern list box on the Patterns tab can be used to shade the contents of cells. You can use this list box also to apply a pattern to a cell or range of cells.

To place an outline around the cells containing the values for the growth rate assumptions:

Select	cells A23:E26
Choose	Format
Choose	Cells
Click	the Border tab

To specify an outline:

Click	the Outline choice in the Border group box
Click	the OK command button

After making cell A21 the active cell, your screen should look like Figure 5-3.

Figure 5-3

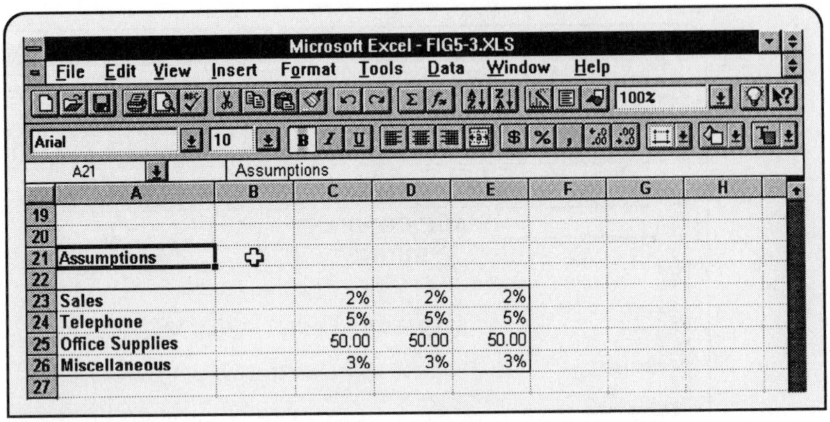

To print the enhanced version of the BUDGET worksheet:

Click   the Print 🖨 button

Your printout should look similar to Figure 5-4.

Figure 5-4

ABC COMPANY BUDGET					
	Q1	**Q2**	**Q3**	**Q4**	**YR TOTAL**
Sales	$60,000	$61,200	$62,424	$63,672	$247,296
Expenses					
Salaries	35,000	35,500	36,200	37,000	143,700
Rent	9,000	9,000	9,000	9,000	36,000
Telephone	1,000	1,050	1,103	1,158	4,311
Office Supplies	750	800	850	900	3,300
Miscellaneous	1,000	1,030	1,061	1,093	4,184
Total Expenses	46,750	47,380	48,214	49,151	191,495
Gross Profit	$13,250	$13,820	$14,210	$14,521	$55,801
Assumptions					
Sales		2%	2%	2%	
Telephone		5%	5%	5%	
Office Supplies		50.00	50.00	50.00	
Miscellaneous		3%	3%	3%	

■ CREATING AND USING STYLES

A **style** is a set of formats that can be applied to one cell or a range of cells. There are three ways to create a style: by example, by definition, or by copying styles from another worksheet. You may use the Style command on the Format menu to create a style name.

Make sure cell A1 is the active cell.

To define a style by example that formats a cell with bold text and light shading:

Click	on cell B5
Choose	Format
Choose	Style

The Style dialog box appears. To give the style a name:

Type	Titles in the Style Name text box

Notice the description of the current format choices in the Style Includes (By Example) box.

To add the style to the list of available styles:

Click	the Add command button

To close the Style dialog box:

Click	the Close command button

To apply the Titles style to the row titles in cells A7 through A26:

Select	cells A7:A26
Choose	Format
Choose	Style
Click	the down arrow on the Style Name drop-down list box
Click	the Titles style in the Style Name list box
Click	the OK command button

The Titles style is applied to cells A7 through A26. After making cell A1 the active cell, your screen should look like Figure 5-5.

Figure 5-5

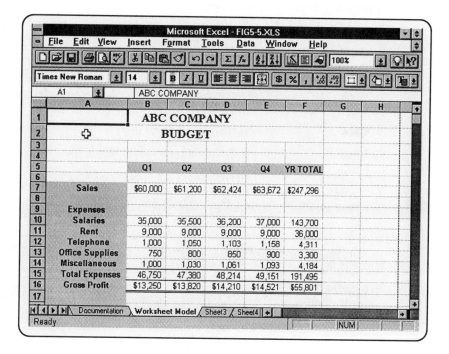

Note that the row title entries in cells A7 through A26 are centered. To left-align the row titles again:

Select	cells A7:A26
Choose	Format
Choose	Cells
Click	the Alignment tab
Click	the Left option button in the Horizontal group box
Click	the OK command button

The row title entries are now left-aligned.

User Tip

An alternative method for left-aligning text with cell(s) is to select the cell(s) and then click the Align Left ▤ button on the Formatting toolbar.

To return the row titles to the "Normal" style:

Select	cells A7:A26 (if necessary)
Choose	Format
Choose	Style
Click	the down arrow on the Style Name drop-down list box
Click	the Normal style choice
Click	the OK command button

The row titles are now left-aligned. The bolding and shading have been removed. After making cell A1 the active cell, your screen should look like Figure 5-6.

Figure 5-6

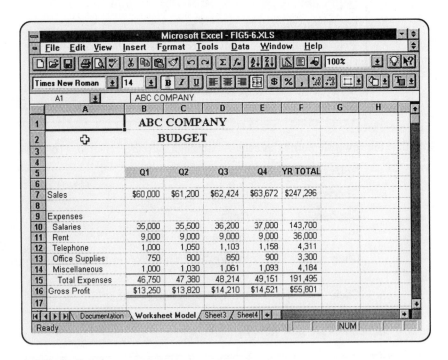

To return cell B5 to normal by applying the "Normal" style to it:

Click	on cell B5
Choose	Format
Choose	Style
Click	the down arrow on the Style Name drop-down list box

Click	the Normal style choice
Click	the OK command button

To format a cell with a style copied from another cell:

Click	on cell C5
Choose	Edit
Choose	Copy
Click	on cell B5
Choose	Edit
Choose	Paste Special

The Paste Special dialog box appears. To paste the formats:

Click	the Formats option button in the Paste group box
Click	the OK command button
Press	Esc to remove the moving border on cell C5

Cell B5 is now properly formatted. Your screen should look Figure 5-7.

Figure 5-7

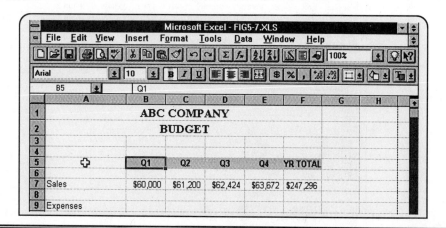

User Tip

An alternative method for copying and pasting the format of a cell to another cell or range of cells is to make the cell that contains the desired format the active cell. Then click the Format Painter ✍ button on the Standard toolbar. Finally, select the cell(s) to which the format is to be pasted.

■ AUTOMATIC FORMATTING

Excel provides some formats for tables of information. These formats can be accessed by using the AutoFormat command on the Format menu. The range of cells in the table must be selected prior to using the available formats.

To examine some of the available formats:

Select	cells A5:F26
Choose	Format
Choose	AutoFormat

The AutoFormat dialog box appears.

To select 3D Effects 1:

Click	on the 3D Effects 1 choice in the Table Format list box (you may have to scroll down to see the option)
Click	the OK command button

After making cell A1 the active cell, your screen should look like Figure 5-8.

Figure 5-8

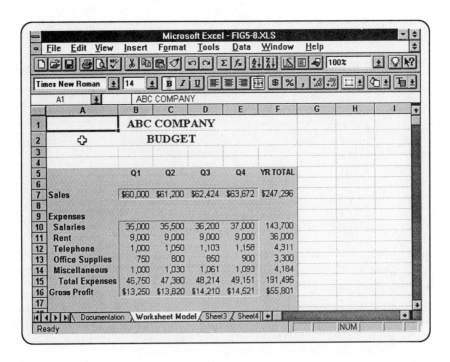

■ REMOVING GRIDLINES

Excel automatically includes gridlines in a worksheet. In some situations, you may not want gridlines on your worksheet. You can use the Options command on the Tools menu to remove the gridlines.

To remove the gridlines:

Choose	Tools
Choose	Options
Click	the View tab (if necessary)

The Window Options box appears on the View tab.

Click	the Gridlines check box in the Window Options group box to remove the X
Click	the OK command button

The gridlines have been removed from the worksheet. Your screen should look like Figure 5-9.

Figure 5-9

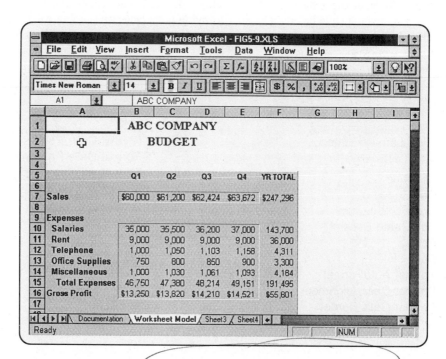

When you print the document, no gridlines will appear on the printout. You can also use the Page Setup command on the File menu to remove the gridlines for printing purposes only.

To place the gridlines on your screen again:

Choose	Tools
Choose	Options
Click	the View tab (if necessary)
Click	the Gridlines check box in the Window Options group box to insert an X
Click	the OK command button

The gridlines appear again.

Save the workbook to a file using the name BUDSTYLE. Close the workbook document.

SUMMARY

Excel provides commands that permit you to improve the appearance of a worksheet. You can include various fonts, boldface the contents of a cell, shade a cell, and include boxes around a cell or range of cells. You can create a style based on a cell's formatting characteristics. You can then apply the style to other cells. Excel also includes features for automatically formatting a table of data and removing the gridlines from a worksheet.

KEY CONCEPTS

Align Left ☰ button
Bold **B** button
Boldface
Cell Shading
Color button
Edit Paste Special
Font
Font Style
Format AutoFormat
Format Cells Alignment
Format Cells Border

Format Cells Font
Format Cells Patterns
Format Painter button
Format Style
Gridlines
Point size
Style
Style Name
Tools Options View
Typeface
Weight

EXERCISE 1

INSTRUCTIONS: Circle T if the statement is true and F if the statement is false.

T   F   1.   Cells that contain letters and numbers can be boldfaced.

T   F   2.   When you use cell shading in Excel, you can shade only one cell at a time.

T   F   3.   You cannot place an outline on a single cell.

T   F   4.   You can use colors in cells.

T   F   5.   You can create custom styles.

EXERCISE 2 -- Improving the Appearance of a Worksheet

INSTRUCTIONS: Open the PRACTICE workbook file. Complete the following items to improve the appearance of the Worksheet Model worksheet:

1. Boldface the worksheet title.
2. Shade the column titles.
3. Boldface the row titles.
4. Create a style using the formats associated with YEAR 1. Name the style *Headings*.
5. Apply the style name created in step 4 to the cells containing row titles.
6. Place an outline around the cells containing the assumptions.
7. Save the workbook to a file using the name PRACTAPP.
8. Print the worksheet.
9. Close the workbook document.

EXERCISE 3 -- Improving the Appearance of a Worksheet

INSTRUCTIONS: Open the SALES workbook file. Complete the following items to improve the appearance of the Worksheet Model worksheet:

1. Change the font for the worksheet title to Times New Roman 12 point.
2. Boldface the worksheet title and the column titles.
3. Boldface the salespersons' names.
4. Shade the cells containing the salespersons' names.

5. Print the worksheet.

6. Close the workbook document. Do not save any changes.

EXERCISE 4 -- Improving the Appearance of a Worksheet

INSTRUCTIONS: Open the PRACTICE workbook file.   Complete the following items to improve the appearance of the Worksheet Model worksheet:

1. Change the font for the worksheet title to Times New Roman 14 point.

2. Boldface the worksheet titles, column titles, and row titles.

3. Select one of the AutoFormat choices and apply it to the worksheet.

4. Print the Worksheet Model worksheet.

5. Close the workbook document. Do not save any changes.

CHAPTER SIX

USEFUL EXCEL COMMANDS

OBJECTIVES

In this chapter, you will learn to:
- Keep a cell reference constant in a formula
- Correct cell entries
- Undo a previous entry
- Format numbers
- Fill a cell with a set of characters
- Move cell contents
- Use the Drag and Drop feature to move and copy data
- Insert and delete columns
- Insert and delete cells
- Set row and column print titles
- Print headers and footers
- Exclude gridlines on printouts
- Insert page breaks
- Print cell formulas of a worksheet in tabular form
- Magnify or shrink the worksheet
- Control the recalculation of a worksheet
- Suppress zeros
- Protect data
- Hide portions of a worksheet
- Create and delete range names
- Find and replace data
- Split windows
- View more than one window
- Size a window
- Move a window

- Customize the toolbar
- Perform worksheet documentation
- Problem solve using the Goal Seek and Solver features
- Use Scenarios

■ CHAPTER OVERVIEW

Chapter 4 provided general procedures for preparing workbooks and worksheets. This chapter describes a variety of Excel commands that are often indispensable when creating and maintaining workbooks and worksheets.

■ ABSOLUTE AND RELATIVE CELL ADDRESSES

Open the SALES workbook file for this example. You created the SALES workbook as an exercise at the end of Chapter 4.

To enter a formula that computes the percentage of total sales by each salesperson:

Click	on cell D6
Type	=
Click	on cell C6
Type	/
Click	on cell C13
Click	the enter box ☑

Cell D6 should display the number 0.146291.

To copy the formula to the remaining cells:

Move	the mouse pointer to the fill handle in cell D6
Drag	the fill handle to cell D12

#DIV/0! appears in cells D7 through D12. After making cell D6 the active cell, your screen should look like Figure 6-1.

Figure 6-1

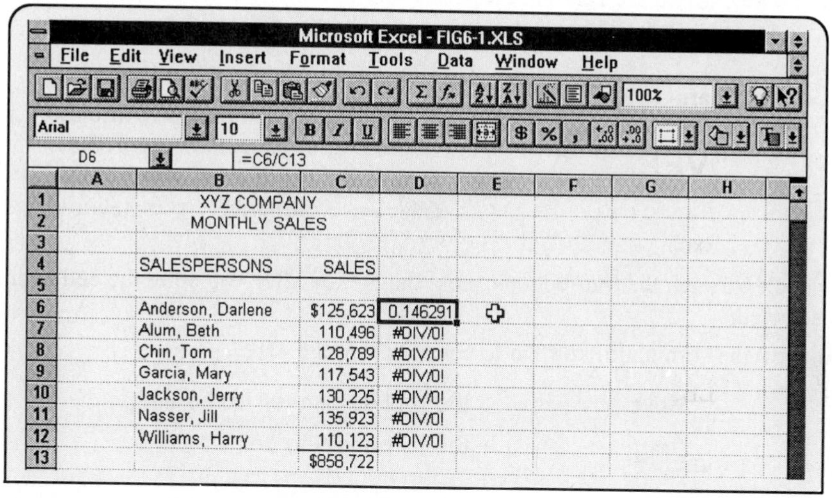

To determine why the formula =C6/C13, when copied, did not compute the expected amount:

Click   on cell D7

Look at the formula in the formula bar. The formula that was *intended* to be copied was =**C7/C13**. However, when the formula =C6/C13 was copied, it became =**C7/C14**. The same results occurred for the formula in cells D8 through D12   (=**C8/C15**, =**C9/C16**, and so on). Formulas are based on **relative location**. Excel interprets the formula that was copied not as =C6/C13 but, rather, as "divide the number one cell to the left by the number to the left one column and seven rows down" for cells D7 through D12.

Since cells C14, C15, and so forth are blank and are interpreted as the number 0 in formula calculations, the message #DIV/0! appears in cells D7 through D12.

To enter a formula that computes the percentage of sales for each salesperson and hold the total sales amount constant when the formula is copied to other cells:

Click   on cell D6

Type   =

Click   on cell C6

Type   /

Click   on cell C13

Press   F4

Click   the enter box ✓

Look at the formula for cell D6 in the formula bar. It should appear as =**C6/$C$13**. The dollar signs in front of the C and the 13 indicate that the column (C) and the row (13) will remain constant, or **absolute**, when copied. Cell D6 should display the number 0.146291.

The F4 key, called the **reference key**, has four options or ways of changing a cell. The following options provide ways to change rows and columns using the reference key:

Option	Example	Column	Row
1	$C$6	Absolute	Absolute
2	C$6	Relative	Absolute
3	$C6	Absolute	Relative
4	C48	Relative	Relative

To cycle through the four options, press the F4 key after you enter the cell address until the proper option is selected.

To copy the formula in cell D6 to cells D7 through D12:

Move the mouse pointer to the fill handle in cell D6

Drag the fill handle to cell D12

The correct computation for cells D7 through D12 occurs. After making cell A1 the active cell, your screen should look like Figure 6-2.

Figure 6-2

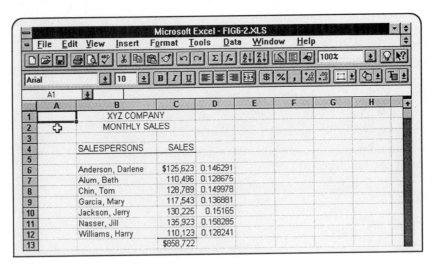

To see how the formula =C6/$C$13 was copied correctly:

Click on cell D7

The formula =C7/$C$13 should appear in the formula bar. If you wish, make cells D8 through D12 the active cell to see that $C$13 is held constant in the formulas for the cells.

Close the SALES workbook document. Do not save any changes.

■ EDITING DATA

Error Correction and Cell Editing

There are several ways to correct errors on a worksheet. Two commonly used methods are illustrated below.

Replacing an Erroneous Entry

First, make sure you have a blank workbook on your screen.

Click	on cell A1
Enter	=100

Your screen should look like Figure 6-3, Part 1.

Figure 6-3
Part 1

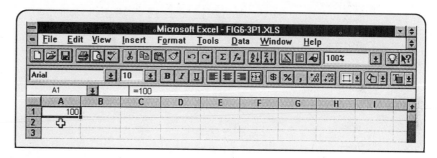

To change the entry to 1000:

Enter	=1000

To replace an item that is incorrect, make sure the cell containing the incorrect entry is the active cell and retype the entry. Your screen should look like Figure 6-3, Part 2.

Figure 6-3
Part 2

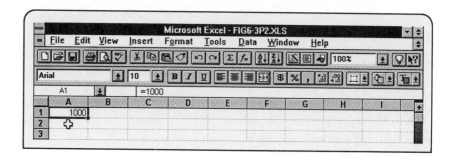

Editing an Entry Using the Formula Bar

To change the cell entry in cell A1 from 1000 to =1000*1.03:

Click	on cell A1
Move	the mouse pointer to the right end of the number in the formula bar
Click	the mouse button

Edit appears on the status bar. Your screen should look like Figure 6-4, Part 1.

Figure 6-4
Part 1

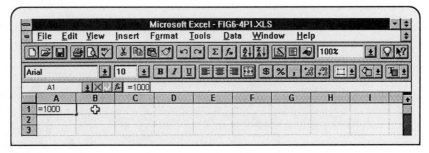

To add the additional characters to the existing entry:

Type	*1.03
Click	the enter box ☑

The contents in cell A1 have now been changed to =1000*1.03 or 1030. Your screen should look like Figure 6-4, Part 2.

Figure 6-4
Part 2

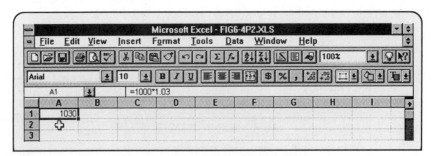

Close the workbook document. Do not save any changes.

Make sure you have a blank workbook on your screen.

You can use the mouse to move the insertion point to different locations in the formula bar. When the Edit mode is activated, you can use the left and right arrow keys as well as the HOME and END keys to move to the beginning and end of an entry, respectively.

Click	on cell C1
Enter	ABC COMPANY
Move	the mouse pointer to the left of the letter A at the beginning of the formula bar
Click	the mouse button
Type	THE
Press	the space bar

When you type the additional text, the remaining text moves to the right so that the new text is inserted. To insert MANUFACTURING:

Move	the mouse pointer to the right of the letter C in ABC
Click	the mouse button
Press	the space bar
Type	MANUFACTURING

To move quickly to the end of the line, so that ", INC." can be inserted:

Move	the mouse pointer to the right of the letter Y in COMPANY
Click	the mouse button
Type	, INC.
Click	the enter box ☑

Your screen should look like Figure 6-5.

Figure 6-5

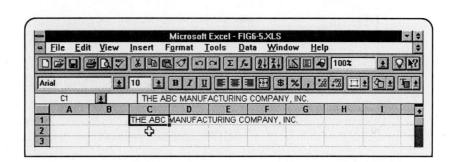

As the previous example illustrates, when you are editing, you can type additional text and the remaining text moves to the right. An alternative approach is to highlight the characters in the formula bar and then type the new characters. For example, to replace the letters ABC with XYZ:

Select	the characters ABC in the formula bar
Type	XYZ
Click	the enter box ☑

The letters ABC have been replaced with the letters XYZ. Your screen should look like Figure 6-6.

Figure 6-6

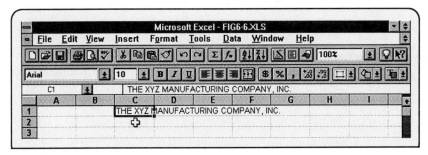

Close the workbook document. Do not save any changes.

■ UNDO

The **Undo** feature creates a temporary copy of both the data and worksheet settings. Excel makes it possible to restore a cell entry to its previous form.

To illustrate the Undo feature, open the BUDGET workbook file.

Click	on cell A7
Enter	Revenues

The text "Sales" has been replaced by "Revenues". Suppose you want to undo the action and have the text "Sales" again appear in cell A7.

Choose	Edit
Choose	Undo Entry

The text "Sales" again appears in cell A7.

User Tip

Alternative procedures for using the Undo Entry command on the View menu are to click the Undo ↶ button on the Standard toolbar or press CTRL+Z.

The Undo Entry command does not work in all situations. For example, you cannot undo a print or file operation.

Close the BUDGET workbook document. Do not save any changes.

■ FORMATTING NUMBERS

Excel allows you to format cells using predefined format codes. You can also create your own number format codes.

Make sure you have a blank workbook on your screen.

To illustrate the two alternative methods:

Enter	25 in cell A3
Enter	50 in cell B3

To use the predefined number format to include two decimal places for the value in cell A3:

Click	on cell A3
Choose	Format
Choose	Cells
Click	the Number tab (if necessary)
Click	the Number choice in the Category list box
Click	the 0.00 choice in the Format codes list box
Click	the OK command button

To format the value in cell B3 with one decimal place, you must create a new number format code.

Click	on cell B3
Choose	Format
Choose	Cells
Click	the Number tab (if necessary)
Click	the Number choice in the Category list box
Double-click	the Code text box
Type	0.0
Click	the OK command button

Your screen should look like Figure 6-7.

Figure 6-7

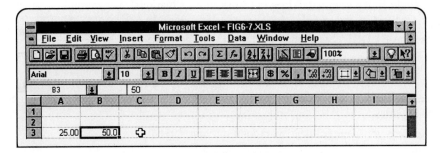

The new format code is added as a choice to the Format Codes list box. You can use the new format code by scrolling to the bottom of the list and clicking the format code.

Close the workbook document. Do not save any changes.

■ FILLING A CELL WITH A SET OF CHARACTERS

In some situations, you may need to fill a cell with a specific character or set of characters. The Format Cells Alignment command can be used to fill a cell.

Make sure you have a blank workbook on your screen.

Suppose you want to fill a cell with the $ character. To illustrate the process for filling a cell with specific characters:

Click	on cell A2
Enter	$

To fill the remaining part of the cell with the $ character:

Choose	Format
Choose	Cells
Click	the Alignment tab
Click	the Fill option button in the Horizontal group box
Click	the OK command button

The $ character now fills cell A2. Your screen should look like Figure 6-8.

Figure 6-8

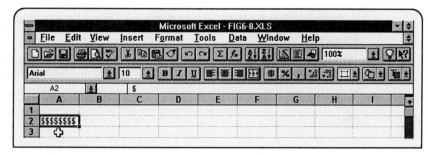

Close the workbook document. Do not save any changes.

■ MOVING CELL CONTENTS

Make sure you have a blank workbook on your screen.

Sometimes, you may want to move information from one location on a worksheet to another area on the worksheet. To illustrate this process:

Enter	20 in cell A1
Enter	50 in cell A3
Enter	100 in cell B3

Using the Edit Cut Command

To move the contents of cell A1 to the clipboard:

Click	on cell A1
Choose	Edit
Choose	Cut

To place the contents of the clipboard in cell H1:

Click	on cell H1
Choose	Edit
Choose	Paste

Your screen should look like Figure 6-9.

Figure 6-9

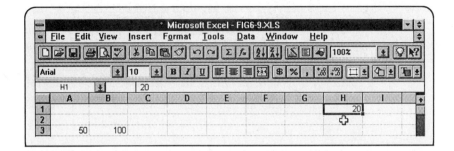

User Tip

An alternative method for cutting the contents of a cell or range of cells to another cell or range of cells is to use the Cut [✂] and Paste [▤] buttons on the Standard toolbar.

Moving the Contents of Several Cells to Another Location on the Worksheet

To move the contents of cell A3 through B3 to cells D5 through E5:

Select	cells A3:B3
Click	the Cut [✂] button
Select	cells D5:E5
Click	the Paste [▤] button

The contents of cells A3 through B3 have been moved to cells D5 through E5. After making cell A1 the active cell, your screen should look like Figure 6-10.

Figure 6-10

![Microsoft Excel - FIG6-10.XLS screenshot showing spreadsheet with 20 in cell H1, and 50 in cell D5 and 100 in cell E5]

Using the Drag and Drop Feature to Move and Copy Data

Moving Cell Contents

To return the contents of cells D5 through E5 to cells A3 through B3:

Select	cells D5:E5
Move	the mouse pointer to a border of cell D5 or E5 until an arrow appears
Drag	the cells to cells A3:B3

The data has been moved. After making cell A1 the active cell, your screen should look like Figure 6-11.

Figure 6-11

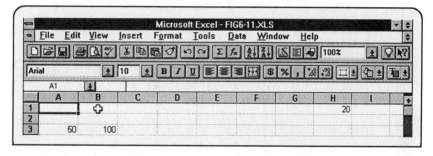

Copying Contents of Cells

To copy the contents of cell H1 to cell A1 so the number 20 appears in both cells:

Select	cell H1
Hold down	the [Ctrl] key
Move	the mouse pointer to a border of cell H1 until an arrow and a plus sign appear
Drag	the mouse pointer to cell A1

The number 20 now appears in cells A1 and H1. Your screen should look like Figure 6-12.

Figure 6-12

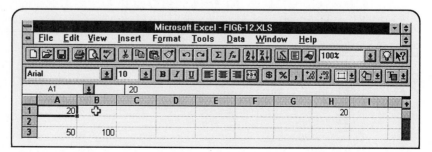

Close the workbook document. Do not save any changes.

■ WORKSHEET INSERTIONS AND DELETIONS

Columns and rows can be inserted into a worksheet after the worksheet is created. You can also delete columns and rows whenever necessary.

To complete the exercise in this section, create the worksheet shown in Figure 6-13. Save the workbook using the name BOATSALE.

Figure 6-13

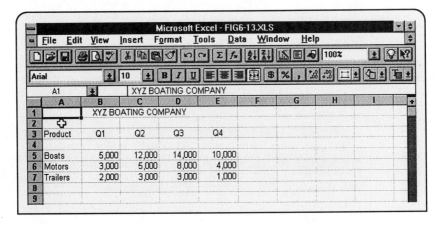

Inserting and Deleting Columns

To insert a column between the Q3 and Q4 columns:

Click	on the column heading E
Choose	Insert
Choose	Columns

After making cell E1 the active cell, your screen should look like Figure 6-14.

Figure 6-14

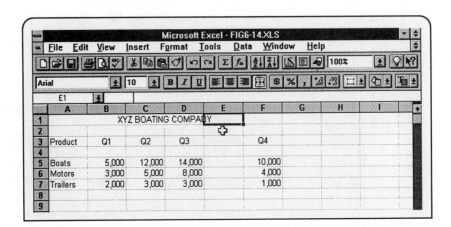

If you want to insert more than one column, you must select the number of columns prior to using the Columns command on the Insert menu.

To remove the blank column E from the worksheet:

Click	on the column heading E
Choose	Edit
Choose	Delete

Your screen should look like Figure 6-13 again.

■ INSERTING AND DELETING CELLS

Suppose you want to insert blank cells to the right of column A and then move the contents of cells B3 through B7 to the right one column.

Select	cells B3:B7
Choose	Insert
Choose	Cells

The Insert dialog box appears.

Click	the Shift Cells Right option button in the Insert group box
Click	the OK command button

After making cell B3 the active cell, your screen should look like Figure 6-15.

Figure 6-15

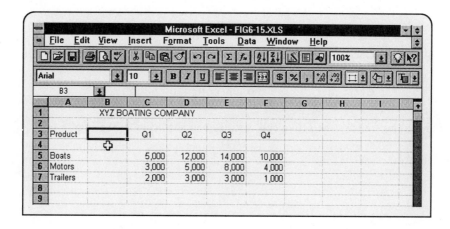

To return the contents of cells C3 through C7 to cells B3 through B7:

Select	cells C3:C7
Move	the mouse pointer to a border of one of the selected cells until an arrow appears
Drag	the cells to B3:B7

After making cell A1 the active cell, your screen should look like Figure 6-16.

Figure 6-16

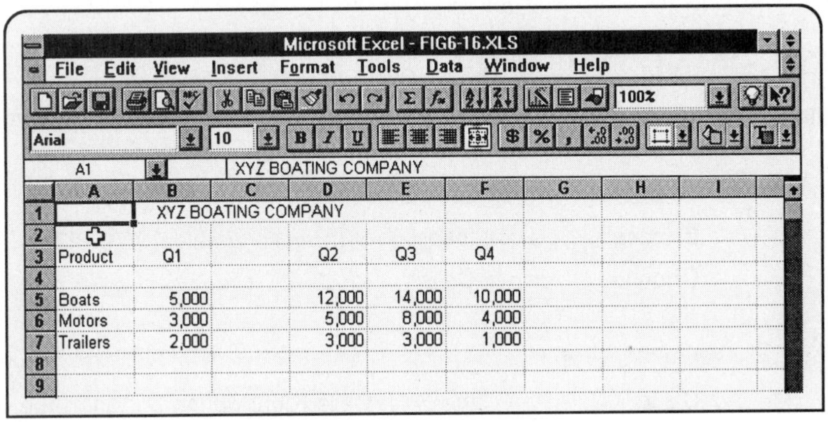

To delete the blank cells in column C and move the remaining cells to their original positions:

Select	cells C3:C7
Choose	Edit
Choose	Delete

The Delete dialog box appears.

Click	the Shift Cells Left option button in the Delete group box
Click	the OK command button

After making cell A1 the active cell, your screen should look like Figure 6-17.

Figure 6-17

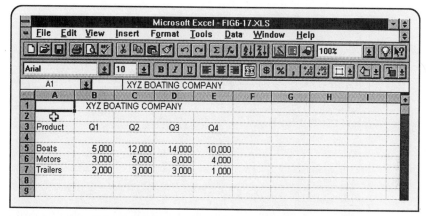

The worksheet appears as it did originally.

Close the BOATSALE workbook document. Do not save any changes.

■ PRINTING

Page Setup

Setting Row and Column Print Titles

Sometimes you may work with large worksheets that contain more than one page. It is useful to include **row print titles** on each page when there are several pages to a report. They provide descriptive information at the top of each page. You can print a **column print title** on the left side of each page for ease in reading the worksheet rows.

Before starting this exercise, open the BUDGET2 workbook file.

To specify the column to repeat at the left of the worksheet:

Choose	File
Choose	Page Setup
Click	the Sheet tab
Click	the Columns to Repeat at Left text box in the Print Titles group box
Type	$A:$A

Your screen should look like Figure 6-18.

Figure 6-18

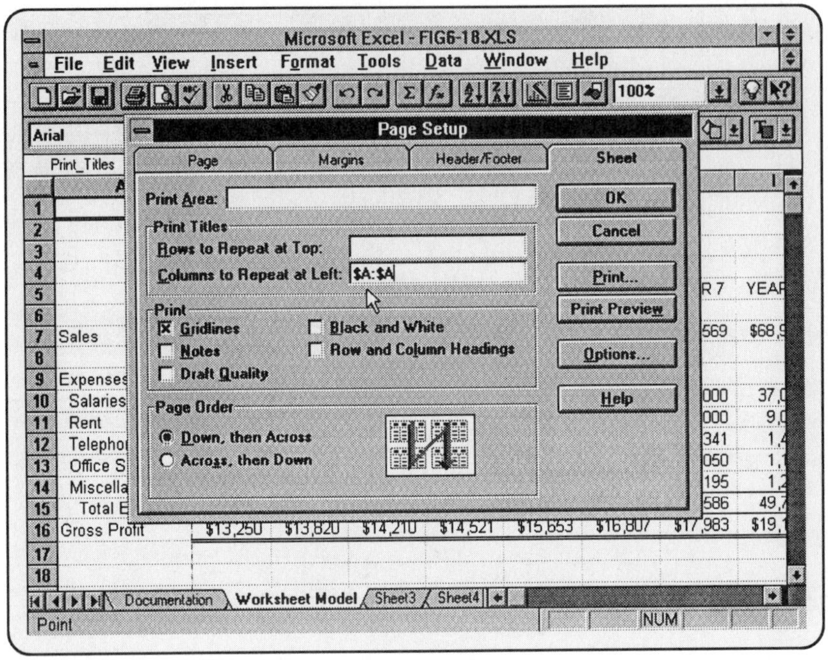

| **Click** | the OK command button |

Headers and Footers

By default, Excel includes the worksheet tab name as the header and the page number as the footer on each printed page. The Page Setup command on the File menu can be used to specify alternative headers, footers, margins, row and column headings, cell gridlines, and other settings.

The **header** is a line of text entered below the top margin of every page. Headers are always printed 0.5" from the top and 0.75" from the side of the page. Headers may be placed at the left margin, right margin, or centered.

To place a header at the top of each page, use the following procedure:

| **Choose** | File |
| **Choose** | Page Setup |

The Page Setup dialog box appears on your screen.

| **Click** | the Header/Footer tab |
| **Click** | the Custom Header command button |

The Header dialog box appears.

Double-click	the text "&[Tab]" in the Center Section edit box
Type	ABC COMPANY in the Center Section edit box
Click	the OK command button

Headers are entered only once, but they are reproduced on each printed page. You can change headers by repeating the procedure. You can delete them by repeating the command sequence, selecting the text in the Center Section edit box, and then pressing the DELETE key.

Footers are always printed 0.5" from the bottom of the page and 0.75" from the side of the page. To create a footer that will result in a right-aligned page number:

| **Click** | the Custom Footer command button |

Headers and footers can also be entered by using the buttons on the Header and Footer dialog boxes. The buttons are explained in the order they appear above the Center Section edit box:

To format the text	[A]
To insert a page number	[#]
To insert the total number of pages	[#]
To insert the current date	[date icon]
To insert the current time	[time icon]
To insert the workbook file name	[file icon]
To insert the worksheet tab name	[tab icon]

The Footer dialog box appears.

| **Delete** | the default text in the Center Section edit box |

To enter the footer:

Click	the Right Section edit box
Type	Page
Press	the space bar once
Click	the Page Number [#] button
Click	the OK command button

Your screen should look like the one in Figure 6-19.

Figure 6-19

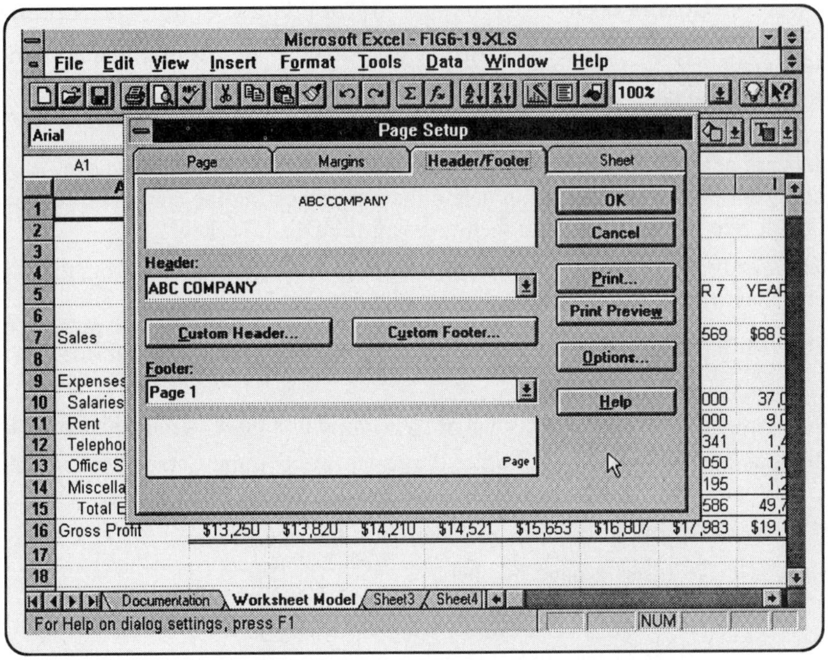

. Note the example header and footer appears in the Header and Footer edit boxes.

Click   the OK command button

To print the Worksheet Model with the column print titles, header, and footer:

Click   the Print 🖨 button

The printout should look like Figure 6-20, Parts 1 and 2.

Figure 6-20
Part 1

		YEAR 1	YEAR 2	YEAR 3	YEAR 4	YEAR 5	YEAR 6	YEAR 7	YEAR 8
ABC COMPANY									
BUDGET									
		YEAR 1	YEAR 2	YEAR 3	YEAR 4	YEAR 5	YEAR 6	YEAR 7	YEAR 8
Sales		$60,000	$61,200	$62,424	$63,672	$64,945	$66,244	$67,569	$68,920
Expenses									
Salaries		35,000	35,500	36,200	37,000	37,000	37,000	37,000	37,000
Rent		9,000	9,000	9,000	9,000	9,000	9,000	9,000	9,000
Telephone		1,000	1,050	1,103	1,158	1,216	1,277	1,341	1,408
Office Supplies		750	800	850	900	950	1,000	1,050	1,100
Miscellaneous		1,000	1,030	1,061	1,093	1,126	1,160	1,195	1,231
Total Expenses		46,750	47,380	48,214	49,151	49,292	49,437	49,586	49,739
Gross Profit		$13,250	$13,820	$14,210	$14,521	$15,653	$16,807	$17,983	$19,181
Assumptions									
Sales			2%	2%	2%	2%	2%	2%	2%
Telephone			5%	5%	5%	5%	5%	5%	5%
Office Supplies			50.00	50.00	50.00	50.00	50.00	50.00	50.00
Miscellaneous			3%	3%	3%	3%	3%	3%	3%

Figure 6-20
Part 2

	YEAR 9	YEAR 10	TOTAL
Sales	$70,298	$71,704	$656,976
Expenses			
Salaries	37,000	37,000	365,700
Rent	9,000	9,000	90,000
Telephone	1,478	1,552	12,583
Office Supplies	1,150	1,200	9,750
Miscellaneous	1,268	1,306	11,470
Total Expenses	49,896	50,058	489,503
Gross Profit	$20,402	$21,646	$167,473
Assumptions			
Sales	2%	2%	
Telephone	5%	5%	
Office Supplies	50.00	50.00	
Miscellaneous	3%	3%	

Gridlines and Row and Column Headings

You can use the check box in the Page Setup dialog box to include or exclude cell gridlines and the row and column headings on your printouts. The default condition is to include gridlines but to exclude row and column headings.

To exclude the gridlines:

Choose	File
Choose	Page Setup
Click	the Sheet tab
Click	the Gridlines check box in the Print group box to remove the X
Click	the OK command button

If you want to print the row and column headings, click the Row and Column Headings check box. To print the Worksheet Model with the column print titles, header, footer, and without gridlines:

Click	the Print 🖨 button

Orientation

In printing operations, the standard orientation for printing a worksheet is **portrait**. To change the orientation to **landscape**:

Choose	File
Choose	Page Setup
Click	the Page tab
Click	the Landscape option button in the Orientation group box
Click	the OK command button

■ PAGE BREAK

Excel has a number of default settings when you print a worksheet. You can change these settings using various print commands. When printing a worksheet in Excel using the default settings, the software prints as much as it can on a single page based on the default page length. The remaining rows are printed on the next page or set of pages. Sometimes, you may wish to specify where you want page breaks to occur. You can use the Page Break command on the Insert menu in such situations.

To insert a page break at cell A12 of the BUDGET2 worksheet:

Click	on cell A12
Choose	Insert
Choose	Page Break

When the worksheet is printed, the data in row 12 (Telephone expenses) will be printed at the top of the second page. Dashes appear on the bottom border for every cell in row 11 to indicate a page break has been set.

After making cell A1 the active cell, your screen should look like Figure 6-21.

Figure 6-21

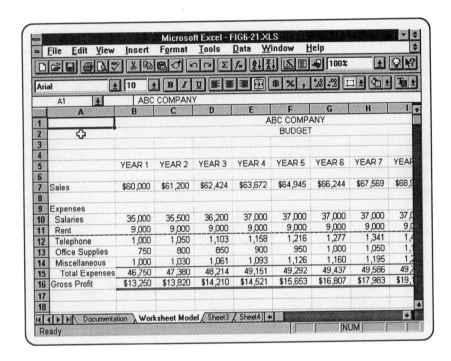

To remove the page break:

Click	on cell A12
Choose	Insert
Choose	Remove Page Break

The dashes no longer appear on the bottom border of every cell in row 11.

Close the workbook document. Do not save any changes.

■ PRINTING THE CELL FORMULAS OF A WORKSHEET IN TABULAR FORM

At times, you may want to see the cell formulas that comprise a worksheet. Open the BUDGET workbook file.

To change the format of the worksheet to see the cell formulas:

Choose	Tools
Choose	Options
Click	the View tab (if necessary)
Click	the Formulas check box in the Window Options group box to insert an X

To view the worksheet and close the Options dialog box:

Click	the OK command button

The formulas that were formatted using the Tools Options command sequence are now displayed on the worksheet itself. However, some cell formulas are not fully displayed because the column width is not wide enough to accommodate them. For example, column C is not wide enough to fully display the formula in cell C12. Your screen should look like Figure 6-22.

Figure 6-22

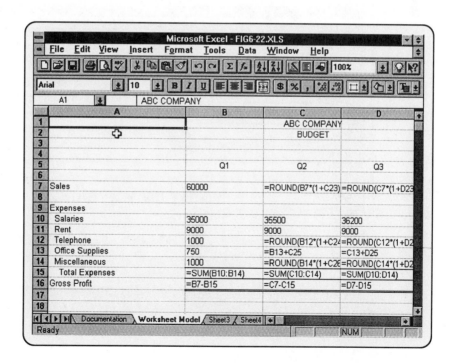

In order to view the full formulas, you need to widen the columns. You can then print the worksheet that includes the formulas by clicking the Print 🖨 button or choosing the Print command on the File menu. Close the workbook document. Do not save any changes.

■ ZOOMING THE WORKSHEET

You can magnify or shrink the worksheet or a portion of the worksheet using the Zoom command on the View menu.

Open the BUDGET2 workbook file.

Choose	View
Choose	Zoom

The Zoom dialog box appears.

Click	the 200% option button in the Magnification group box
Click	the OK command button

Your screen should look like Figure 6-23.

Figure 6-23

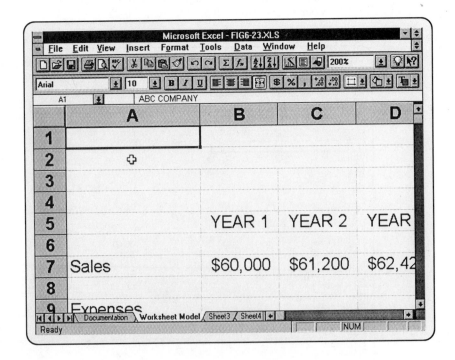

To restore the selected screen to normal size:

Choose	View
Choose	Zoom
Click	the 100% option button in the Magnification group box
Click	the OK command button

The worksheet can be made smaller in size. You can also specify your own factor by typing the desired percentage in the Custom text box. The size of the worksheet on your screen does not affect the size of the worksheet when it is printed.

User Tip

An alternative method to "zoom" in on a worksheet is to click the down arrow on the Zoom Control `100%` ± button on the Standard toolbar. Then choose the desired magnification.

■ RECALCULATION OF A WORKSHEET

To change the value of a cell on the worksheet:

Click	on cell B7
Enter	70,000

The worksheet is automatically recalculated with the new entry $70,000 for Sales in YEAR 1. Your screen should look like Figure 6-24. The initial setting for recalculation is Automatic; the worksheet recalculates automatically and in natural order every time any cell is changed. When a worksheet is large and new data are input, it may take several seconds or even minutes for the worksheet to recalculate. If you have several changes to make, time will be wasted while you wait for Excel to make the change individually. A way to reduce the time is to set the Recalculation option to Manual.

Figure 6-24

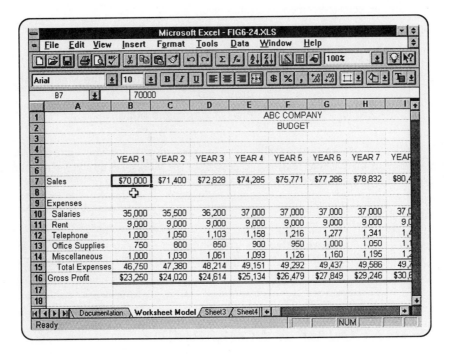

To control the recalculation in a worksheet manually:

Choose	Tools
Choose	Options
Click	the Calculation tab
Click	the Manual option button in the Calculation group box
Click	the OK command button

To change the Sales amount in cell B7 again:

Enter	80,000

Note that when the number 80,000 was entered, the worksheet was not recalculated and the word Calculate appears on the status bar. Your screen should look like Figure 6-25.

Figure 6-25

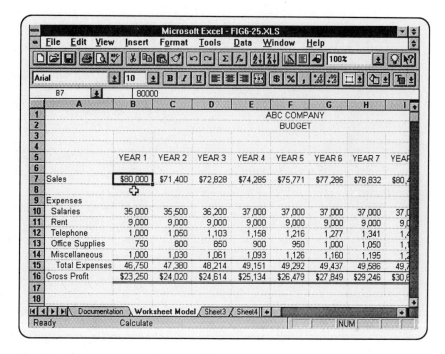

To recalculate the worksheet:

Choose	Tools
Choose	Options
Click	the Calculation tab (if necessary)
Click	the Calc Now (F9) command button

The word Calculate no longer appears on the status bar.

Your worksheet is now recalculated. If another number is changed at this point, the Calculate message will reappear on the status bar. Multiple entries can be made without the worksheet recalculating after each entry. Your screen should look like Figure 6-26.

Figure 6-26

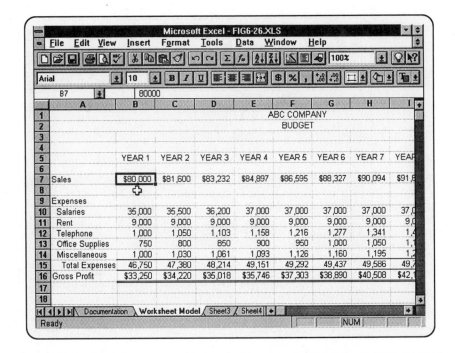

User Tip

An alternative method for recalculating the worksheet is to press the F9 key after you input the appropriate number(s) in the worksheet.

To return to automatic calculation:

Choose	Tools
Choose	Options
Click	the Calculation tab (if necessary)
Click	the Automatic option button in the Calculation group box
Click	the OK command button

Your worksheet will now recalculate automatically with any change made to it.

■ ZERO VALUE SUPPRESSION

There may be times when you wish to eliminate the display of all zeros in a worksheet. Instead of a zero, a blank will appear in any cells containing zeros or a formula that currently evaluates to zero.

For the purposes of this example, a zero will be placed in the entry for Sales in YEAR 1. All of the projections for Sales in the following years are based on this number, and therefore, will also display zeros.

Click	on cell B7 (if necessary)
Type	0
Click	the enter box ✓

The row displaying the Sales data now contains zeros. Your screen should look like Figure 6-27.

Figure 6-27

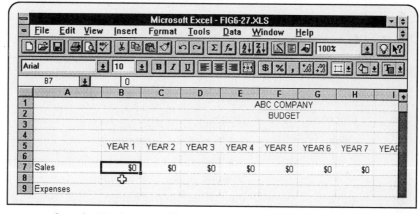

The Options command on the Tools menu allows you to suppress zeros from the worksheet. To suppress the zeros:

Choose	Tools
Choose	Options
Click	the View tab
Click	the Zero Values check box in the Window Options group box to remove the X
Click	the OK command button

The zeros are now suppressed. Notice that even though the zero value is suppressed, the formula in cell C7 still appears in the formula bar when you select cell C7. Your screen should look like Figure 6-28.

Figure 6-28

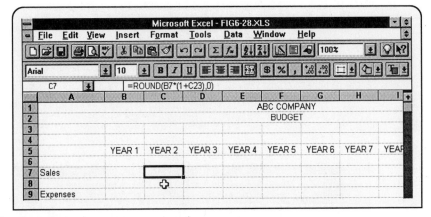

To make the zeros appear on your screen again:

Choose	Tools
Choose	Options
Click	the View tab (if necessary)
Click	the Zero Values check box in the Window Options group box to insert an X
Click	the OK command button

The zeros should be visible again.

Close the workbook document. Do not save any changes.

■ PROTECTING DATA

You can protect your worksheet data by restricting access to the worksheet or to parts of the worksheet. Excel allows you to protect cells, use passwords, and hide data in order to prevent changes.

Cell Protection

Cells can be "locked" to prevent changes from being made to them.

The Protect Sheet command turns on worksheet protection. You can also protect the entire workbook by using the Protect Workbook command. You can change cells only if they were previously unprotected using the Protection tab associated with the Cells command on the Format menu. When you try to enter data or make changes in protected cells, a dialog box appears reminding you that the cells are locked.

Saving files with a password is an alternate method for limiting access to files. This method of file protection is discussed later in this chapter.

Open the BUDGET workbook file.

To unprotect only cells B7 through B14:

Select	cells B7:B14
Choose	Format
Choose	Cells
Click	the Protection tab
Click	the Locked check box to remove the X
Click	the OK command button

To protect the worksheet:

Choose	Tools
Choose	Protection
Choose	Protect Sheet

The Protect Sheet dialog box appears on your screen. Notice that you may enter a password. Unlike a password created when the file is saved, this password will allow anyone to open the workbook file but will prevent them from unlocking the workbook.

To skip creating a password and simply accept protecting the workbook:

Click	the OK command button

Now all cells in the worksheet except B7 through B14 are protected.

Click	on cell C7
Type	3

A dialog box appears in the worksheet window to indicate the cell is protected. To remove the dialog box:

Click	the OK command button
Click	on cell B10
Enter	36000

Notice that you are able to change the data in the unprotected cells and the worksheet recalculates.
To unprotect the worksheet:

Choose	Tools
Choose	Protection
Choose	Unprotect Sheet

> *Design Tip*
> Use the cell-protection capabilities of Excel liberally in your worksheet. For
> example, protect all cells that include formulas. By protecting such cells, you can
> avoid accidental changes to your worksheet.

Close the BUDGET workbook document. Do not save any changes.

Workbook File Protection

You can create a password for a workbook file using the Save As command. Only users who know the password can open the file. The password can be up to 15 characters in length and is case sensitive. It is important to remember to keep a record of the exact password and the combination of upper- or lowercase characters that you used.

When a password is entered in the Protection Password text box, Excel displays an asterisk for each character. Once you have entered the password, Excel asks you to verify the password. You must enter the exact password again.

Open the BUDGET workbook file.

To create a password for the workbook file:

Choose	File
Choose	Save As
Click	the Options command button

The Save Options dialog box appears.

Type	the desired password in the Protection Password text box
Click	the OK command button
Retype	the password
Click	the OK command button
Click	the OK command button
Click	the Yes command button

Close the BUDGET workbook document.

To remove a password from a file, first open the BUDGET workbook file.

The Password dialog box appears.

Enter	the password
Click	the OK command button

Then:

Choose	File
Choose	Save As
Click	the Options command button
Double-click	the asterisks in the Protection Password box (if necessary)
Press	[Delete]
Click	the OK command button
Click	the OK command button
Click	the Yes command button

Close the BUDGET workbook document.

■ HIDING PORTIONS OF A WORKSHEET

Excel allows you to hide columns and rows in a worksheet so they are not visible on your screen.

Hiding Columns

One or more columns of a worksheet can be suppressed so that any data in them is not displayed or printed, but the data continues to be used in calculations.

Open the BUDGET2 workbook file. To hide column E:

Click	on cell E1
Choose	Format
Choose	Column
Choose	Hide

Column E is no longer visible on the screen. Notice that the letter E is gone from the column headings and is replaced now by a slightly thicker line. Your screen should look like Figure 6-29.

Figure 6-29

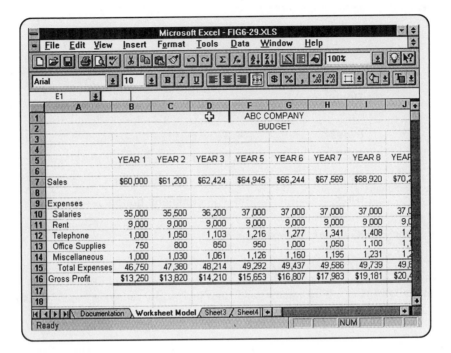

To make column E visible on your screen again:

Select	cells D1:F1
Choose	Format
Choose	Column
Choose	Unhide

Column E appears on your screen again.

Hiding Rows

You can suppress one or more rows of a worksheet so that any data in them is not displayed or printed, but the data continues to be used in calculations.

To hide rows 7 and 16 so that the Sales and Gross Profit values are invisible:

Select	rows 7 and 16
Choose	Format
Choose	Row
Choose	Hide

Rows 7 and 16 no longer appear on your screen. Notice that the numbers are gone from the row headings and are replaced by a slightly thicker line.

To make rows 7 and 16 visible on your screen again:

Select	rows 6 through 8 and rows 15 through 17
Choose	Format
Choose	Row
Choose	Unhide

The hidden rows reappear on your screen.

Close the BUDGET2 workbook document. Do not save any changes.

■ RANGE NAMES

Creating Range Names

Range names can be used rather than cell addresses to make it easier to remember the location of cells. A range name is associated with the cell addresses.

Open the BUDGET workbook file. To assign a range name to the cells containing the values of Sales for the four quarters:

Select	cells B7:E7
Choose	Insert
Choose	Name
Choose	Define

Notice the default text in the Names in Workbook text box is the row title. You can accept this name or change to some other text.

To accept the name Sales:

Click	the OK command button

User Tip

An alternative method for defining a name is to select the range of cells. Then double-click the name box in the left side of the formula bar. Type the name and press ENTER. To see the list of names defined in the workbook, click the arrow on the name box drop-down list box.

You can use range names in formulas in place of cell addresses. Cell addresses in formulas can be changed to reflect that you have defined a name for the range of cells.

> *Design Tip*
> In some situations, you may need to specify several ranges of cells to print for a worksheet. By defining and using range names, you do not need to remember the cell ranges, but rather can refer to the range names.

Deleting a Range Name

When you delete a range name, the contents of the cell or range of cells do not change.

To delete the range name Sales you created:

Choose	Insert
Choose	Name
Choose	Define
Click	on the Sales name in the Names in Workbook list box
Click	the Delete command button
Click	the OK command button

"Sales" in the name box has been replaced by "B7."

■ FIND AND REPLACE

The Find command on the Edit menu finds a string of characters in a cell and highlights the cell containing the string. Unless the Match Case box is marked, uppercase and lowercase characters are treated without sensitivity. You can search all or part of the worksheet. To search a portion of a worksheet, highlight a specific range of cells to search.

The Replace command on the Edit menu finds a string of characters in a label or formula and then replaces it with the exact string of characters that you designate. The matching cell is highlighted. The following four options are available:

Find Next:	skips the current occurrence and highlights the next one
Close:	quits the procedure
Replace:	inserts the replacement and automatically moves to the next occurrence
Replace All:	replaces all occurrences of the string

When there are no further strings of characters that match, another cell is not made active.

Suppose you need to change the word *Sales* to *Revenue*.

To search for the word *Sales*:

Click	on cell A1
Choose	Edit
Choose	Replace
Type	Sales in the Find What text box
Click	the Replace with text box
Type	Revenue
Click	the Find Next command button

The cell containing the first occurrence of the word *Sales* is highlighted. To replace *Sales* with the word *Revenue*:

Click	the Replace command button

The cell containing the next occurrence of the word *Sales* becomes the active cell. You may accept replacement by selecting the Replace command button, or skip the occurrence by selecting the Find Next command. Continue to click the Replace command button until a dialog box appears indicating Excel can find no additional matching data. Since there are no more occurrences of Sales in the worksheet, cell A23 remains the active cell.

Once the process is completed, to close the Replace dialog box:

Click	the OK command button when the message "Cannot find matching data" appears in a dialog box
Click	the Close command button

Close the BUDGET workbook document. Do not save any changes.

■ MANIPULATING DATA

Freezing and Unfreezing Panes

When working on a large worksheet and moving to a distant row or column, your column and row titles may disappear from the screen. When this happens, it can be difficult to understand the data. The following example demonstrates how such a problem can occur and how to solve the problem. Open the BUDGET2 workbook file.

Make cell I24 the active cell. Your screen should look like Figure 6-30.

Figure 6-30

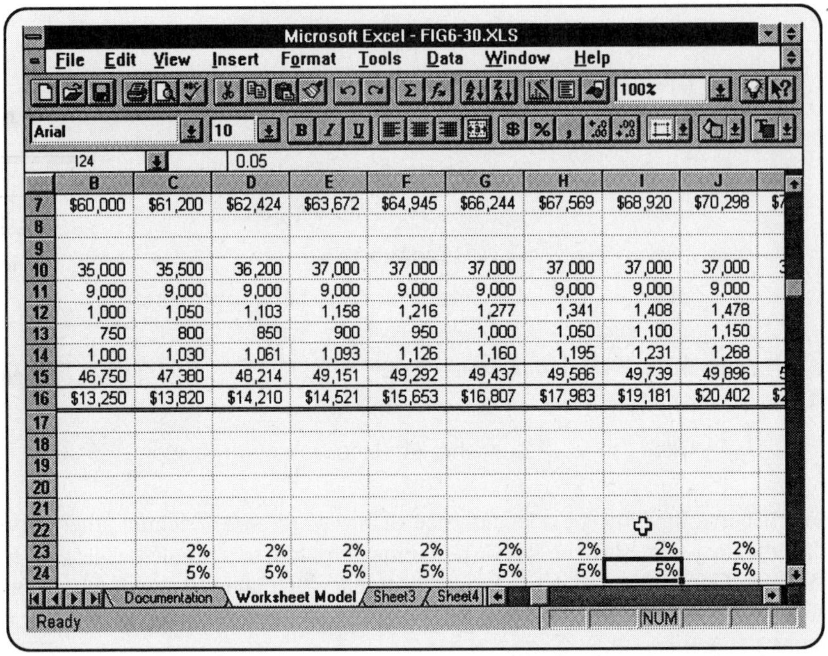

Note that the column titles and row titles are not visible, thus making it difficult to interpret the data.

Before you use the menu to freeze the panes, the active cell must be in the correct position as described below:

> The column(s) you wish to keep displayed must be displayed directly to the left of the active cell (in this example, column A will remain on the screen because the active cell will be in column B).

> The row(s) you wish to keep displayed must be directly above the active cell (in this example, row 5 will remain on the screen because the active cell will be in row 6).

To position the cell pointer so that the appropriate column and row titles are visible on the screen:

Press	Ctrl + Home
Click	on cell B6

To access the menu commands to freeze the column and row titles:

Choose	Window
Choose	Freeze Panes

To see the results of freezing the first column and rows 1 through 5, make cell I28 the active cell. Your screen should look like Figure 6-31.

Figure 6-31

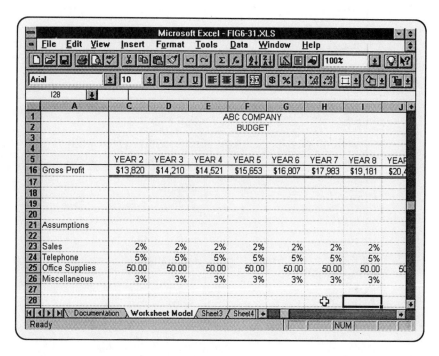

Note that even though the cell pointer has been moved to a "distant" area of the worksheet, rows 1 through 5 and column A remain visible on the screen. By using this option, it is possible to see the column and row titles and understand the content of the worksheet.

To remove the freeze settings:

Choose	Window
Choose	Unfreeze Panes

Splitting a Window into Panes

An alternative to freezing panes is to use Excel's Splitting feature. Excel allows you to view different areas of the worksheet at the same time by splitting the worksheet window into panes. A worksheet window can be split into panes by using the horizontal and vertical split bar or by choosing the Split command on the Window menu. The vertical split bar appears at the right edge of the horizontal scroll bar. The horizontal split bar appears at the top of the vertical scroll bar.

To split the screen vertically to aid in viewing row titles:

Press	Ctrl + Home
Click	the vertical split box

| **Drag** | the gray split bar to the boundary line between columns C and D |
| **Release** | the mouse button |

Two vertical windows are visible on the screen. You can use the same steps to view horizontally split windows aiding in viewing column titles. Your screen should look like Figure 6-32.

Figure 6-32

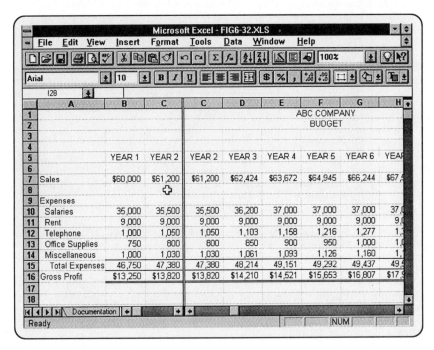

Notice that column C appears in each window.

To move to the right window:

| **Click** | on any cell in the right window |
| **Click** | on cell L7 |

Any cell in either window can be accessed. To move to the left window:

| **Click** | on cell B7 in the left window |
| **Enter** | 65000 |

By splitting the window into panes, you are able to see the effect of changing Sales in YEAR 1 on another area of the worksheet. In this example, you can see the updated amount for the TOTAL of Sales when the value of Sales in YEAR 1 is changed. Your worksheet should look like Figure 6-33.

Figure 6-33

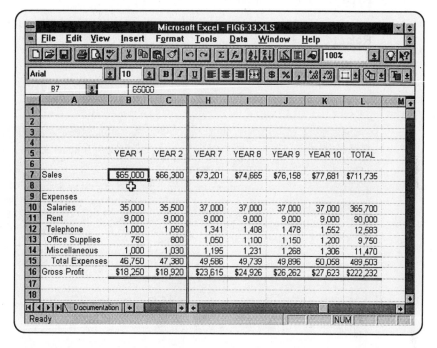

To clear the window panes:

Click	the vertical split bar
Drag	the gray split bar to the right edge of the workbook document window

The split view of the worksheet is removed from your screen. Splitting windows can also be achieved with the Split command on the Window menu. By default, Excel splits the window above and to the left of the active cell.

Close the BUDGET2 workbook document. Do not save any changes.

Viewing More Than One Window

Depending on the capabilities of your computer and the size of the workbooks, Excel allows you to have as many workbook files open at one time as your computer's memory allows. You may view small portions of each workbook file simultaneously with the Arrange command on the Window menu.

First, make sure no workbook files are open. Then open the BUDGET workbook file and the SALES workbook file. You can only see the SALES workbook or the last workbook opened.

The Arrange command on the Window menu allows you to see all of your open workbooks by dividing the screen into various parts. To see vertical portions of both workbooks:

Choose	Window
Choose	Arrange

The Arrange Windows dialog box appears.

Click the Tiled option button in the Arrange group box

Click the OK command button

Your screen should look like Figure 6-34.

Figure 6-34

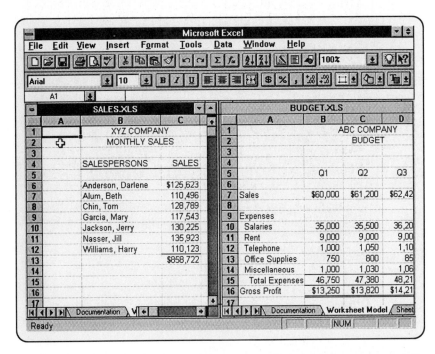

Notice that the SALES workbook appears on the left and is the active window. When the Arrange command is issued, the currently active workbook always appears in the left-uppermost window.

To make the BUDGET workbook the active window:

Click anywhere in the BUDGET window

Your screen should look similar to Figure 6-35.

Figure 6-35

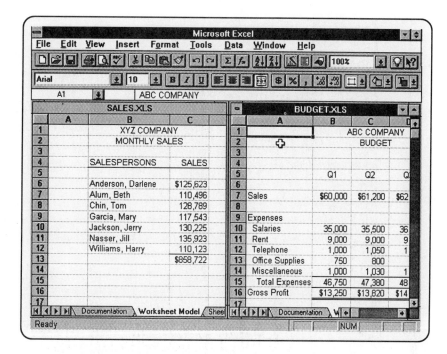

Only one window can be active at a time. When a window is active, you can see the active cell in the worksheet. Also, scroll bars and the document Control-menu box are visible. The title bar should also change color when the window is active. Changes made to the active window do not affect the other window(s).

Close the SALES workbook document. Do not save any changes. The BUDGET workbook document remains on your screen and is used in the next section.

Sizing a Window

You can change the size of a window by changing the size of the window frame.

Move	the mouse pointer to the bottom border of the BUDGET workbook window until it becomes a double-pointing arrow
Press and Drag	the frame up to make the window smaller

Your screen should look similar to Figure 6-36.

Figure 6-36

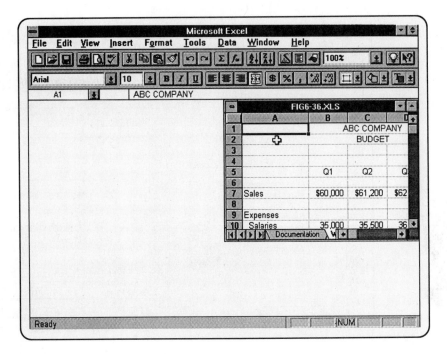

Any one of the four frame sides may be used to change the window size. If you move to a corner of the window frame, you may size the window proportionally.

Moving a Window

At times, you may want to move a window. To move the BUDGET workbook to the middle of the workbook window:

Move	the mouse pointer to the BUDGET.XLS title bar
Drag	the title bar toward the middle of the screen
Release	the mouse button to accept the new window position

Your screen should look similar to Figure 6-37.

Figure 6-37

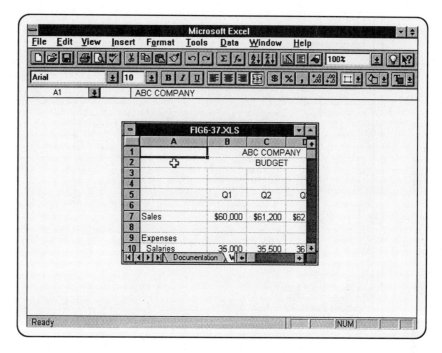

A dialog box can be moved in the same manner as a workbook window. This is sometimes necessary to view data hidden by the dialog box.

Close the BUDGET workbook document. Do not save any changes.

■ CUSTOMIZING THE TOOLBAR

The buttons on the toolbars allow you to quickly perform commands using the mouse without accessing the menu. You may also customize a toolbar and choose from a variety of available toolbars.

Before starting this exercise, make sure you have a blank workbook document on your screen. If necessary, maximize the workbook window.

To view different toolbars:

Choose	View
Choose	Toolbars

The Toolbars dialog box appears on your screen. Your screen should look like Figure 6-38.

Figure 6-38

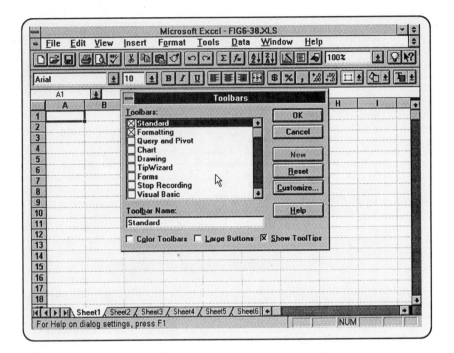

To select the Chart toolbar:

Click   the Chart check box in the Toolbars list box to
            insert an X

Click   the OK command button

Your screen should look like Figure 6-39.

Figure 6-39

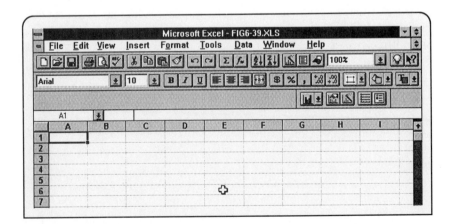

If the Chart toolbar does not appear below the Standard and Formatting toolbars, it can be placed there by dragging it above the column headings. Once a toolbar has been placed below the Standard and Formatting toolbars, it will return to that position the next time it is used.

To remove the Chart toolbar:

Choose	View
Choose	Toolbars
Click	the Chart check box in the Toolbars list box to remove the X
Click	the OK command button

Toolbars may also be altered with the Customize command button in the Toolbars dialog box. The picture of the tool may be changed and tools may be copied from one toolbar to another. See the Help feature or consult the Excel User's Guide for more details.

User Tip

An alternative method for selecting other toolbars is to move the mouse pointer anywhere in the toolbar area and click the alternate mouse button. The other toolbar choices appear in the menu. You can make selections by clicking any toolbar name in the menu.

■ WORKSHEET DOCUMENTATION

After a worksheet is completed, it should be documented. Minimum documentation should include: (1) a printout of the worksheet, (2) a printout of the worksheet cell formulas, (3) a copy of the worksheet on a diskette, (4) information on the purpose of the worksheet, (5) source of the input data, and (6) destination and users of the output information. Documentation is particularly useful when a worksheet must be changed or a workbook file is destroyed.

It is a good idea to keep the documentation in a fireproof file cabinet or in a separate location. You can usually obtain additional assistance on documentation and backup precautions from the information systems department in an organization.

■ PROBLEM SOLVING

Excel provides methods for performing complex problem solving analysis through the Goal Seek and Solver commands on the Tools menu.

Goal Seek

The Goal Seek command feature helps you calculate a particular goal by changing one variable. For example, suppose you want to determine how to reach Total Sales in Q1 of $73,000 for the ABC Company. Total Sales are based on the sales of two products, Product A and Product B. Of the products, assume that only Product A can change.

To determine the answer manually, you may have to perform a series of guesses for Product A sales. However by using the Goal Seek command on the Tools menu, you can calculate the answer very easily.

To initiate this exercise:

Open	the BUDGET workbook file

To add the titles for the product information:

Enter	QTY in cell B34
Enter	PRICE in cell C34
Enter	SALES in cell D34
Right-align	the contents of cells B34:D34

To place the data for Product A on the worksheet:

Enter	Product A in cell A35
Enter	5,000 in cell B35
Enter	$2.00 in cell C35

To add the data for Product B:

Enter	Product B in cell A36
Enter	10,000 in cell B36
Enter	$5.00 in cell C36

To compute the sales for each product:

Click	on cell D35
Enter	the formula =B35*C35
Copy	the formula in cell D35 to D36

Format cells C35 and C36 to insert dollar signs and two decimal places.

Your screen should look like Figure 6-40.

Figure 6-40

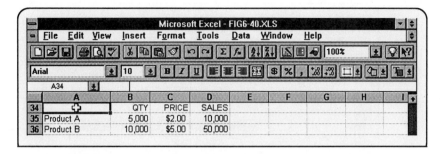

The entry for Q1 Sales in cell B7 must be a formula that reflects the sales of Product A and Product B. To change Q1 Sales to a formula:

| **Click** | on cell B7 |
| **Enter** | the formula =D35+D36 |

Save the workbook document to a file using the name PRODUCT.

To solve the problem using the Goal Seek command:

| **Choose** | Tools |
| **Choose** | Goal Seek |

The Goal Seek dialog box appears.

To specify the cell to set to a particular value and the desired value:

Click	on cell B7 (if necessary)
Click	the To value text box
Enter	73,000

To indicate the cell to change:

| **Click** | the By changing cell text box |
| **Click** | on cell B35 |

Your screen should look like Figure 6-41.

Figure 6-41

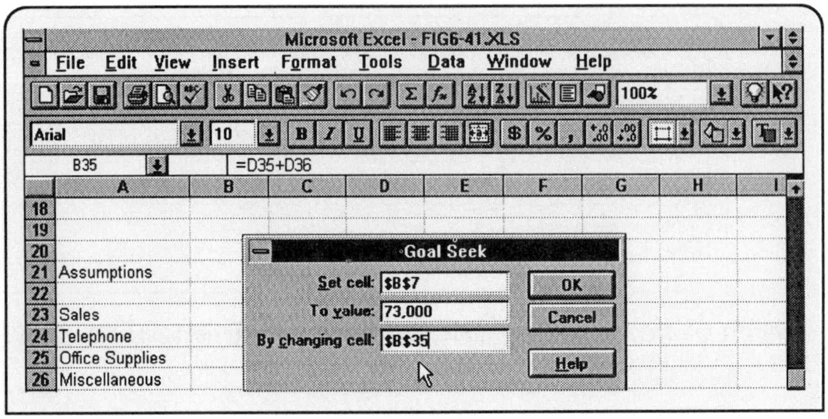

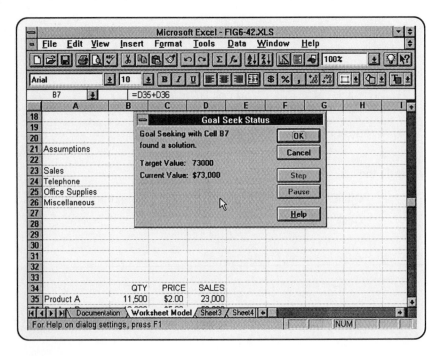

To determine the appropriate quantity of Product A and complete the Goal Seek command:

Click   the OK command button

The Goal Seek Status dialog box appears. The message indicates that Excel has found a solution. Your screen should look like Figure 6-42.

Figure 6-42

To view the solution:

Click   the OK command button

Examine the contents of cell B35. Notice that it has changed from 5,000 to 11,500.

Your screen should look like Figure 6-43.

Figure 6-43

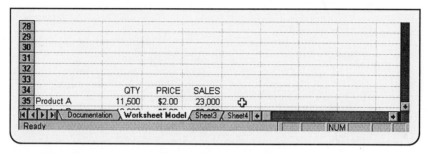

Click on cell B7. Note that the new Q1 Sales value is $73,000.

Close the PRODUCT workbook document. Do not save any changes.

Solver

The Solver command on the Tools menu allows you to determine the maximum, minimum, or specified value for a cell based on a set of constraints. For example, you can compute the maximum value for Q1 sales when both Products A and B change.

Because there are limits to how much you can possibly sell in one quarter, the Solver command allows you to specify constraints. To determine the answer to this problem, you will use the following constraints:

> Q1 Sales can be greater than or equal to $65,000.
>
> Q1 Sales can be less than or equal to $80,000.
>
> Production of Product A can be greater than or equal to 6,000 units.
>
> Production of Product B can be less than or equal to 12,000 units.

To begin the example:

> **Open**   the PRODUCT workbook file

To use the Solver command to find the product values that maximize Q1 Sales:

> **Choose**   Tools
>
> **Choose**   Solver

The Solver Parameters dialog box appears.

To specify Q1 Sales is the target cell:

> **Click**   on cell B7

Since the Max option button is selected, the next step is to specify what cells can change.

Click	the By Changing Cells text box
Select	cells B35:B36

To include the first constraint:

Click	the Add command button

The Add Constraint dialog box appears.

To specify the constraint:

Click	on cell B7
Click	the arrow on the Operator symbol drop-down list box
Select	the >= option
Click	the Constraint text box
Enter	65,000

The first constraint is specified. Your screen should look like Figure 6-44.

Figure 6-44

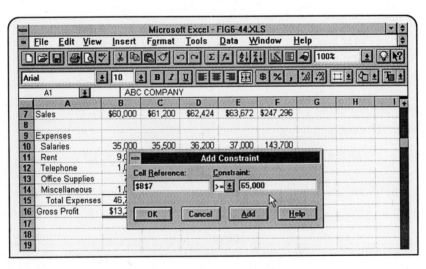

To enter the second constraint:

Click	the Add command button
Click	on cell B7
Click	the arrow on the Operator symbol drop-down list box

Select	the <= option
Click	the Constraint text box
Enter	80,000

To specify the third constraint:

Click	the Add command button
Click	on cell B35
Click	the arrow on the Operator symbol drop-down list box
Select	the >= option
Click	the Constraint text box
Enter	6,000

To include a fourth constraint:

Click	the Add command button
Click	on cell B35
Click	the arrow on the Operator symbol drop-down list box
Select	the <= option
Click	the Constraint text box
Enter	12,000

To stop adding constraints:

Click	the OK command button

The Solver Parameters dialog box appears again. Your screen should look like Figure 6-45.

Figure 6-45

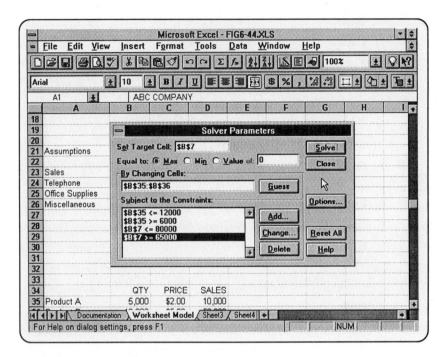

Note that the constraints you entered are displayed in the Subject to the Constraints list box. To solve the problem:

Click   the Solve command button

The Solver Results dialog box appears. Your screen should look like Figure 6-46.

Figure 6-46

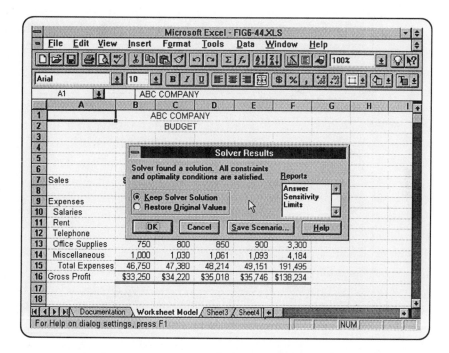

The message in the dialog box indicates that Solver has found an optimal solution. The Keep Solver Solution option button is selected. If you select the Restore Original Values option button, the original values are placed in the worksheet.

To create the report including the answers to the problem:

Select   Answer in the Reports list box

Click   the OK command button

Excel places the Answer Report on the sheet immediately to the left of the active sheet. Note that the new values for production of Product A and Product B appear in cells B35 and B36.

To view the Answer Report sheet that includes additional information:

Click   the Answer Report 1 tab name

The Answer Report appears. Your screen should look like Figure 6-47.

Figure 6-47

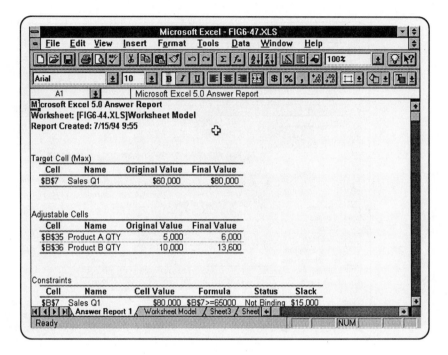

Note that the final values for Product A QTY and Product B QTY are the values appearing in cells B35 and B36.

Close the PRODUCT workbook document. Do not save any changes.

■ USING SCENARIOS

As noted earlier in this book, Excel allows you to complete "what-if" analysis. In such a situation, you change the values of one or more cells to see the impact of the changes on a worksheet. For example, you might change the growth rate for Sales.

You can also create scenarios. In this case, you can create range names associated with one or more cells to specify a scenario. Then you can add the named scenario to the Scenario Manager and then recall the a specific scenario whenever it is appropriate.

Earlier in this chapter, you created the BOATSALE workbook.

Open	the BOATSALE workbook file
Save	the BOATSALE workbook to another file using the name BOATSCEN

Your screen should look like Figure 6-48.

Figure 6-48

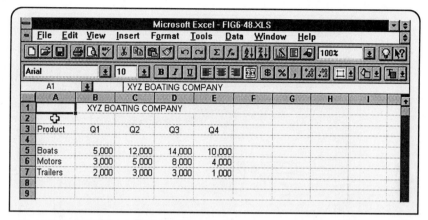

Suppose you are not certain of the values for Motor sales. You can use the Scenario Manager to prepare multiple versions of the Motor sales data and construct scenarios using the different versions. You can use the scenarios and versions to analyze the impact of the various values for Motor sales.

To illustrate the process for using the Scenario Manager, you will assign the current values for Motors to the scenario name CURRENT. Then you will create another version for higher Motor sales and assign the scenario name HIGH SALES.

To add the CURRENT name to the Scenario Manager:

Select	cells B6:E6
Choose	Tools
Choose	Scenarios

The Scenario Manager dialog box appears.

Click	the Add command button

The Add Scenario dialog box appears.

Type	CURRENT in the Scenario Name text box
Click	the OK command button

The Scenario Values dialog box appears.

To accept the existing values for the cells as the current cells scenario:

Click	the OK command button

The Scenario Manager dialog box appears again. Your screen should look like Figure 6-49.

Figure 6-49

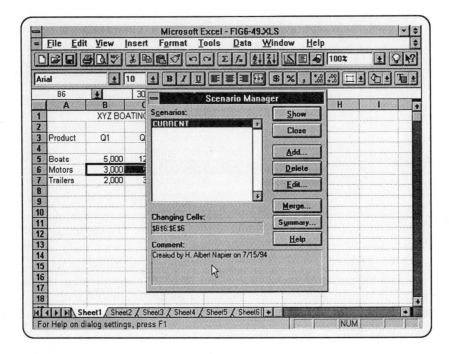

Note that the CURRENT name appears in the Scenarios list box.

To add the HIGH SALES scenario name:

Click	the Add command button
Type	HIGH SALES in the Scenario Name text box
Click	the OK command button

The Scenario Values dialog box appears.

To place the values in the Motor sales cells:

Double-click	the first value text box (if necessary)
Type	4500
Double-click	the second value text box
Type	7000
Double-click	the third value text box
Type	10000
Double-click	the fourth value text box
Type	5000

Your screen should look like Figure 6-50.

Figure 6-50

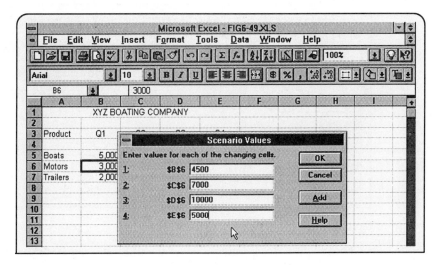

To accept the new values:

Click   the OK command button

The Scenario Manager dialog box appears. Note that the CURRENT and HIGH SALES scenario names appear.

To stop adding scenarios to the Scenario Manager:

Click   the Close command button

The original BOATSCEN worksheet appears on your screen. At this point, you must save the workbook document. The names will remain for you to use.

Click   the Save 🖫 button

To show the HIGH SALES values for Motor sales:

Choose   Tools

Choose   Scenarios

Select   the HIGH SALES scenario in the Scenarios list
                   box

Click   the Show command button

To view the worksheet containing the HIGH SALES values for Motor sales and close the Scenario Manager:

Click   the Close command button

Your screen should look like Figure 6-51.

Figure 6-51

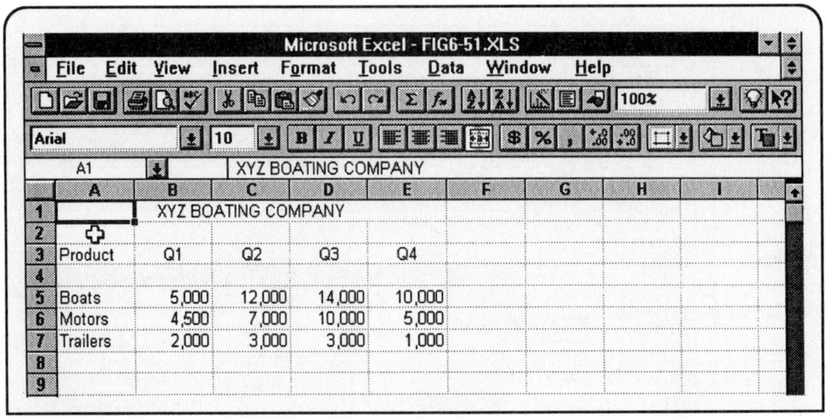

To return to the original values using the CURRENT scenario:

Choose	Tools
Choose	Scenarios
Select	the CURRENT scenario in the Scenarios list box
Click	the Show command button

To view the worksheet containing the CURRENT values for Motor sales and close the Scenario **Manager**:

Click	the Close command button

The original Motor sales appear in the worksheet.

You can modify the values in a scenario. Suppose the values for Motors sales in Q4 should have been 6,500.

To edit the HIGH SALES scenario:

Choose	Tools
Choose	Scenarios
Select	the HIGH SALES scenario
Click	the Edit command button

The Edit Scenario dialog box appears. To accept the HIGH SALES scenario name:

Click	the OK command button

The Scenario Values dialog box appears. To change the Q4 value for Motor sales from 5,000 to 6,500:

Double-click	the fourth value text box
Type	6500
Click	the OK command button

To see the new value and remove the Scenario Manager dialog box:

| **Click** | the Show command button |
| **Click** | the Close command button |

Your screen should look like Figure 6-52.

Figure 6-52

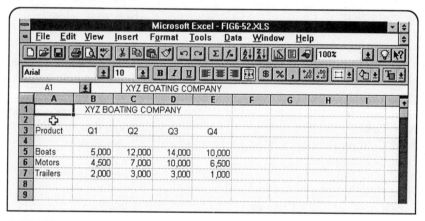

Close the BOATSCEN workbook document. Do not save any changes.

SUMMARY

With the various menu commands and features of Excel, you can control how data is entered and viewed. There are many Excel commands that allow you to work more effectively and efficiently when you are creating, editing, or analyzing worksheets.

KEY CONCEPTS

Absolute cell reference
Cell protection
Column print titles
Customizing the toolbar
Cut ✄ button
Edit Cut
Edit Delete
Edit Find
Edit Paste
Edit Replace
Edit Undo Entry
Error correction
File Page Setup Header/Footer
File Page Setup Page
File Page Setup Sheet
Footers
Format Cells Alignment Fill
Format Cells Number
Format Cells Protection
Format Column Hide
Format Column Unhide
Format Row Hide
Format Row Unhide
Freezing and unfreezing panes
Gridlines
Headers
Hiding columns
Hiding rows
Insert Cells
Insert Columns
Insert Name Define
Insert Page Break
Insert Remove Page Break

Landscape
Moving cell contents
Moving a window
Orientation
Page break
Paste 📋 button
Portrait
Range names
Recalculation
Relative cell reference
Reference key F4
Row print titles
Sizing a window
Tools Goal Seek
Tools Options Calculation
Tools Options View
Tools Protection Protect Sheet
Tools Protection Unprotect Sheet
Tools Scenarios
Tools Solver
Undo
Vertical split box
View Toolbars
View Zoom
Viewing more than one window
Window Arrange Tiled
Window Freeze Panes
Window Unfreeze Panes
Workbook file protection
Worksheet documentation
Zero value suppression
Zoom Control 100% ⬇ button

EXERCISE 1

INSTRUCTIONS: Circle T if the statement is true and F if the statement is false.

T   F   1.   An absolute cell reference means that the reference is kept constant, even when copied.

T   F   2.   The formula bar allows you to correct a cell entry without retyping the entire entry.

T   F   3.   The Freeze Panes command on the Window menu allows you to center titles on a worksheet.

T   F   4.   The vertical split box allows you to view two different areas of a worksheet at the same time.

T   F   5.   The Page Break command on the Insert menu creates a page break in a worksheet.

T   F   6.   If column D is hidden on a worksheet using the Column Hide command on the Format menu, column D will not appear if the worksheet is printed.

T   F   7.   With Tools Options Calculation Manual, you can enter data without the worksheet recalculating after each new entry.

EXERCISE 2

INSTRUCTIONS: Explain a typical situation when the following items are used:

Problem 1: `F4`	*Problem 10:* `F9`
Problem 2: Window Freeze Panes	*Problem 11:* Window Arrange Tiled
Problem 3: Vertical split box	*Problem 12:* View Toolbars
Problem 4: Format Cells Alignment Fill	*Problem 13:* Edit Undo Entry
Problem 5: Insert Cells	*Problem 14:* Insert Page Break
Problem 6: Insert Columns	*Problem 15:* Edit Replace
Problem 7: Edit Cut	*Problem 16:* File Page Setup Header/Footer
Problem 8: Edit Delete	*Problem 17:* View Zoom
Problem 9: Tools Options Calculation Manual	

EXERCISE 3 -- Making a Cell Entry Absolute

INSTRUCTIONS: The following example illustrates a common error. Follow the instructions below to create the error and solve the problem:

Make sure you have a blank workbook on your screen.

In cell A1, enter Revenue.

In cell A2, enter Assumed Rev Rate.

Widen column A to 18 characters.

In cell B1, enter 10000.

In cell B2, enter .15.

In cell C1, enter =B1*(1+B2).

Copy the formula in cell C1 to cells D1 and E1.

After making cell A1 the active cell, your screen should look like Figure 6-53.

Figure 6-53

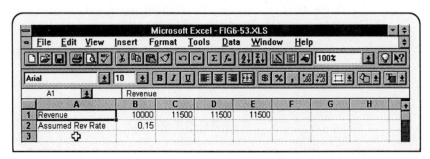

Change the formula in cell C1 and recopy it so that the formulas in cells D1 and E1 also refer to cell B2 for the projected revenue rate.

Print the worksheet.

Close the workbook document. Do not save any changes.

EXERCISE 4 -- Protecting Cells in a Worksheet

INSTRUCTIONS: Open the PRACTICE workbook file you created as an exercise in Chapter 4.

Unprotect the cells containing the Revenue Growth Rates.

Protect all cells in the worksheet.

Change the revenue growth rates to 8%, 5%, 10%, and 7%, respectively, for YEAR 2 through YEAR 5.

Print the worksheet after you have changed the growth rates.

Close the PRACTICE workbook document. Do not save any changes.

EXERCISE 5 -- Hiding and Displaying a Column

INSTRUCTIONS: Open the BUDGET workbook file that you created in Chapter 4.

Hide columns B and F.

Print the worksheet.

Display columns B and F on the screen.

Print the worksheet.

Close the BUDGET workbook document. Do not save any changes.

EXERCISE 6 -- Entering Page Breaks in a Worksheet

INSTRUCTIONS: Open the BUDGET workbook file.

Create a page break after Total Expenses.

Print the worksheet.

Close the BUDGET workbook document. Do not save any changes.

EXERCISE 7 -- Printing Headers and Footers

INSTRUCTIONS: Open the SALES workbook file.

Create the following header and footer:

Header:

SALES RESULTS

Footer:

ANNUAL SALES--CURRENT YEAR

Center the header and footer. Include the current date to the right of the text information of the footer.
Print the worksheet.

Close the SALES workbook document. Do not save any changes.

EXERCISE 8 -- Range Names

INSTRUCTIONS: Open the BUDGET2 workbook file.

Create the range name "Sales" and include the cells containing the Sales amounts for the ten years.

Create the range name "Total_Expenses" and include the cells containing the Total Expenses values for the ten years.

Create the range name "Gross_Profit" and include the cells containing the Gross Profit amounts for the ten years.

Close the BUDGET2 workbook document. Do not save any changes.

EXERCISE 9 -- Replacing Text

INSTRUCTIONS: Open the BUDGET workbook file.

Use the Replace command on the Edit menu to change the name ABC COMPANY to ABC, INC.

Change the word *Sales* to *Revenues* using the Replace command.

Print the worksheet.

Close the BUDGET workbook document. Do not save any changes.

EXERCISE 10 -- Inserting and Deleting Rows and Columns

INSTRUCTIONS: Open the SALES workbook file.

Insert a column at column C.

Insert two rows at row 12.

Print the worksheet.

Delete the column you inserted.

Delete the rows you inserted.

Print the worksheet.

Close the SALES workbook document. Do not save any changes.

EXERCISE 11 -- Suppressing Zero Values

INSTRUCTIONS: Open the PRACTICE workbook file.

Enter the value 0 for the Revenue value in YEAR 1.

Suppress the zero values in the worksheet so that no zeros appear.

Print the worksheet.

Close the PRACTICE workbook document. Do not save any changes.

EXERCISE 12 -- Printing Cell Formulas

INSTRUCTIONS: Open the PRACTICE workbook file.

Change the format of the worksheet to see the cell formulas.

Widen the columns as necessary in order to view the full formulas.

Print the worksheet.

Close the PRACTICE workbook document. Do not save any changes.

CHAPTER SEVEN

CREATING AND PRINTING CHARTS

OBJECTIVES

In this chapter, you will learn to:
- Identify parts of a chart
- Create a column chart
- Create a line chart
- Create a bar chart
- Create a combination chart
- Create a stacked column chart
- Create a pie chart
- Create an XY (Scatter) chart
- Create an area chart
- Create a doughnut chart
- Create a radar chart
- Print a chart document
- Create an embedded chart in a worksheet with the ChartWizard
- Print an embedded chart
- Print an embedded chart and a worksheet
- Delete an embedded chart from a worksheet

■ CHAPTER OVERVIEW

If a worksheet contains a large amount of data, it can be very difficult to detect trends and see relationships among various values. A **chart** depicting key elements of a worksheet can facilitate a more accurate analysis. You can use Excel to create charts using the worksheet data. The chart image can be viewed on your screen and may also be printed. The data points, selected from values on a worksheet, are grouped together into a data series. Each data series has a distinguishing pattern or color.

Excel has 9 two-dimensional chart types and 6 three-dimensional chart types. Excel also provides a number of chart formats for the various chart types.

The 9 two-dimensional chart types available are: area, bar, column, line, pie, doughnut, radar, XY (scatter), and combination. The 6 three-dimensional chart types include: 3-D Area, 3-D Bar, 3-D Column, 3-D Line, 3-D Pie, and 3-D Surface.

Excel provides a tool named ChartWizard to assist you in creating a chart. ChartWizard is a series of five dialog boxes that guide you through the process for preparing a chart.

The ChartWizard has five steps:

1. Specify the range of cells you want to include in the chart.

2. Select the chart type to include on the worksheet.

3. Select the chart format.

4. Indicate whether the data series are in rows or columns and specify the data series on the worksheet to include as category (X) and value (Y) axis.

5. Specify whether to include a legend, input the chart title, or enter the axis title information.

If you modify a data series in the worksheet containing the values for the chart, the chart is automatically updated.

This chapter covers most of the available two-dimensional chart types. The three-dimensional chart types and some additional chart commands are discussed in Chapter 8.

■ IDENTIFYING PARTS OF THE CHART

Figure 7-1 includes a column chart in a chart sheet and identifies the various parts of the chart.

Figure 7-1

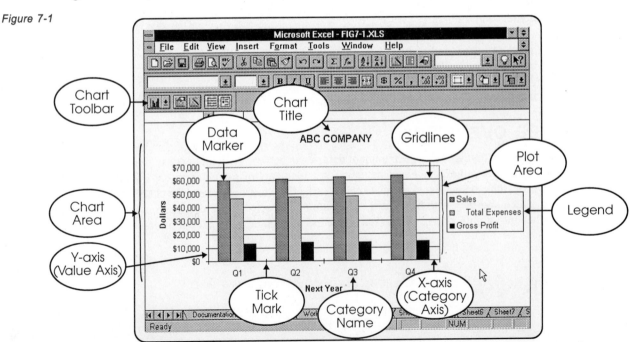

You will create this chart as you work through the remainder of this chapter.

Chart Area

The chart area includes all of the area in the chart sheet and all the elements in the chart.

Chart Toolbar

The Chart toolbar displays some tools for working with charts. With these tools, you can change the chart type, utilize the default chart type, use the ChartWizard, add or delete horizontal gridlines, and include or delete a legend.

Chart Title

The chart title describes the content of the chart.

Data Marker

The data marker is an item such as a bar, dot, area, or other symbol that marks an individual data value.

X-axis (Category Axis)

The x-axis, or category axis, is the horizontal axis along which you normally plot categories of data.

Y-axis (Value Axis)

The Y-axis, or value axis, is the vertical axis you usually use to plot the values associated with various categories.

Category Name

The category names are labels associated with a specific category on the x-axis.

Chart Data Series

A chart data series is a group of related data, such as the values in a single row or column of a worksheet. In this case, Sales for the various quarters is an example of a chart data series.

Gridlines

These lines are optional and are included to make a chart easier to view and understand. Horizontal and/or vertical gridlines can appear on a chart.

Tick Mark

Tick marks are small lines that appear on an axis. Use them to delineate a category, scale, or chart data series.

Data Label

A data label value or label is used to identify a data series or a chart.

Plot Area

The plot area includes the plotted data. The x-axis, y-axis, and data markers are located in the plot area.

Attached Text

Attached text is text associated with a specific object on the chart. For example, the chart title is considered attached text.

Unattached Text

You can include text on the chart outside the plot area. Also, you can place graphics such as arrows on a chart.

Legend

A legend is a key that you use to identify the patterns, colors, or symbols associated with the markers for a chart data series. The chart data series name appears in the legend.

■ CREATING A COLUMN CHART

A column chart is useful for depicting changes in data series that cover a few time periods.

The first chart that you will create in this chapter is based on data in the BUDGET workbook that you created in Chapter 4. To begin the exercise, open the BUDGET workbook file. Your screen should look like Figure 7-2.

Figure 7-2

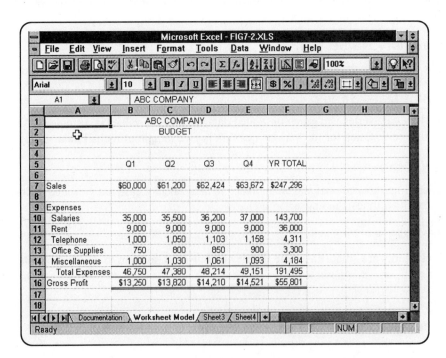

You will create a chart using the Sales, Total Expenses, and Gross Profit values for the four quarters in the BUDGET worksheet. When you finish the chart, your screen will look like Figure 7-3.

Figure 7-3

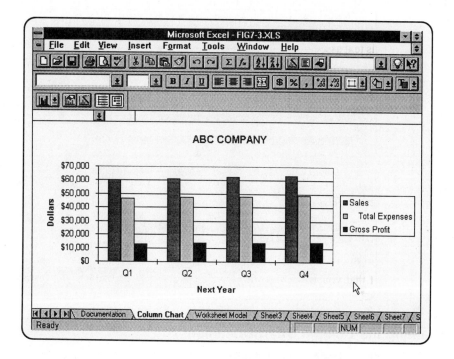

Selecting the Chart Data

You specify the data to chart by selecting it before you create the chart.

Suppose you want to chart the Sales, Total Expenses, and Gross Profit values for the four quarters. You also need to include the column headings (Q1, Q2, Q3, and Q4) in your selection so that they will appear on the x-axis (category axis).

Select	cells A5:E5
Hold down	the Ctrl key and select cells A7:E7, A15:E15, and A16:E16

Your screen should look like Figure 7-4.

Figure 7-4

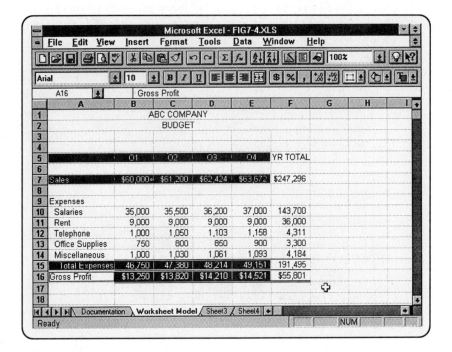

Creating the Column Chart Document

To create a chart using the selected data:

Choose	Insert
Choose	Chart
Choose	As New Sheet

The first dialog box associated with the ChartWizard appears.

Notice the command buttons at the bottom of the dialog box. The buttons and the action associated with each one are:

Help	Access the Help feature
Cancel	Cancel the ChartWizard tool and return to the worksheet
< Back	Return to the previous ChartWizard dialog box
Next >	Proceed to the next ChartWizard dialog box
Finish	Create a chart with the options selected at this point and terminate the usage of ChartWizard

The first dialog box is used to specify the data series to include in the chart.

Since you have already selected the data series for the chart:

Click   the Next command button

The second ChartWizard dialog box appears. Use this dialog box to specify the chart type.
Since the Column chart type is already selected:

Click   the Next command button

The third ChartWizard dialog box appears. This dialog box allow you to select the format for the Column
chart. To accept the default selection format number 6:

Click   the Next command button

The fourth ChartWizard dialog box appears. A sample chart appears in the dialog box. If there is a
problem, you can trace back through the ChartWizard dialog boxes to correct any errors by clicking the
Back command button. If you want to start over, click the Cancel command button or press the ESC key.

In this dialog box, you indicate whether the data series are in rows or columns. Since you are using rows,
you can indicate which rows are used to specify the category (X) axis labels and which columns are used
to define the legend text. Excel assumes that the first row selected specifies the category (X) axis labels.
The software assumes that the first column includes the legend text.

Since the data series you selected are consistent with these assumptions:

Click   the Next command button

The fifth ChartWizard dialog box appears. In this dialog box, you indicate whether a legend should be
placed on the chart. You also can include a chart title and axis titles to make the chart easier to understand.

Excel assumes that you want to include a legend. If you do not desire for a legend to appear on your
screen, click the No option button below the Add a Legend question.

To specify the chart title and include a title for the category and value axis:

Click   the Chart Title text box

Type   ABC COMPANY

Click   the Category (X) text box in the Axis Titles
                     group box

Type   Next Year

Click   the Value (Y) text box in the Axis Titles group
                     box

Type   Dollars

Notice that the sample chart changes to include the information.

To complete the chart-creation process:

Click   the Finish command button

The chart is placed on a chart sheet. Your screen should look like Figure 7-5.

Figure 7-5

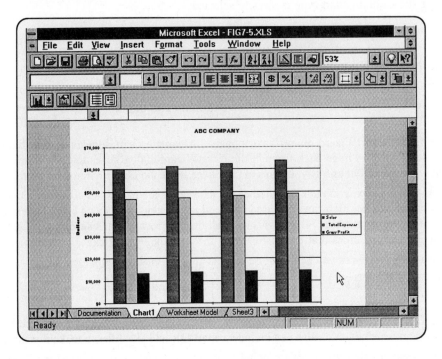

By default, a new chart sheet is independent of the window size. This allows you to see what the chart will look like when it is printed. You can use the Zoom command on the View menu to change the size of the chart.

In order to view the entire chart on the screen, use the Sized with Window command on the View menu. The chart fills the entire window. This display makes it easier to view and edit the chart, but does not show how the chart will print. To view the chart before printing, use the Print Preview command on the File menu or click the Print Preview 🔍 button on the Standard toolbar. You cannot use the Zoom command on the View menu when your chart has been sized with the window.

To view the entire chart:

Choose   View

Choose   Sized with Window

Your screen should look like Figure 7-6.

Figure 7-6

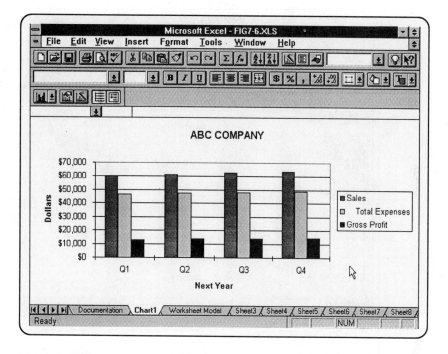

To name the chart sheet:

Double-click	the Chart1 tab
Type	Column Chart
Click	the OK command button

Your screen should look like Figure 7-7.

Figure 7-7

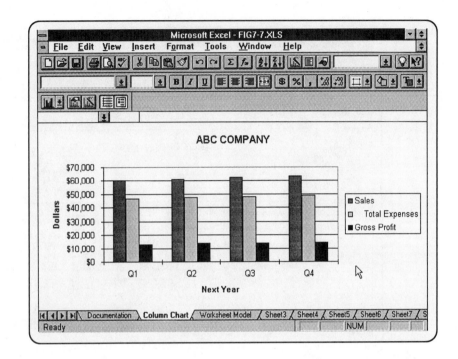

In This Book

The patterns and background on your screen may not look exactly like those in the text. The patterns of charts in the text were chosen because they present a clear illustration.

The Total Expenses legend on the chart is indented. If you choose to remove the indention, you must delete the four leading spaces in cell A15 in the Worksheet Model.

Save the BUDGET workbook to a file using the name BUDCOL. Close the workbook document.

■ CREATING A LINE CHART

When you want to portray changes over time with data series or many time periods, a line chart is appropriate.

Before creating a line chart for the Sales, Total Expenses, and Gross Profit variables:

Open	the BUDGET workbook file
Select	cells A5:E5, A7:E7, A15:E15, and A16:E16

To create a line chart:

Choose	Insert
Choose	Chart
Choose	As New Sheet

The first ChartWizard dialog box appears. Since you have already selected the data series for the chart:

Click	the Next command button

The second ChartWizard dialog box appears. To select the Line chart type:

Click	the Line chart type
Click	the Next command button

The third ChartWizard dialog box appears. To specify format 1 for the Line chart:

Click	format number 1 for the Line chart
Click	the Next command button

The fourth ChartWizard dialog box appears. A sample chart appears in the dialog box.

In this dialog box, you indicate whether the data series are in rows or columns. Since you are using rows, you can indicate which rows are used to specify the category (X) axis labels and which columns are used to define the legend text. Excel assumes that the first row selected specifies the category (X) axis labels. The software also assumes that the first column includes the legend text.

Since the data series you selected are consistent with these assumptions:

Click	the Next command button

The fifth ChartWizard dialog box appears. Excel assumes that you want to include a legend. To specify the chart title and include a title for the category and value axis:

Click	the Chart Title text box
Type	ABC COMPANY
Click	the Category (X) text box in the Axis Titles group box
Type	Next Year
Click	the Value (Y) text box in the Axis Titles group box
Type	Dollars

Notice that the sample chart changes to include the information.

To complete the chart-creation process:

Click   the Finish command button

The chart is placed on a chart sheet.

> *In This Book*
> For Chapters 7, 8, and 9 change the size of the chart to fit the window by choosing the Sized with Window command on the View menu.

To name the chart sheet:

Double-click   the Chart1 tab

Type   Line Chart

Click   the OK command button

Your screen should look like Figure 7-8.

Figure 7-8

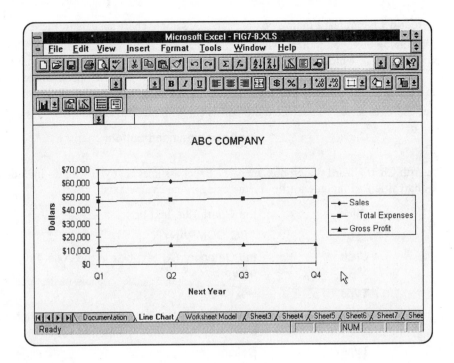

Save the BUDGET workbook to a file using the name BUDLINE. Close the workbook document.

◼ CREATING A BAR CHART

A bar chart is useful for illustrating the values at a specific time or to illustrate comparisons between items. Before creating a bar chart for the Sales, Total Expenses, and Gross Profit variables:

Open	the BUDGET workbook file
Select	cells A5:E5, A7:E7, A15:E15, and A16:E16

To create a bar chart:

Choose	Insert
Choose	Chart
Choose	As New Sheet

The first ChartWizard dialog box appears. Since you have already selected the data series for the chart:

Click	the Next command button

The second ChartWizard dialog box appears. To select the Bar chart type:

Click	the Bar chart type
Click	the Next command button

The third ChartWizard dialog box appears. To accept the default format for the Bar chart:

Click	the Next command button

The fourth ChartWizard dialog box appears. A sample chart appears in the dialog box.

In this dialog box, you indicate whether the data series are in rows or columns. Since you are using rows, you can indicate which rows are used to specify the category (X) axis labels and which columns are used to define the legend text. Excel assumes that the first row selected specifies the category (X) axis labels. The software also assumes that the first column includes the legend text.

Since the data series you selected are consistent with these assumptions:

Click	the Next command button

The fifth ChartWizard dialog box appears. Excel assumes that you want to include a legend. To specify the chart title and include a title for the category and value axis:

Click	the Chart Title text box
Type	ABC COMPANY
Click	the Category (X) text box in the Axis Titles group box
Type	Next Year
Click	the Value (Y) text box in the Axis Titles group box
Type	Dollars

Notice that the sample chart changes to include the information.

To complete the chart-creation process:

Click	the Finish command button

The chart is placed on a chart sheet.

To name the chart sheet:

Double-click	the Chart1 tab
Type	Bar Chart
Click	the OK command button

Your screen should look like Figure 7-9.

Figure 7-9

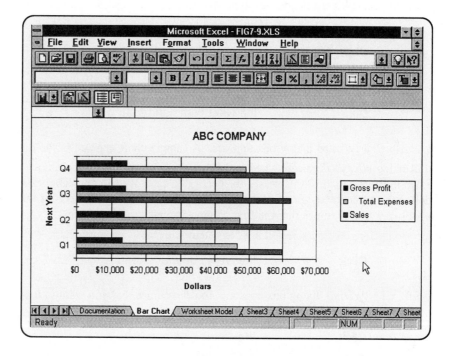

Save the BUDGET workbook to a file using the name BUDBAR. Close the workbook document.

■ CREATING A COMBINATION CHART

In some situations, you may want to use lines and columns to represent data on a chart. You can use a combination chart to create such a chart.

Suppose you need to create a chart that depicts the Total Expenses data series using a line and the Sales data series as a column:

Open	the BUDGET workbook file
Select	cells A5:E5, A7:E7, and A15:E15

To create a combination chart:

Choose	Insert
Choose	Chart
Choose	As New Sheet

The first ChartWizard dialog box appears. Since you have already selected the data series for the chart:

Click	the Next command button

The second ChartWizard dialog box appears. To select the Combination chart type:

Click	the Combination chart type
Click	the Next command button

The third ChartWizard dialog box appears.   To accept the default format for the Combination chart:

Click	the Next command button

The fourth ChartWizard dialog box appears. A sample chart appears in the dialog box.

In this dialog box, you indicate whether the data series are in rows or columns. Since you are using rows, you can indicate which rows are used to specify the category (X) axis labels and which columns are used to define the legend text. Excel assumes that the first row selected specifies the category (X) axis labels. The software also assumes that the first column includes the legend text.

Since the data series you selected are consistent with these assumptions:

Click	the Next command button

The fifth ChartWizard dialog box appears. Excel assumes that you want to include a legend. To specify the chart title and include a title for the category and two value axes:

Click	the Chart Title text box
Type	ABC COMPANY
Click	the Category (X) text box in the Axis Titles group box
Type	Next Year
Click	the Value (Y) text box in the Axis Titles group box
Type	Dollars
Click	the Second Y text box in the Axis Titles group box
Type	Dollars

Notice that the sample chart changes to include the information.

To complete the chart-creation process:

Click	the Finish command button

The chart is placed on a chart sheet.

To name the chart sheet:

Double-click	the Chart1 tab
Type	Combination Chart
Click	the OK command button

Your screen should look like Figure 7-10.

Figure 7-10

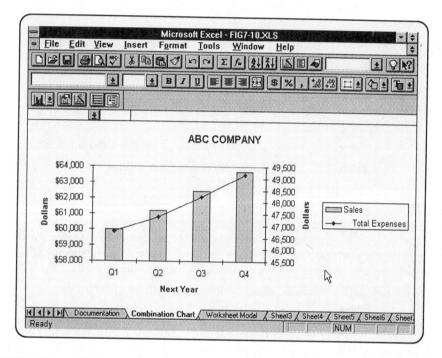

Save the BUDGET workbook to a file using the name BUDCOMB. Close the workbook document.

■ CREATING A STACKED COLUMN CHART

Rather than have separate columns to represent data, you may need to show the data series columns stacked on top of each other in one column.

Before creating a stacked column chart for the Sales, Total Expenses, and Gross Profit variables:

Open	the BUDGET workbook file
Select	cells A5:E5, A7:E7, A15:E15, and A16:E16

To create a stacked column chart:

Choose	Insert
Choose	Chart
Choose	As New Sheet

The first ChartWizard dialog box appears. Since you have already selected the data series for the chart:

Click	the Next command button

The second ChartWizard dialog box appears. To accept the Column chart type:

Click	the Next command button

The third ChartWizard dialog box appears.   To select a format for the Column chart that will result in a Stacked Column chart:

Click	format number 3 for the Column chart
Click	the Next command button

The fourth ChartWizard dialog box appears. A sample chart appears in the dialog box.

In this dialog box, you indicate whether the data series are in rows or columns. Since you are using rows, you can indicate which rows are used to specify the category (X) axis labels and which columns are used to define the legend text. Excel assumes that the first row selected specifies the category (X) axis labels. The software also assumes that the first column includes the legend text.

Since the data series you selected are consistent with these assumptions:

Click	the Next command button

The fifth ChartWizard dialog box appears. Excel assumes that you want to include a legend. To specify the chart title and include a title for the category and value axis:

Click	the Chart Title text box
Type	ABC COMPANY
Click	the Category (X) text box in the Axis Titles group box
Type	Next Year
Click	the Value (Y) text box in the Axis Titles group box
Type	Dollars

Notice that the sample chart changes to include the information.

To complete the chart-creation process:

Click   the Finish command button

The chart is placed on a chart sheet.

Your screen should look like Figure 7-11.

Figure 7-11

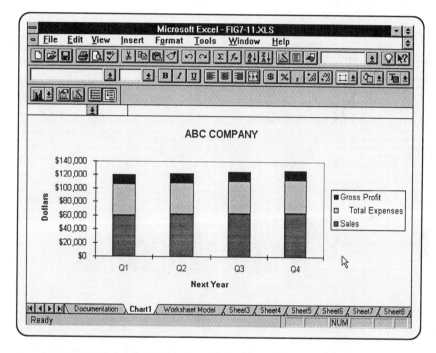

The settings are not appropriate, however, for a stacked column chart. You need to change the selected data so the stacked column chart more accurately depicts the data in the BUDGET Worksheet Model. Close the workbook document and do not save any changes.

To properly illustrate the data in the BUDGET Worksheet Model, you need only include the Total Expenses and Gross Profit data series on the chart. The sum of these items is equal to Sales.

To prepare the appropriate stacked column chart:

Open   the BUDGET workbook file

Select   cells A5:E5, A15:E15, and A16:E16

Repeat the instructions for creating a stacked column chart. A stacked column chart appears on your screen.

To name the chart sheet:

Double-click	the Chart1 tab
Type	Stacked Column
Click	the OK command button

When you have finished, your screen should look like Figure 7-12.

Figure 7-12

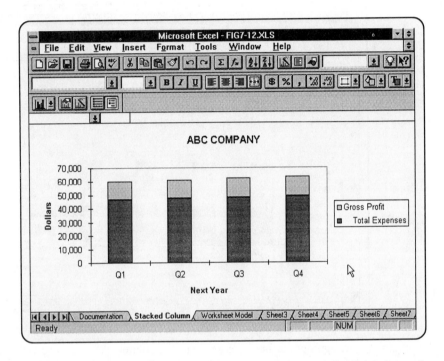

Notice that the Total Expenses plus Gross Profit for each quarter equal the Sales for each quarter.

Save the BUDGET workbook to a file using the name BUDSTCOL. Close the workbook document.

■ CREATING A PIE CHART

A pie chart is useful for portraying the relationship or proportion of one item to a whole.

Suppose you want to create a pie chart for some of the expense categories for the first quarter in the BUDGET worksheet model.

Before creating the pie chart:

Open	the BUDGET workbook file
Select	cells A10:A12 and B10:B12

To create a pie chart:

Choose	Insert
Choose	Chart
Choose	As New Sheet

The first ChartWizard dialog box appears. Since you have already selected the data series for the chart:

Click	the Next command button

The second ChartWizard dialog box appears. To select the Pie chart type:

Click	the Pie chart type
Click	the Next command button

The third ChartWizard dialog box appears. To accept the default format for the Pie chart type:

Click	the Next command button

The fourth ChartWizard dialog box appears. A sample chart appears in the dialog box.

In this dialog box, you indicate whether the data series are in rows or columns. Since you are using data from a column, Excel selects the Columns option button. Since you included two columns in the data series, Excel assumes that the first column contains the pie slice labels.

To accept the specified parameters:

Click	the Next command button

The fifth ChartWizard dialog box appears. Excel assumes that you do not want to include a legend because you included the row labels for use as the pie slice labels. Since there are no axes in a pie chart, you are not allowed to enter data for these items in the dialog box. To specify the chart title:

Click	the Chart Title text box
Type	ABC COMPANY

Notice that the sample chart changes to include the information.

To complete the chart-creation process:

Click	the Finish command button

The chart is placed on a chart sheet.

To name the chart sheet:

Double-click	the Chart1 tab
Type	Pie Chart
Click	the OK command button

Your screen should look like Figure 7-13.

Figure 7-13

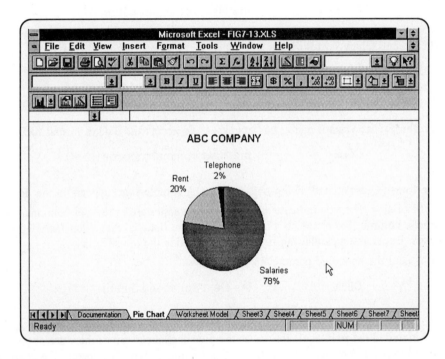

Save the BUDGET workbook to a file using the name BUDPIE. Close the workbook document.

■ CREATING AN XY (SCATTER) CHART

XY (Scatter) charts show the relationship between the values for several variables. This type of chart can also be used to show two data series as one data series of xy coordinates.

Before creating the XY (Scatter) chart:

Open	the UNITPROD workbook file
Select	cells C5:C11 and D5:D11

To create an XY (Scatter) chart:

Choose	Insert
Choose	Chart
Choose	As New Sheet

The first ChartWizard dialog box appears. Since you have already selected the data series for the chart:

Click	the Next command button

The second ChartWizard dialog box appears. To select the XY (Scatter) chart type:

Click	the XY (Scatter) chart type
Click	the Next command button

The third ChartWizard dialog box appears. To accept the default format for the XY (Scatter) chart:

Click	the Next command button

The fourth ChartWizard dialog box appears. A sample chart appears in the dialog box.

In this dialog box, you indicate whether the data series are in rows or columns. Since you are using columns, Excel selects the Column option button.

Excel assumes that the first column includes the X data series and the remaining columns include the Y data series.

In this case, the X data are the products. The number 1 represents Regular Coffee, 2 represents Decaffeinated Coffee, and so on for the product names. The second and third columns include the Y data series associated with each product. For this example, you are charting the number of units produced and sold for each product. Note that when you create XY (Scatter) charts, the software assumes that the first row includes the legend text.

Since the data series you selected are consistent with these assumptions:

Click	the Next command button

The fifth ChartWizard dialog box appears. Excel assumes that you want to include a legend. To specify the chart title and include a title for the category and value axis:

Click	the Chart Title text box
Type	ABC COMPANY
Click	the Category (X) text box in the Axis Titles group box
Type	Product

Click	the Value (Y) text box in the Axis Titles group box
Type	Units

Notice that the sample chart changes to include the information.

To complete the chart-creation process:

Click	the Finish command button

The chart is placed on a chart sheet.

To name the chart sheet:

Double-click	the Chart1 tab
Type	XY (Scatter) Chart
Click	the OK command button

Your screen should look like Figure 7-14.

Figure 7-14

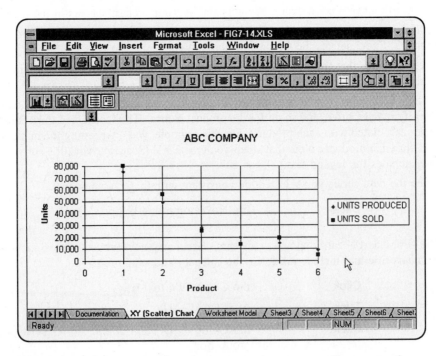

Save the UNITPROD workbook to a file using the name XYSCATT. Close the workbook document.

■ CREATING AN AREA CHART

You can use an area chart to illustrate the relative importance of various items during a period of time.

Suppose you want to show the amount of change in values over a period of time. In this case, you want to create an area chart.

Before creating the area chart:

Open	the BOATSALE workbook file
Select	cells A3:E3, A5:E5, A6:E6, and A7:E7

To create an area chart:

Choose	Insert
Choose	Chart
Choose	As New Sheet

The first ChartWizard dialog box appears. Since you have already selected the data series for the chart:

Click	the Next command button

The second ChartWizard dialog box appears. To select the Area chart type:

Click	the Area chart type
Click	the Next command button

The third ChartWizard dialog box appears. To accept the default format for the Area chart:

Click	the Next command button

The fourth ChartWizard dialog box appears. A sample chart appears in the dialog box.

In this dialog box, you indicate whether the data series are in rows or columns. Since you are using rows, you can indicate which rows are used to specify the category (X) axis labels and which columns are used to define the legend text. Excel assumes that the first row selected specifies the category (X) axis labels. The software also assumes that the first column includes the legend text.

Since the data series you selected are consistent with these assumptions:

Click	the Next command button

The fifth ChartWizard dialog box appears. Excel assumes that you want to include a legend. To specify the chart title and include a title for the category and value axis:

Click	the Chart Title text box
Type	XYZ BOATING COMPANY

Click	the Category (X) text box in the Axis Titles group box
Type	Quarters
Click	the Value (Y) text box in the Axis Titles group box
Type	Dollars

Notice that the sample chart changes to include the information.

To complete the chart-creation process:

| **Click** | the Finish command button |

The chart is placed on a chart sheet.

To name the chart sheet:

Double-click	the Chart1 tab
Type	Area Chart
Click	the OK command button

Your screen should look like Figure 7-15.

Figure 7-15

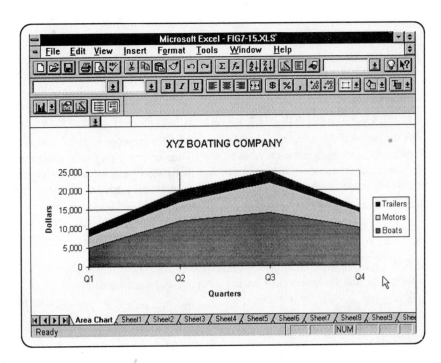

Save the BOATSALE workbook to a file using the name BOATAREA. Close the workbook document.

■ CREATING A DOUGHNUT CHART

A doughnut chart is similar to a pie chart. The main difference is that you can show more than one data series.

Before creating a doughnut chart:

Open	the BOATSALE workbook file
Select	cells A3:E3, A5:E5, A6:E6, and A7:E7

To create a doughnut chart:

Choose	Insert
Choose	Chart
Choose	As New Sheet

The first ChartWizard dialog box appears. Since you have already selected the data series for the chart:

Click	the Next command button

The second ChartWizard dialog box appears. To select the Doughnut chart type:

Click	the Doughnut chart type
Click	the Next command button

The third ChartWizard dialog box appears. To accept the default format for the Doughnut chart:

Click	the Next command button

The fourth ChartWizard dialog box appears. A sample chart appears in the dialog box.

In this dialog box, you indicate whether the data series are in rows or columns. Since you are using rows, you can indicate which rows are used to specify the Doughnut Slice Labels and which columns are used to define the Series Titles. Excel assumes that the first row selected specifies the Doughnut Slice Labels. The software also assumes that the first column includes the Series Titles.

Since the data series you selected are consistent with these assumptions:

Click	the Next command button

The fifth ChartWizard dialog box appears. Excel assumes that you do not want to include a legend for a doughnut chart. Since you are creating a doughnut chart, you are not allowed to include Category (X) or Value (Y) titles for these axes.

To include a legend and specify the chart title:

Click	the Yes option button under Add a Legend? to include a Legend
Click	the Chart Title text box
Type	Sales of Boats, Motors, and Trailers

Notice that the sample chart changes to include the information.

To complete the chart-creation process:

Click	the Finish command button

The chart is placed on a chart sheet.

To name the chart sheet:

Double-click	the Chart1 tab
Type	Doughnut Chart
Click	the OK command button

Your screen should look like Figure 7-16.

Figure 7-16

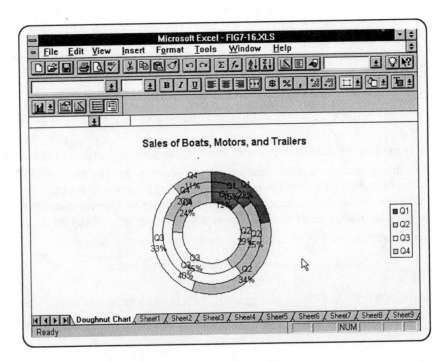

Save the BOATSALE workbook to a file using the name BOATDNUT. Close the workbook document.

■ CREATING A RADAR CHART

You can use a radar chart to show changes in various sets of data series relative to a center point and to each other.

Before creating a radar chart:

Open	the BOATSALE workbook file
Select	cells A3:E3, A5:E5, A6:E6, and A7:E7

To create a radar chart:

Choose	Insert
Choose	Chart
Choose	As New Sheet

The first ChartWizard dialog box appears. Since you have already selected the data series for the chart:

Click	the Next command button

The second ChartWizard dialog box appears. To select the Radar chart type:

Click	the Radar chart type
Click	the Next command button

The third ChartWizard dialog box appears. To accept the default format for the Radar chart:

Click	the Next command button

The fourth ChartWizard dialog box appears. A sample chart appears in the dialog box.

In this dialog box, you indicate whether the data series are in rows or columns. Since you are using rows, you can indicate which rows are used to specify the radar axis labels and which columns are used to define the legend text. Excel assumes that the first row selected specifies the radar axis labels. The software also assumes that the first column includes the legend text.

Since the data series you selected are consistent with these assumptions:

Click	the Next command button

The fifth ChartWizard dialog box appears. Excel assumes that you want to include a legend. To specify the chart title:

Click	the Chart Title text box
Type	Sales Analysis by Product

Notice that the sample chart changes to include the information.

To complete the chart-creation process:

Click	the Finish command button

The chart is placed on a chart sheet.
To name the chart sheet:

Double-click	the Chart1 tab
Type	Radar Chart
Click	the OK command button

Your screen should look like Figure 7-17.

Figure 7-17

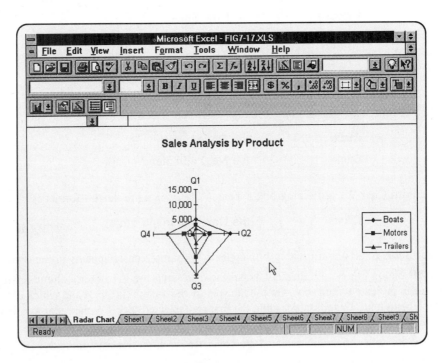

Save the BOATSALE workbook to a file using the name BOATRAD. Close the workbook document.

■ PRINTING A CHART DOCUMENT

After you create a chart, you will most likely want to print it. In some instances, you may want to print a chart that you created in an earlier Excel session.

To print the column chart you prepared earlier in this chapter, open the BUDCOL workbook file. To print the BUDCOL chart:

Click	the Column Chart tab (if necessary)
Click	the Print 🖨 button

Your printout should look similar to Figure 7-18.

Figure 7-18

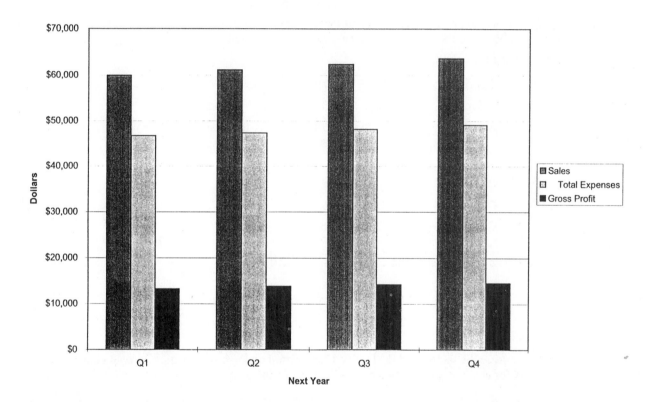

ABC COMPANY

Unless you are using a color printer, notice that Excel uses various shades of black, white, and gray for the colors of the columns. In Chapter 9, you will learn to change column colors as well as specify hatch patterns.

Excel includes the chart tab name as the header and page number as the footer for the chart. You may remove or modify the header and footer by using the Page Setup command on the File menu.

Close the workbook document. Do not save any changes.

■ CREATING AN EMBEDDED CHART

Earlier in this chapter, you learned to create a chart as a separate sheet in a document. In this section, you learn to use the ChartWizard to embed a chart in a worksheet.

Suppose you want to prepare a column chart that includes the Revenue, Profit Before Tax, and Profit After Tax data series in the PRACTICE Worksheet Model you created in Chapter 4.

Before creating the column chart:

Open	the PRACTICE workbook file
Select	cells A5:F5, A7:F7, A9:F9, and A11:F11
Scroll	to make sure row 20 is the first row and column A is the first column on your screen

To create a column chart:

Choose	Insert
Choose	Chart
Choose	On This Sheet

The mouse pointer changes shapes and appears as a chart icon ⊞. To place the chart in an appropriate location:

Move	the mouse pointer to the middle of cell A20
Drag	the mouse pointer to the middle of cell G35

When you release the mouse button, the first ChartWizard dialog box appears. Once you have completed the process for creating a chart, the chart will appear in the area you designated.

User Tip

An alternative method for selecting the area for an embedded chart is to choose the ChartWizard 📊 button on the Standard toolbar. The mouse pointer changes shapes and appears as a chart icon. Drag the chart icon over the selected chart area and release the mouse button.

Since you have already selected the data series for the chart:

Click	the Next command button

The second ChartWizard dialog box appears. To accept the default chart type as a column chart:

Click   the Next command button

The third ChartWizard dialog box appears. To accept the default selection format number 6:

Click   the Next command button

The fourth ChartWizard dialog box appears. To accept the default Excel assumptions that the first row selected specifies the category (X) axis labels and the first column includes the legend text:

Click   the Next command button

The fifth ChartWizard dialog box appears.

To specify the chart title and include a title for the category and value axes:

Click	the Chart Title text box
Type	EAZY DISTRIBUTION COMPANY
Click	the Category (X) text box in the Axis Titles group box
Type	Next Five Years
Click	the Value (Y) text box in the Axis Titles group box
Type	Dollars

Notice that the sample chart changes to include the information.

To complete the chart-creation process:

Click   the Finish command button

The chart is placed in the area you designate in the worksheet. After making row 20 the first row on your screen, your screen should look like Figure 7-19.

Figure 7-19

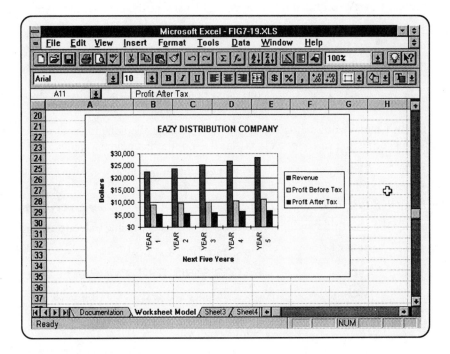

Save the PRACTICE workbook to a file using the name PRACTCHT.

■ PRINTING AN EMBEDDED CHART

You can print an embedded chart.

To print only the embedded chart you created in the last section:

Double-click	the chart to display the chart in a chart window
Choose	File
Choose	Print
Click	the Selected Chart option button in the Print What box (if necessary)
Click	the OK command button

Notice only the embedded chart is printed. The Worksheet Model tab name appears as the header along with the characters "Chart 1."

■ PRINTING AN EMBEDDED CHART AND WORKSHEET

You can print the worksheet model and chart at the same time by selecting the Selected Sheet(s) option button in the Print What box within the Print dialog box.

To print the worksheet model and chart:

Click	anywhere in the worksheet outside the chart
Choose	File
Choose	Print
Click	the Selected Sheet(s) option button in the Print What box (if necessary)
Click	the OK command button

The worksheet model and chart are printed. The Worksheet Model tab name appears as the header.

■ DELETING AN EMBEDDED CHART FROM A WORKSHEET

You can delete an embedded chart from a worksheet by selecting the chart and pressing the DELETE key.
To delete the embedded chart from the PRACTCHT Worksheet Model:

Click	anywhere in the embedded chart to select the chart
Press	Delete

The chart no longer appears on your worksheet. Close the workbook document. Do not save any changes.

SUMMARY

Excel allows you to create a chart on a separate sheet or as an embedded chart on a worksheet document. Creating charts using data series from a worksheet is easy because the data does not need to be entered again before the chart is prepared. The ChartWizard tool leads you through the process for constructing a chart. If the data in the worksheet is recalculated, the chart reflects the modifications in the data the next time the chart is viewed.

Charts can assist you in analyzing data in a worksheet as well as in presenting the data to other individuals.

KEY CONCEPTS

Area chart
Attached text
Bar chart
Category axis
Chart
Chart data series name
Chart [+] icon
Chart menu bar
Chart title
Chart toolbar
Chart Type [🔅] button
ChartWizard
ChartWizard [📊] button
Column chart
Combination chart
Data label
Data marker

Doughnut chart
Embedded chart
Gridlines
Legend
Line chart
Pie chart
Plot area
Radar chart
Stacked column chart
Tick mark
Unattached text
Value axis
View Sized with Window
X-axis (Category Axis)
XY (Scatter) chart
Y-axis (Value Axis)

EXERCISE 1

INSTRUCTIONS: Circle T if the statement is true and F if the statement is incorrect.

T   F   1.   There are only eight types of charts available in Excel.

T   F   2.   If you change values on the worksheet, the chart can reflect the changes when the chart is viewed again on the screen.

T   F   3.   You cannot create three completely different charts with data from one worksheet.

T   F   4.   If you do not save a chart document, it will not be available to use at a later time.

T   F   5.   A pie chart displays only one range of data.

T   F   6.   If you create a chart with the ChartWizard, you can only print it with a worksheet.

T   F   7.   You cannot remove an embedded chart from a worksheet document.

T   F   8.   You can combine column and line charts on one chart.

T   F   9.   You must select data to include on a chart prior to using the ChartWizard button.

T   F   10.   When the Chart toolbar is activated while you are creating a chart document, it normally appears immediately above the status bar.

EXERCISE 2

INSTRUCTIONS: Describe a typical situation when the following Excel commands are used.

Problem 1:   Insert Chart On This Sheet
Problem 2:   Insert Chart As New Sheet

EXERCISE 3 -- Creating a Line Chart

INSTRUCTIONS: Open the PRACTICE workbook file created in Chapter 4.

Create a line chart using the default format selection that includes Revenue, Expenses, and Profit Before Tax for 5 years. Place the chart on a new sheet.

Include YEAR 1 through YEAR 5 as the categories on the X-axis.

Place a legend on the chart and include the chart title, "PROJECTED PROFITS". Include "Dollars" as the Value (Y) axis title.

Name the chart sheet "Line Chart".

Print the chart.

Save the PRACTICE workbook to a file using the name PRACTLNE.

Close the PRACTLNE workbook document.

EXERCISE 4 -- Creating a Bar Chart

INSTRUCTIONS: Open the PRACTICE workbook file.

Create a bar chart using the instructions in Exercise 3.

Name the chart sheet "Bar Sheet".

Print the chart.

Save the PRACTICE workbook to a file using the name PRACTBAR.

Close the PRACTBAR workbook document.

EXERCISE 5 -- Creating a Stacked Column Chart

INSTRUCTIONS: Open the PRACTICE workbook file.

Create a stacked column chart using format number 3 that includes Expenses, Profit Before Tax, and Profit After Tax data for 5 years. Place the chart on a new sheet.

Place a legend on the chart and include the chart title, "PROJECTED PROFITS". Include "Dollars" as the Value (Y) axis title.

Name the chart sheet "Stacked Column Chart".

Print the chart.

Save the PRACTICE workbook to a file using the name PRACSTBR.

Close the PRACSTBR workbook document.

EXERCISE 6 -- Creating a Pie Chart

INSTRUCTIONS: Open the SALES workbook file.

Create a pie chart using the default format selection that includes the data for the individual salespersons. Place the chart on a new sheet.

Include the chart title, "ABC COMPANY SALES".

Name the chart sheet "Pie Chart".

Print the chart.

Save the SALES workbook to a file using the name SALESPCT.

Close the SALESPCT workbook document.

EXERCISE 7 -- Creating a Combination Chart

INSTRUCTIONS: Open the PRACTICE workbook file.

Create a combination chart using the default format selection that includes the Profit Before Tax and Profit After Tax data for 5 years. Place the chart on a new sheet.

Place a legend on the chart and include the chart title, "PROJECTED PROFITS". Include "Dollars" as the Value (Y) and Second Y axis titles.

Name the chart sheet "Combination Chart".

Print the chart.

Save the PRACTICE workbook to a file using the name COMBINE.

Close the COMBINE workbook document.

EXERCISE 8 -- Creating an Area Chart

INSTRUCTIONS: Create the worksheet in Figure 7-20 and save it to a file using the name XYZSALES.

Figure 7-20

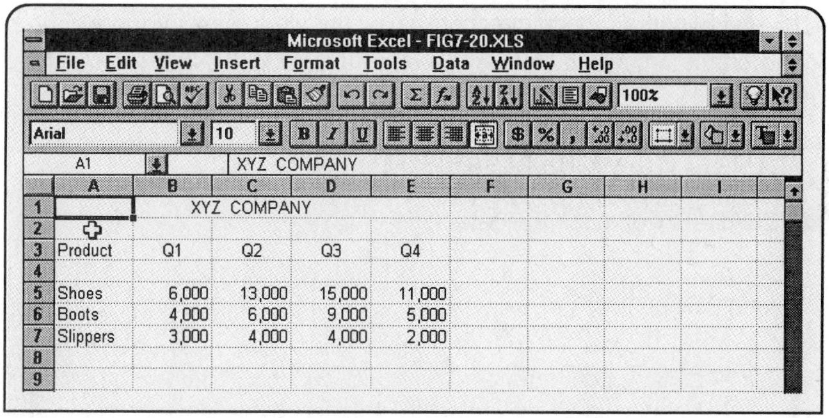

Create an area chart using the default format selection that includes the sales for the four quarters for Shoes, Boots, and Slippers. Place the chart below the worksheet information in cells A9 through E22.

Place a legend on the chart and include the chart title, "XYZ COMPANY SALES". Include "Next Year" as the Category (X) axis title and "Dollars" as the Value (Y) axis title.

Print only the chart.

Print the worksheet and chart together.

Save the XYZSALES workbook to a file using the name XYZEMBED.

Close the XYZEMBED workbook document.

EXERCISE 9 -- Creating a Doughnut Chart

INSTRUCTIONS: Open the XYZSALES workbook file.

Create a doughnut chart using the default format selection that includes the sales for the four quarters for Shoes, Boots, and Slippers. Place the chart below the worksheet information in cells A9 through E22.

Include the chart title, "XYZ DOUGHNUT CHART".

Print only the chart.

Print the worksheet and chart together.

Save the XYZSALES workbook to a file using the name XYZDONUT.

Close the XYZDONUT workbook document.

EXERCISE 10 -- Creating a Radar Chart

INSTRUCTIONS: Open the XYZSALES workbook file.

Create a radar chart using the default format selection that includes the sales for the four quarters for Shoes, Boots, and Slippers. Place the chart below the worksheet information in cells A9 through E22.

Place a legend on the chart and include the chart title, "XYZ RADAR CHART".

Print only the chart.

Print the worksheet and chart together.

Save the XYZSALES workbook to a file using the name XYZRADAR.

Close the XYZRADAR workbook document.

CHAPTER EIGHT

ADDITIONAL CHART TOPICS

OBJECTIVES

In this chapter, you will learn to:
- Create 3-D charts
- Create an open-high-low-close chart
- Use additional chart commands

■ CHAPTER OVERVIEW

The previous chapter covered the basics of creating charts. This chapter includes instructions for completing most of the various 3-D charts available in Excel. Some additional useful chart commands are also discussed.

■ CREATING A 3-D AREA CHART

An area chart stacks the chart areas for the various data series on top of one another. You can also create a 3-D area chart, which makes each variable's area three-dimensional.

To create a 3-D area chart using the data in the BOATSALE workbook:

Open	the BOATSALE workbook file
Select	cells A3:E3, A5:E5, A6:E6, and A7:E7

To create a 3-D area chart:

Choose	Insert
Choose	Chart
Choose	As New Sheet

The first ChartWizard dialog box appears. To accept the range of cells you selected as the range of cells to chart:

Click	the Next command button

The second ChartWizard dialog box appears. To specify that you want to use a 3-D Area chart type:

Click	the 3-D Area chart type
Click	the Next command button

The third ChartWizard dialog box appears. To accept the default format for the 3-D Area chart type:

Click	the Next command button

The fourth ChartWizard dialog box appears. An example of the chart appears.

Based on the data you selected, Excel has made some choices for using rows for the data series, the first selected row for the category (X) axis labels, and the first selected column for the legend text. To accept the default choices made by Excel:

Click	the Next command button

The fifth ChartWizard dialog box appears. To accept the default setting of including a legend and to specify the appropriate chart title, category (X), and value (Z) information:

Click	the Chart Title text box
Type	XYZ BOATING SALES
Click	the Category (X) text box in the Axis Titles group box
Type	Quarters
Click	the Value (Z) text box in the Axis Titles group box
Type	Dollars
Click	the Finish command button

The chart appears on your screen.

To complete the process for creating the 3-D area chart:

Name	the Chart1 tab "3-D Area Chart"

Your screen should look like Figure 8-1.

Figure 8-1

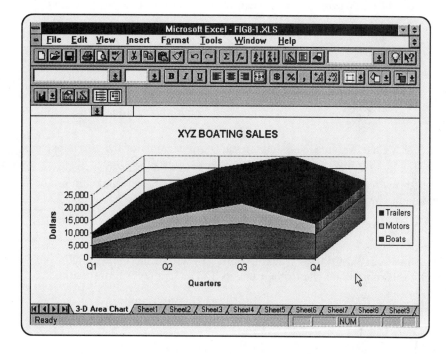

Save the BOATSALE workbook to a file using the name BT3DAREA. Close the workbook document.

■ CREATING A 3-D BAR CHART

In some situations, you may want to create a 3-D bar chart. Suppose you need a 3-D bar chart for the Sales, Total Expenses, and Gross Profit data in the BUDGET workbook.

Before creating the 3-D bar chart:

Open	the BUDGET workbook file
Select	cells A5:E5, A7:E7, A15:E15, and A16:E16

To create a 3-D bar chart:

Choose	Insert
Choose	Chart
Choose	As New Sheet

The first ChartWizard dialog box appears. To accept the range of cells you selected as the range of cells to chart:

Click	the Next command button

The second ChartWizard dialog box appears. To specify that you want to use a 3-D Bar chart type:

Click	the 3-D Bar chart type
Click	the Next command button

The third ChartWizard dialog box appears. To accept the default format for the 3-D Bar chart type:

Click	the Next command button

The fourth ChartWizard dialog box appears. An example of the chart appears.

Based on the data you selected, Excel has made some choices for using rows for the data series, the first selected row for the category (X) axis labels, and the first selected column for the legend text. To accept the default choices made by Excel:

Click	the Next command button

The fifth ChartWizard dialog box appears. To accept the default setting of including a legend and to specify the appropriate chart title, category (X) and value (Y) information:

Click	the Chart Title text box
Type	ABC COMPANY
Click	the Category (X) text box in the Axis Titles group box
Type	Next Year
Click	the Value (Y) text box in the Axis Titles group box
Type	Dollars
Click	the Finish command button

The chart appears on your screen.

To complete the process for creating the 3-D bar chart:

Name	the Chart1 tab "3-D Bar Chart"

Your screen should look like Figure 8-2.

Figure 8-2

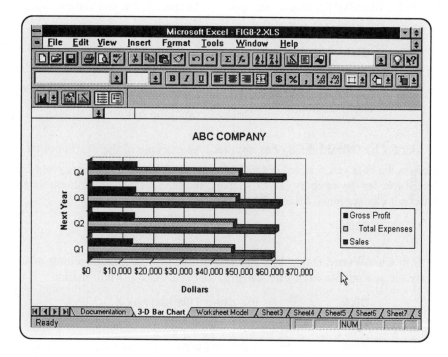

Save the BUDGET workbook to the file using the name BUD3DBAR. Close the workbook document.

■ CREATING A 3-D COLUMN CHART

Sometimes you may want to create a 3-D column chart. Suppose you need to develop a 3-D column chart for the Sales, Total Expenses, and Gross Profit data in the BUDGET workbook.

Before creating the 3-D column chart:

Open	the BUDGET workbook file
Select	cells A5:E5, A7:E7, A15:E15, and A16:E16

To create the 3-D column chart:

Choose	Insert
Choose	Chart
Choose	As New Sheet

The first ChartWizard dialog box appears. To accept the range of cells you selected as the range of cells to chart:

Click	the Next command button

The second ChartWizard dialog box appears. To specify that you want to use a 3-D Column chart type:

Click	the 3-D Column chart type
Click	the Next command button

The third ChartWizard dialog box appears. To accept the default format for the 3-D Column chart type:

Click	the Next command button

The fourth ChartWizard dialog box appears. An example of the chart appears.

Based on the data you selected, Excel has made some choices for using rows for the data series, the first selected row for the category (X) axis labels, and the first selected column for the legend text. To accept the default choices made by Excel:

Click	the Next command button

The fifth ChartWizard dialog box appears. To accept the default setting of including a legend and to specify the appropriate chart title, category (X) and value (Z) information:

Click	the Chart Title text box
Type	ABC COMPANY
Click	the Category (X) text box in the Axis Titles group box
Type	Next Year
Click	the Value (Z) text box in the Axis Titles group box
Type	Dollars
Click	the Finish command button

The chart appears on your screen.

To complete the process for creating the 3-D column chart:

Name	the Chart1 tab "3-D Column Chart"

Your screen should look like Figure 8-3.

Figure 8-3

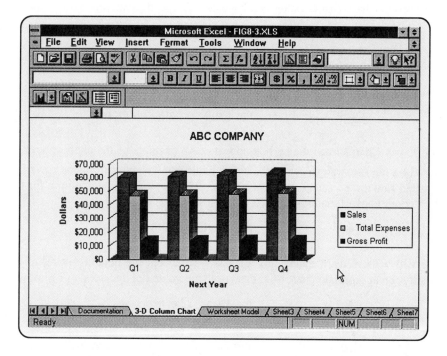

Save the BUDGET workbook to the file using the name BUD3DCOL. Close the workbook document.

■ CREATING A 3-D LINE CHART

Sometimes you may want to create a 3-D line chart. Suppose you need to develop a 3-D line chart for the Sales, Total Expenses, and Gross Profit data in the BUDGET workbook.

Before creating the 3-D line chart:

Open	the BUDGET workbook file
Select	cells A5:E5, A7:E7, A15:E15, and A16:E16

To create the 3-D line chart:

Choose	Insert
Choose	Chart
Choose	As New Sheet

The first ChartWizard dialog box appears. To accept the range of cells you selected as the range of cells to chart:

Click	the Next command button

The second ChartWizard dialog box appears. To specify that you want to use a 3-D Line chart type:

Click	the 3-D Line chart type
Click	the Next command button

The third ChartWizard dialog box appears. To accept the default format for the 3-D Line chart type:

Click	the Next command button

The fourth ChartWizard dialog box appears. An example of the chart appears.

Based on the data you selected, Excel has made some choices for using rows for the data series, the first selected row for the category (X) axis labels, and the first selected column for the legend text. To accept the default choices made by Excel:

Click	the Next command button

The fifth ChartWizard dialog box appears. To accept the default setting of including a legend and to specify the appropriate chart title, category (X), value (Z) and series (Y) information:

Click	the Chart Title text box
Type	ABC COMPANY
Click	the Category (X) text box in the Axis Titles group box
Type	Next Year
Click	the Value (Z) text box in the Axis Titles group box
Type	Dollars
Click	the Series (Y) text box in the Axis Titles group box
Type	Item
Click	the Finish command button

The chart appears on your screen.

To complete the process for creating the 3-D line chart:

Name	the Chart1 tab "3-D Line Chart"

Your screen should look like Figure 8-4.

Figure 8-4

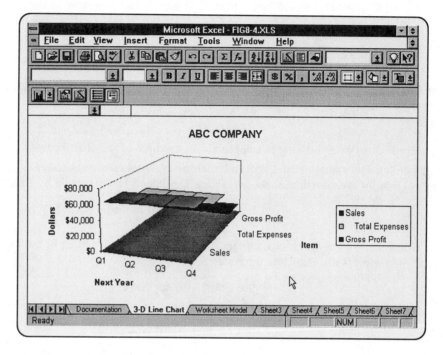

Save the BUDGET workbook to the file using the name BUD3DLNE. Close the workbook document.

■ CREATING A 3-D PIE CHART

Sometimes you may want to create a 3-D pie chart. Suppose you need to develop a 3-D pie chart for some of the expense categories in the BUDGET workbook.

Before creating the 3-D pie chart:

Open	the BUDGET workbook file
Select	cells A10:B12

To create the 3-D pie chart:

Choose	Insert
Choose	Chart
Choose	As New Sheet

The first ChartWizard dialog box appears. To accept the range of cells you selected as the range of cells to chart:

Click	the Next command button

The second ChartWizard dialog box appears. To specify that you want to use a 3-D Pie chart type:

| **Click** | the 3-D Pie chart type |
| **Click** | the Next command button |

The third ChartWizard dialog box appears. To accept the default format for the 3-D Pie chart type:

| **Click** | the Next command button |

The fourth ChartWizard dialog box appears. An example of the chart appears.

Based on the data you selected, Excel has made some choices for using columns as the data series and the first column for the pie slice labels. To accept the default choices made by Excel:

| **Click** | the Next command button |

The fifth ChartWizard dialog box appears. To accept the default setting of not including a legend and to specify the appropriate chart title information:

Click	the Chart Title text box
Type	ABC COMPANY
Click	the Finish command button

The chart appears on your screen.

To complete the process for creating the 3-D pie chart:

| **Name** | the Chart1 tab "3-D Pie Chart" |

Your screen should look like Figure 8-5.

Figure 8-5

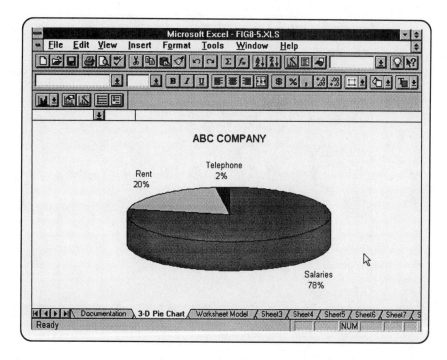

Save the BUDGET workbook to the file using the name BUD3DPIE. Close the workbook document.

■ CREATING AN OPEN-HIGH-LOW-CLOSE CHART

You can use Excel to track investments in stocks and bonds. Investors are often interested in comparing the prices for an individual stock or bond.

Suppose you receive the information shown in Figure 8-6.

Figure 8-6

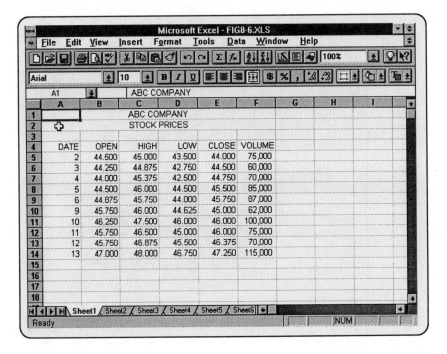

Assume that you have purchased ABC Company stock and wish to follow the price of the stock using an open-high-low-close chart.

Before creating the chart, you will need to construct a worksheet like the one shown in Figure 8-6. Save the workbook to a file using the name ABCOHLC.

To create an open-high-low-close chart:

Select	cells A4:E14
Choose	Insert
Choose	Chart
Choose	As New Sheet

The first ChartWizard dialog box appears. To accept the range of cells you selected as the range of cells to chart:

Click	the Next command button

The second ChartWizard dialog box appears. To specify that you want to use a Line chart type:

Click	the Line chart type
Click	the Next command button

The third ChartWizard dialog box appears. To specify the open-high-low-close chart type:

Click	format number 9 for the open-high-low-close chart type
Click	the Next command button

The fourth ChartWizard dialog box appears. Another dialog box is displayed indicating that only four data series can appear in an open-high-low-close chart. This second dialog box appears, because you have selected five series (date, open, high, low, and close). The first data series, date is assigned to the category (X) axis labels.

To remove the Warning dialog box:

Click	the OK command button

Based on the data you selected, Excel has made some choices for using columns and what data series to include as the legend text. To specify that the first column contains the category (X) axis labels and accept the other choices made by Excel:

Double-click	the Use First Column(s) for Category (X) Axis Labels text box
Type	1 (if necessary)
Click	the Next command button

The fifth ChartWizard dialog box appears. To accept the default setting of including a legend and to specify the appropriate chart title and axis title information:

Click	the Chart Title text box
Type	ABC COMPANY STOCK PRICE
Click	the Category (X) text box in the Axis Titles group box
Type	Date
Click	the Value (Y) text box in the Axis Titles group box
Type	Dollars
Click	the Finish command button

The chart appears on your screen.

To complete the process for creating the open-high-low-close chart:

Name	the Chart1 tab "Open-High-Low-Close Chart"

Your screen should look like Figure 8-7.

Figure 8-7

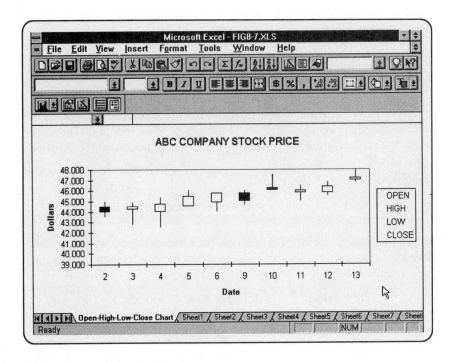

Save the ABCOHLC workbook to the file using the name STKPOHLC. Close the workbook document.

In some cases, you may want to include only high-low-close information on a chart. For example, you might want to record the high-low-close information on the temperature or the humidity in a room for a particular date. In this case, the "open" information is not selected when you create the chart. Use the Line chart type and choose format number 8.

■ ADDING AND DELETING DATA IN A CHART

After you have created a chart, you may want to add or delete a data series.

In the last chapter, you created a line chart that includes Sales, Total Expenses, and Gross Profit during the forecast period. Suppose you want to drop the Total Expenses category and add the Salaries expenses category.

Before you modify the line chart:

Open	the BUDLINE workbook file

The BUDLINE chart appears on your screen.

To add Salaries expenses to the chart:

Click	the Worksheet Model tab
Select	cells A10:E10
Choose	Edit

Choose	Copy
Click	the Line Chart tab
Choose	Edit
Choose	Paste

The chart is updated and the appropriate Salaries expenses data series appears on the chart.

To remove the Total Expenses data series:

Click	the Total Expenses line to select it
Press	Delete

The Total Expenses data series is deleted from the chart. The new chart includes the Sales, Salaries expenses, and Gross Profit data series information. Your screen should look like Figure 8-8.

Figure 8-8

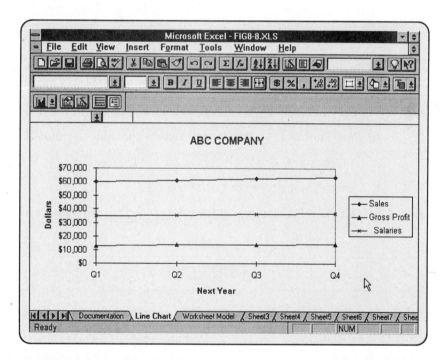

Save the BUDLINE workbook containing the updated chart to a file using the name BUDLNECG. Close the workbook document.

SUMMARY

Various types of 3-D charts are available in Excel, including 3-D Area, 3-D Bar, 3-D Column, 3-D Line, 3-D Pie, and 3-D Surface. You also can create open-high-low-close and high-low-close charts. Also, you can add data series to a chart or delete them.

KEY CONCEPTS

3-D Area chart   Adding data series to a chart
3-D Bar chart   Deleting data series from a chart
3-D Column chart   High-Low-Close chart
3-D Line chart   Open-High-Low-Close chart
3-D Pie chart

EXERCISE 1

INSTRUCTIONS: Circle T if the statement is true and F if the statement is incorrect.

T   F   1.   Only one data series can be added or deleted from a chart.

T   F   2.   You cannot use a previously created pie chart to create a 3-D pie chart.

T   F   3.   There is only one chart format for a 3-D area chart.

T   F   4.   There are six types of 3-D charts.

T   F   5.   An individual can plot stock prices using the high-low-close chart type.

EXERCISE 2

INSTRUCTIONS: Describe a typical situation when you use the following Excel commands:

Problem 1:   3-D Column chart   *Problem 4:*   3-D Bar chart

Problem 2:   3-D Area chart   *Problem 5:*   Open-High-Low-Close chart

Problem 3:   3-D Pie chart

EXERCISE 3 -- Creating a 3-D Area Chart

INSTRUCTIONS: Open the PRACTICE workbook file.

Create a 3-D area chart that includes the Revenue, Profit Before Tax, and Profit After Tax data series. Place the chart on a new sheet.

Include YEAR 1 through YEAR 5 as the category (X) axis labels.

Select format 2 for the 3-D Area chart type.

Use the row labels for Revenue, Profit Before Tax, and Profit After Tax as the legend text.

Use "EAZY DISTRIBUTION COMPANY" as the chart title. Include "Five Year Forecast" as the category (X) axis title and "Dollars" as the value (Z) axis title.

Name the chart sheet "3-D Area Chart".

Print the chart.

Save the PRACTICE workbook to a file using the name PR3DAREA.

Close the PR3DAREA workbook document.

EXERCISE 4 -- Creating a 3-D Bar Chart

INSTRUCTIONS: Open the PRACTICE workbook file.

Create a 3-D bar chart that includes the Revenue, Profit Before Tax, and Profit After Tax data series. Place the chart on a new sheet.

Include YEAR 1 through YEAR 5 as the category (X) axis labels.

Select format 5 for the 3-D Bar chart type.

Use the row labels for Revenue, Profit Before Tax, and Profit After Tax as the legend text.

Use "EAZY DISTRIBUTION COMPANY" as the chart title. Include "Five Year Forecast" as the category (X) axis title and "Dollars" as the value (Y) axis title.

Name the chart sheet "3-D Bar Chart".

Print the chart.

Save the PRACTICE workbook to a file using the name PRA3DBAR.

Close the PRA3DBAR workbook document.

EXERCISE 5 -- Creating a 3-D Column Chart

INSTRUCTIONS: Open the PRACTICE workbook file.

Create a 3-D column chart that includes the Revenue, Profit Before Tax, and Profit After Tax data series. Place the chart below the worksheet information in cells A20 through G35.

Include YEAR 1 through YEAR 5 as the category (X) axis labels.

Select format 8 for the 3-D Column chart type.

Use the row labels for Revenue, Profit Before Tax, and Profit After Tax as the legend text.

Use "EAZY DISTRIBUTION COMPANY" as the chart title. Include "Five Year Forecast" as the category (X) axis title, "Dollars" as the value (Z) axis title, and omit the series (Y) axis title.

Print the chart.

Save the PRACTICE workbook to a file using the name PRA3DCOL.

Close the PRA3DCOL workbook document.

EXERCISE 6 -- Creating a 3-D Line Chart

INSTRUCTIONS: Open the PRACTICE workbook file.

Create a 3-D line chart that includes the Revenue, Profit Before Tax, and Profit After Tax data series. Place the chart below the worksheet information in cells A20 through G35.

Include YEAR 1 through YEAR 5 as the category (X) axis labels.

Select format 2 for the 3-D Line chart type.

Use the row labels for Revenue, Profit Before Tax, and Profit After Tax as the legend text and the series (Y) axis labels.

Use "EAZY DISTRIBUTION COMPANY" as the chart title. Include "Five Year Forecast" as the category (X) axis title, "Dollars" as the value (Z) axis title, and omit the series (Y) axis title.

Print the chart.

Save the PRACTICE workbook to a file using the name PR3DLINE.

Close the PR3DLINE workbook document.

EXERCISE 7 -- Creating a 3-D Pie Chart

INSTRUCTIONS: Open the SALES workbook file.

Create a 3-D pie chart that includes the salesperson's data series. Place the chart on a new sheet.

Select format 7 for the 3-D Pie chart type.

Use the salesperson's names as the pie slice labels. Use "SALES" as the chart title.

Name the chart sheet "3-D Pie Chart".

Print the chart.

Save the SALES workbook to a file using the name SAL3DPIE.

Close the SAL3DPIE workbook document.

EXERCISE 8 -- Creating an Open-High-Low-Close Chart

INSTRUCTIONS: Create the worksheet shown in Figure 8-9 and save it to a file using the name XYZOHLC.

Figure 8-9

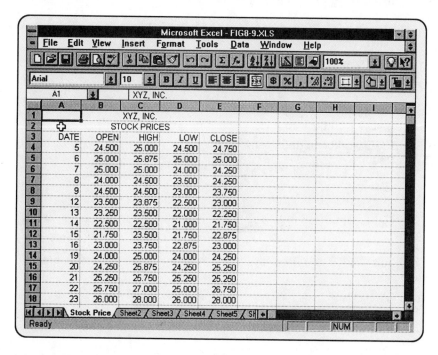

Create an open-high-low-close chart for the stock price data series of XYZ, Inc. Place the chart below the information in cells A20 through G35.

Include the Date data series as the category (X) axis labels. Use the column labels that include the items "DATE", "OPEN", "HIGH", "LOW", and "CLOSE" as the legend text.

Select format 9 for the Line chart type.

Use the first selected column, the dates, as category (X) axis labels.

Use "XYZ, INC." as the chart title, "Date" as the category (X) axis title, and "Stock Price" as the value (Y) axis title.

Print the chart.

Save the XYZOHLC workbook to a file using the name XYZSTOCK.

Close the XYZSTOCK workbook document.

EXERCISE 9 -- Modifying the Data in an Existing Chart

INSTRUCTIONS: Open the SAL3DPIE chart.

Add the following salesperson to the worksheet model:

      Zumalt, Mary   113,542

Note that you will have to move the underline below Zumalt and change the formula for summing the sales amounts.

Save the SAL3DPIE workbook to a file using the name SALESADD.

Add Mary Zumalt to the chart.

Print the chart.

Save the SALESADD workbook to a file using the name SALES3D.

Close the SALES3D workbook document.

CHAPTER NINE

ENHANCING THE APPEARANCE OF A CHART

OBJECTIVES

In this chapter, you will learn to:
- Change the location of a legend
- Remove and change the axes scales
- Change the fonts of chart text
- Change colors and hatch patterns
- Insert gridlines
- Add unattached text and graphic objects
- Size and move an embedded chart

■ CHAPTER OVERVIEW

In some situations, you may need to change or enhance the appearance of a chart. With the options available in Excel, you can change the location of a legend on a chart, remove and modify the axes scales, and change the fonts of text appearing on the chart. You can modify the chart colors, hatch patterns, gridlines, and borders. Text and graphic objects can be added to a chart. Finally, you can move and size embedded charts.

■ CHANGING THE LOCATION OF A LEGEND

The default location of a legend is on the right side of the chart. Sometimes, you may want the legend to appear in a different location on the chart.

Suppose you wish to place the legend on a bar chart at the bottom of the chart. To illustrate the process for placing the legend in a new location:

Open	the BUDBAR workbook file
Click	the Legend object in the chart
Choose	Format
Choose	Selected Legend

The Format Legend dialog box appears. To place the legend at the bottom of the chart:

Click	the Placement tab
Click	the Bottom option button in the Type group box
Click	the OK command button

The legend appears below the chart. Deselect the legend. Your screen should look like Figure 9-1.

Figure 9-1

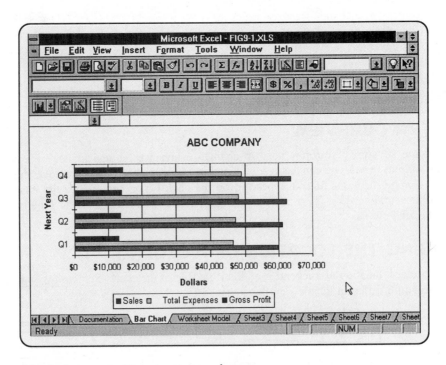

Close the workbook document. Do not save any changes.

■ REMOVING AND CHANGING AXES SCALES

Excel allows you to remove the category (X) axis or value (Y) axis scales. If necessary, you can also change the scales of the axes.

Suppose you want to remove the value (Y) axis scale from the column chart you created in the BUDCOL workbook. To delete the value (Y) scale:

Open	the BUDCOL workbook file
Choose	Insert
Choose	Axes

The Axes dialog box appears.

Click	the Value (Y) Axis check box in the Primary Axis group box to remove the X
Click	the OK command button

The value (Y) axis disappears. Your screen should look like Figure 9-2.

Figure 9-2

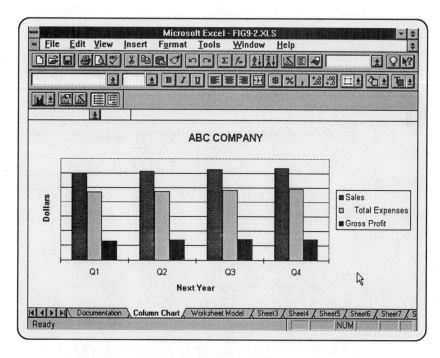

Suppose you want to change the scale for the value (Y) axis on the BUDCOL chart.
To place the scale on the chart again:

Choose	Insert
Choose	Axes

Click	the Value (Y) Axis check box in the Primary Axis group box to insert an X
Click	the OK command button

Assume you want the value (Y) axis increment to be 12,000 instead of 10,000.

Select	the Value (Y) Axis
Choose	Format
Choose	Selected Axis

The Format Axis dialog box appears.

Click	the Scale tab
Double-click	the Major Unit text box
Type	12000
Click	the OK command button

The scale for the value (Y) axis is changed. Notice that the maximum value is now $72,000 instead of the $70,000. Deselect the value (Y) axis. Your screen should look like Figure 9-3.

Figure 9-3

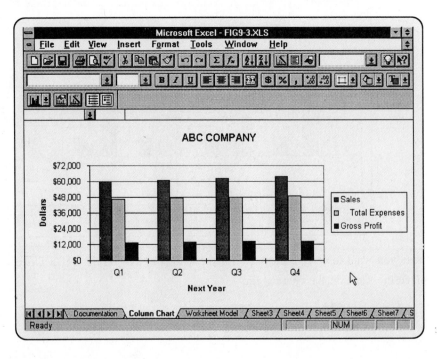

Close the workbook document. Do not save any changes.

■ CHANGING THE FONTS OF CHART TEXT

You can change or modify the font of the text appearing on a chart, including the actual font, font style, size, and color. You can also underline the selected chart text. Effects such as strike through, superscript, and subscript are available.

Suppose you need to change the font and size of the title on the BUDCOL chart. To complete the modifications for the chart title:

Open	the BUDCOL workbook file
Select	the chart title
Choose	Format
Choose	Selected Chart Title

The Format Chart Title dialog box appears.

Click	the Font tab
Click	the Times New Roman option in the Font list box
Click	the Bold Italic option in the Font Style list box
Click	the 14 option in the Size list box
Click	the OK command button

Various font-related items for the chart title have been changed. Deselect the chart title. Your screen should look like Figure 9-4.

Figure 9-4

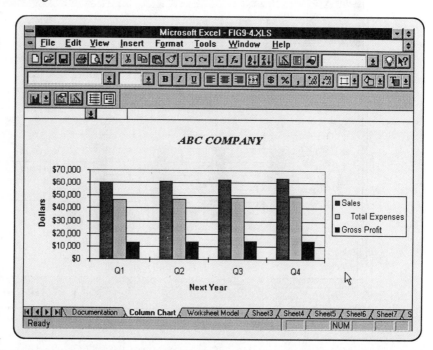

Close the workbook document. Do not save any changes.

■ CHANGING COLORS AND HATCH PATTERNS

In some situations, you may want to change the color or hatch pattern for a data marker (category) on a chart. You can modify the border color, area cover, and pattern used for a data marker.

Suppose you want to use a different color for the Sales data marker in the BUDCOL chart.

To change the color:

Open	the BUDCOL workbook file
Select	the Sales category data marker
Choose	Format
Choose	Selected Data Series

The Format Data Series dialog box appears.

Click	the Red color option in the first row of the Color palette in the Area group box
Click	the OK command button

The Sales category data marker now has a red color. Deselect the Sales data marker. Your screen should look like Figure 9-5, except for the color, which is not visible in this text.

Figure 9-5

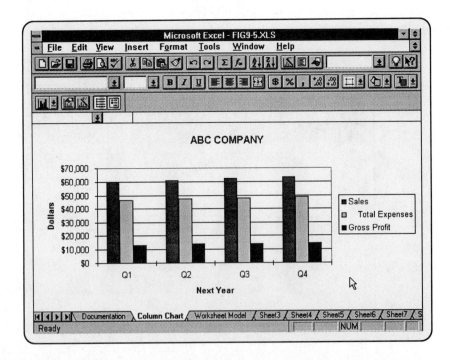

In some instances, you may want to use a hatch pattern rather than a solid color for a data marker. To illustrate the use of a hatch pattern:

Select	the Sales category data marker
Choose	Format
Choose	Selected Data Series
Click	the Black color on the color palette in the Area group box
Click	the arrow on the Pattern drop-down list box
Click	the last pattern on the first row of the pattern palette
Click	the OK command button

The red color has changed to black, and a pattern appears. Deselect the Sales data marker. Your screen should look like Figure 9-6.

Figure 9-6

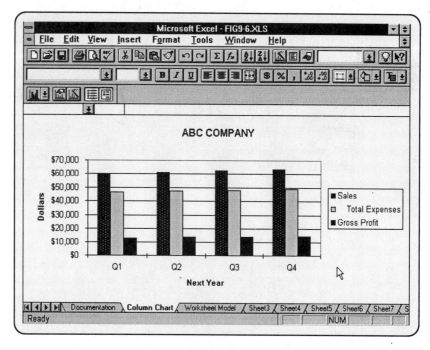

Close the workbook document. Do not save any changes.

■ INSERTING GRIDLINES

When you select the format for a chart type, some of the formats include gridlines and some do not. You can insert category (vertical) and/or value (horizontal) gridlines. Also, you can modify the format of existing gridlines.

To illustrate the process for including horizontal gridlines on a chart:

Open	the BUDSTCOL workbook file
Choose	Insert
Choose	Gridlines

The Gridlines dialog box appears. Note that you may include gridlines at major and minor units on the chart.

To include value (horizontal) gridlines at major units on the chart:

Click	the Major Gridlines check box in the Value (Y) Axis group box to insert an X
Click	the OK command button

Horizontal gridlines appear on your screen. Your screen should look like Figure 9-7.

Figure 9-7

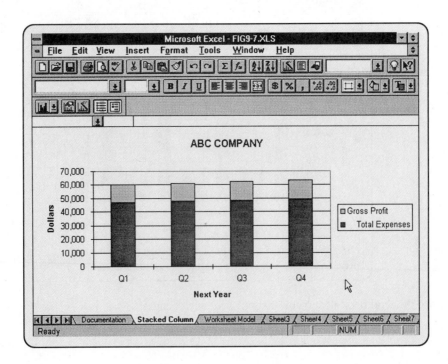

User Tip

An alternative method for inserting or deleting horizontal gridlines is to click the Horizontal Gridlines ▤ button on the Chart toolbar.

Close the workbook document. Do not save any changes.

■ ADDING UNATTACHED TEXT AND GRAPHIC OBJECTS TO A CHART

Excel allows you to include additional text on a chart. Such text is sometimes called **unattached text**. You can also place graphic objects such as arrows on a chart.

Suppose you want to place the words "Actual" above the first-quarter information and "Projected" above the remaining quarters' information on the chart in the BUDCOL workbook.

To illustrate the process for including text on a chart:

Open	the BUDCOL workbook file
Choose	View
Choose	Sized with Window
Select	the 75% option in the Zoom Control pull-down list box on the Standard toolbar
Type	Actual
Click	the enter box ☑

The word "Actual" appears in the middle of the chart.

Drag	the text box containing "Actual" above the first-quarter data

The text appears in the proper location.

To deselect the text:

Press	Esc

Your screen should look similar to Figure 9-8.

Figure 9-8

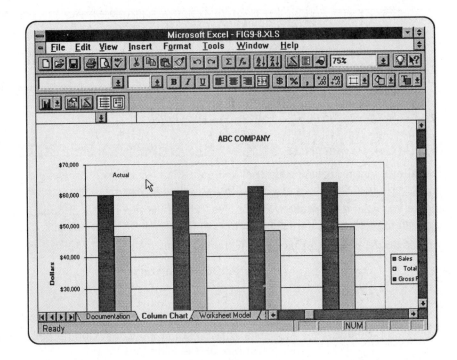

To place additional text above the second-quarter information:

Type	Projected
Click	the enter box ☑
Drag	the text box containing "Projected" above the second-quarter data

The text appears in the proper location. Deselect the text. Your screen should look similar to Figure 9-9.

Figure 9-9

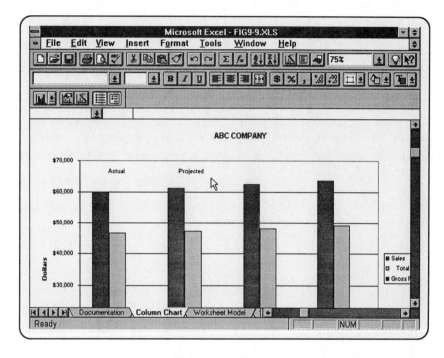

Repeat the process above to place the word "Projected" above the data for the third and fourth quarters. When you have finished this activity, your screen should look similar to Figure 9-10.

Figure 9-10

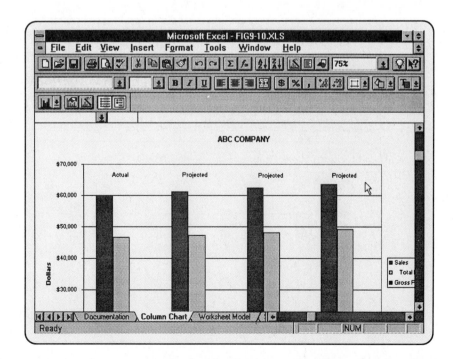

> *User Tip*
> You can use the Copy and Paste commands to copy the text "Projected". Select the text box. Then choose the Copy 📋 and Paste 📋 buttons on the Standard toolbar. Once the text box appears, drag the text box to the appropriate location.

You can place graphic objects on a chart. Suppose that the fourth-quarter sales value will set a record. To indicate this situation, you can place an arrow and some text on the chart.

Before starting, make sure nothing is selected on your chart. To add the arrow:

Click   the Drawing 🖉 button on the Standard toolbar

The Drawing toolbar appears on your screen.

Click   the Arrow 🖉 button on the Drawing toolbar

Move   the cross-hair pointer to where you want the
         end of the arrow

Drag   the cross-hair pointer where you want the head
         of the arrow

When you release the mouse button, the arrow will appear on your chart. Place the text "Record Sales" on the chart so your screen looks similar to Figure 9-11.

Figure 9-11

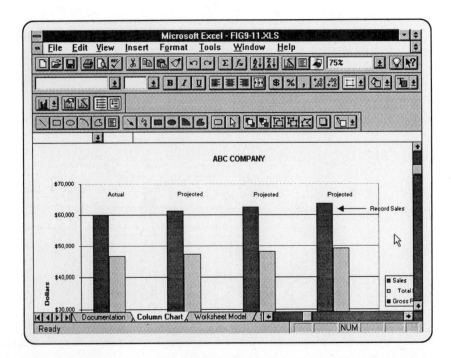

Close the workbook document. Do not save any changes.

Remove the Drawing toolbar.

■ SIZING AND MOVING AN EMBEDDED CHART

In Chapter 7, you included an embedded chart on a worksheet. You also can change the size of an embedded chart and move the chart on a worksheet.

Suppose you want to change the size of the embedded chart in the PRACTCHT workbook you created in Chapter 7 and move the chart to a different location on the worksheet.

To change the size of the embedded chart:

Open	the PRACTCHT workbook file
Click	anywhere on the chart to select the chart
Move	the mouse pointer to the sizing handle at the bottom right corner of the chart until it becomes a double-headed arrow
Drag	the cross-hair pointer until the pointer is in the middle of column F
Move	the mouse pointer to the sizing handle at the middle left border of the chart until it becomes a double-headed arrow
Drag	the cross-hair pointer until the pointer is at the left side of column A

The size of the chart is now changed.

To move the chart to a new location:

Move	the mouse pointer to the top edge of the embedded chart
Drag	the pointer until the pointer is in the middle of row 25

Deselect the chart.

After making row 24 the first row on your screen, your screen should look similar to Figure 9-12.

Figure 9-12

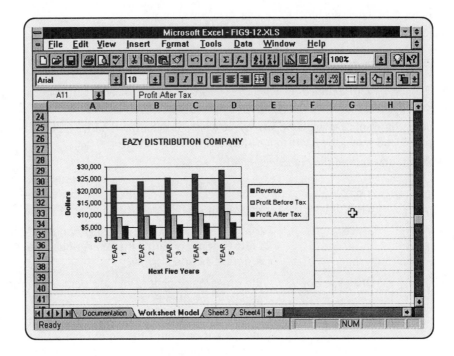

Close the workbook document. Do not save any changes.

SUMMARY

With Excel, you can enhance the appearance of charts that you create. For example, you can remove or change the axes scales, change the font of chart text, change colors and hatch patterns, and include or exclude gridlines. You can also add unattached text and graphic objects to a chart. Finally, you can change the size of an embedded chart on a worksheet or move a chart to a different location.

KEY CONCEPTS

Axes scales
Colors
Font
Graphic objects
Gridlines

Hatch patterns
Move an embedded chart
Size an embedded chart
Unattached text

EXERCISE 1

INSTRUCTIONS: Circle T if the statement is true and F if the statement is false.

T	F	1. You can vary the appearance of text on a chart.
T	F	2. It is possible to change both the color and patterns of each data series.
T	F	3. Ten font choices are available for each group of chart text.
T	F	4. Arrows, rectangles, lines, and ellipses are the only graphic objects that you may place on an Excel chart.
T	F	5. You can change the Y-axis scale manually.

EXERCISE 2

INSTRUCTIONS: Explain a typical situation when the following Excel commands are used:

Problem 1:   Format Select Chart Title   *Problem 4:*   Insert Axes

Problem 2:   Insert Gridlines   *Problem 5:*   Format Selected Data Series

Problem 3:   Format Selected Legend

EXERCISE 3

INSTRUCTIONS: Open the PRACSTBR workbook file.

Change the font for the chart title to Times New Roman, bold italic, and 14 point.

Remove the Y-axis scale.

Place horizontal gridlines on the chart.

Place the word "Actual" over the YEAR 1 data series. Place the word "Forecast" over the data series for YEAR 2 through YEAR 5.

Print the chart.

Save the PRACSTBR workbook document.

Close the PRACSTBR workbook document.

EXERCISE 4

INSTRUCTIONS: Open the PRACTBAR workbook file.

Change the color and hatch patterns of each data series.
Print the chart.
Save the PRACTBAR workbook document.
Close the PRACTBAR workbook document.

EXERCISE 5

INSTRUCTIONS: Open the XYZEMBED workbook file.

Change the size of the embedded chart so that it appears in cells A9 through E19.
Move the chart so the top border of the chart is in the middle of row 11.
Print the chart.
Print the worksheet and chart together.
Save the XYZEMBED workbook document.
Close the XYZEMBED workbook document.

CHAPTER TEN

CREATING AND USING A TEMPLATE WORKBOOK

OBJECTIVES

In this chapter, you will learn to:
- Create a template workbook
- Save a template workbook
- Use a template workbook

■ CHAPTER OVERVIEW

In Excel, the term **template** describes a worksheet that you can use to create a series of other workbooks. A template usually consists of the general format (column titles, row titles, and numeric format) and formulas that are common to all of the worksheets. When you enter data in the template workbook, the worksheet formulas calculate accordingly. The new data is then saved using a different workbook file name. Using a template can save you hours of time and effort in creating worksheets. A template is sometimes referred to as a **shell document**.

The template workbook you create in this chapter computes the total salaries for employees in various divisions of the ABC Company example used earlier. Since the salaries for each division are on a separate workbook, you build a template that can be used to create the workbooks for the various divisions of ABC Company. When you have completed the template workbook, your screen will look like Figure 10-1.

Figure 10-1

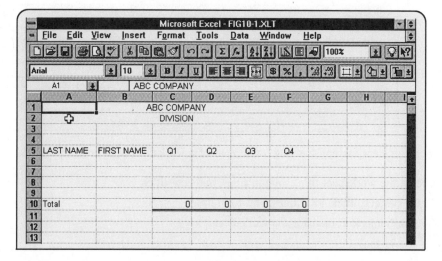

■ CREATING A TEMPLATE WORKBOOK

Before creating the actual template workbook, make sure there is a blank workbook document on your screen. Then enter the documentation information in Figure 10-2, Parts 1 and 2 on Sheet1. Change the tab name to "Documentation."

Figure 10-2
Part 1

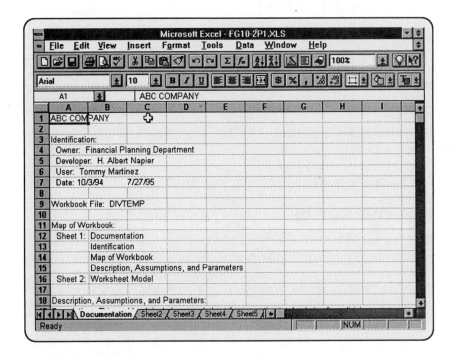

Figure 10-2
Part 2

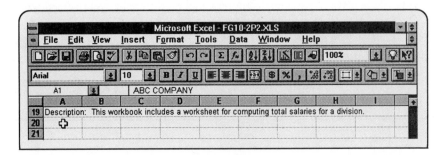

There are three steps for constructing a template of a worksheet contained in a workbook:

1. Create the worksheet title, column titles, and row titles.

2. Enter subtotal lines, total lines, and formulas.

3. Set the numeric format for the worksheet.

Entering the Worksheet Title, Column Titles, and Row Titles

To enter the column titles for the template:

Click	on the Sheet2 tab
Click	on cell A1 (if necessary)
Enter	ABC COMPANY
Click	on cell A2
Enter	DIVISION

To center the contents of cells A1 and A2 over columns A through F:

Select	cells A1:F2
Click	the Center Across Columns ⊞ button

To place the titles for columns A and B on the worksheet:

Click	on cell A5
Enter	LAST NAME
Click	on cell B5
Enter	FIRST NAME

To view the contents of cells A5 and B5, widen columns A and B to 12 characters.
To enter the titles for columns C through F:

Enter	Q1 in cell C5
Enter	Q2 in cell D5
Enter	Q3 in cell E5
Enter	Q4 in cell F5

Center the column titles in cells C5 through F5.
To enter the row title for total salaries:

Click	on cell A10
Enter	Total

Your screen should look like Figure 10-3.

Figure 10-3

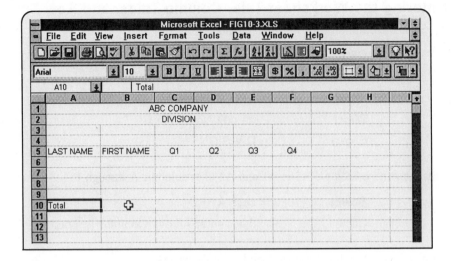

Entering Subtotal Lines, Total Lines, and Formulas

To enter subtotal lines:

Select	cells C9:F9
Click	the Borders button

Design Tip

You use the SUM function to add values in contiguous cells in a column. Later, after completing a worksheet, you may need to insert a row at the beginning or end of the range of cells included in a SUM function cell entry. To make sure you include the new cells in the SUM cell entry, you must include the cell above and below the actual cells you want to include in the SUM function cell entry. Otherwise, the cells in the row you insert will not be included in the SUM function cell entry. You can use a similar approach if you are summing cell entries for a group of contiguous columns.

To enter the formula to sum the salaries:

Click	on cell C10
Click	the AutoSum ∑ button
Click	on cell C5
Drag	the mouse pointer to cell C9
Click	the enter box

A zero (0) should appear in cell C10 because the template does not contain any numbers to add. Including one row above and below where data will be input allows the SUM formula to adjust correctly in the event rows of data are inserted or deleted. In this example, there is no salary information that will be included in the ninth row. Since the cells in the fifth and ninth rows contain text or a blank, their values are assumed to be zero and, therefore, will not cause the SUM formula results to be incorrect.

To copy the SUM formula to cells D10 through F10:

Click	on cell C10
Drag	the fill handle to cell F10

To place double underlines on the worksheet:

Select	cells C10:F10 (if necessary)
Click	the down arrow on the Borders ⊡▾ button
Click	on the double underline border

Setting the Numeric Format for the Worksheet

To set the format for the numeric data on the template worksheet:

Select	cells C6:F10
Choose	Format
Choose	Cells
Click	the Number tab (if necessary)
Click	the Number option in the Category list box
Click	the #,##0 format choice in the Format Codes list box
Click	the OK command button

When you enter numbers, they will be formatted with commas and zero decimal places. Change the Sheet2 tab name to "Worksheet Model." The template worksheet is now complete. After making cell A1 the active cell, your screen should look like Figure 10-4.

Figure 10-4

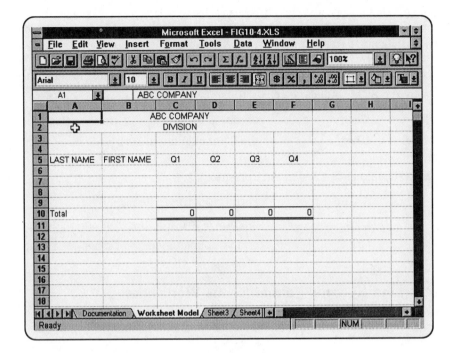

■ SAVING THE TEMPLATE WORKBOOK TO A TEMPLATE FILE

To save the workbook document to a file for later use:

Choose	File
Choose	Save As
Type	DIVTEMP
Click	the down arrow on the Save File as Type drop-down list box
Click	the Template choice
Click	the OK command button

Note that the file has an extension of .XLT rather than .XLS to designate the DIVTEMP file as a template file.

Alternatively, you can create a template workbook by first creating a worksheet for a division. After creating the worksheet, make sure that all the formulas and other elements of the worksheet are correct. Then erase the data for all cells that will be different for the other similar worksheets, and save the shell to a template workbook file. In this example, the names, salary data, and division number would be erased. This method may be preferable in some cases because it eases the checking of worksheet appearance and accuracy.

Close the DIVTEMP template workbook document.

■ USING A TEMPLATE WORKBOOK

The purpose of having a template is to use it as a shell for other workbooks. In this section, you use the DIVTEMP template workbook created in the previous section to create the worksheet for Division 1 of ABC Company.

Open the Template Workbook File

To use the template worksheet, open the DIVTEMP workbook file.

Enter Data into the Template Worksheet

Click	on cell A2
Move	the mouse pointer to the formula bar and click the mouse button with the I-beam at the end of the word DIVISION
Press	the space bar
Type	1
Click	the enter box ☑

Using the data in Figure 10-5 as a reference, enter the names and the quarterly salary information. The formulas in the Total row compute the totals as the salary data for each person is input. Notice that the appropriate numeric format is used for the values. Change the "Worksheet Model" tab name to "Division 1."

Figure 10-5

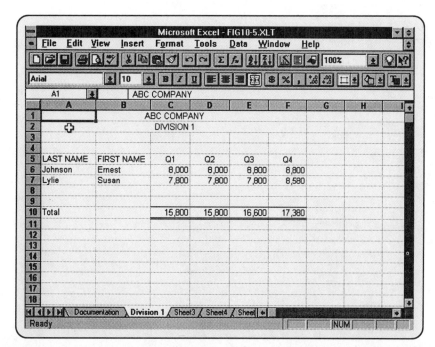

Save the Template Workbook Using Another Name

To save the template workbook using another name:

Click	on cell A1
Choose	File
Choose	Save As
Type	DIV1
Click	the OK command button

Close the DIV1 workbook document.

SUMMARY

A template workbook document is a shell document that you can use to create multiple worksheets that have the same basic format. The template contains features that are common to all other worksheets having a similar appearance. For example, worksheet titles, row titles, column titles, formulas, formats, defined names, and print settings may be created in a template workbook document. When data is entered into the template workbook, the results are saved to a file with a different name than the template workbook file.

KEY CONCEPTS

Shell document
Template
Template workbook document
Template workbook file

EXERCISE 1

INSTRUCTIONS: Circle T if the statement is true and F if the statement is false.

    T   F   1.   In Excel, you must combine a template workbook file with another file containing data to generate a new workbook.

    T   F   2.   Using a template workbook is a good way to keep workbooks standardized.

    T   F   3.   When you add data to a template in memory, it is automatically added to the template workbook file on the disk.

    T   F   4.   You can use a template workbook to create multiple workbooks.

    T   F   5.   After you have added data to a template workbook in order to create a new workbook, you should save the workbook using a name other than the template workbook name.

EXERCISE 2 -- Creating a Template Workbook from an Existing Workbook

---

INSTRUCTIONS: Open the DIV1 workbook file. Erase the number 1 from the worksheet title DIVISION 1.

Erase the data for LAST NAME, FIRST NAME, and all four quarters for Ernest Johnson and Susan Lylie to create a template workbook. Change the worksheet tab name "Division 1" to "Worksheet Model".

Save the template workbook to a template file using the name DIVTEMP2. The DIVTEMP2 workbook file should be identical to the DIVTEMP workbook file that you created in this chapter. Your screen should look like Figure 10-6.

Figure 10-6

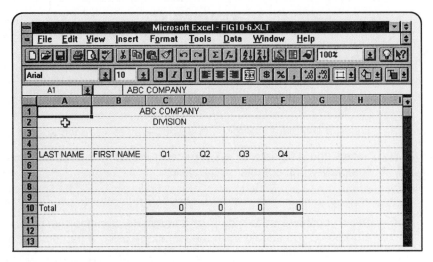

Close the DIVTEMP2 template workbook document.

EXERCISE 3 -- Creating a Template

INSTRUCTIONS: Create the template workbook displayed in Figure 10-7. Place appropriate information on the Documentation worksheet, and put the worksheet itself on the Worksheet Model worksheet.

Figure 10-7

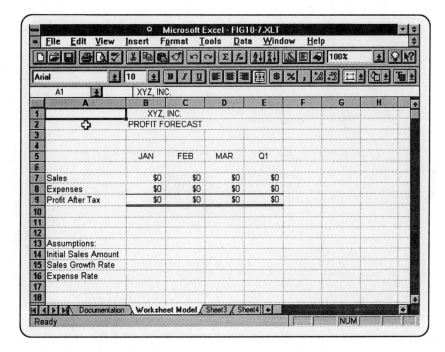

Sales for the month of January are determined from the amount entered in cell B14 by placing the formula =B14 in cell B7. You compute the values for Sales in February and March by multiplying the Sales amount for the previous month times 1 plus the Growth Rate for the current month.

Calculate Expenses by multiplying the Expense Rate for each month times the Sales amount for the month.

Save the template workbook to a file using the name PROFTEMP.

Print the template worksheet model.

Once you have placed the values in the appropriate Assumptions cells, your screen should look like Figure 10-8.

Figure 10-8

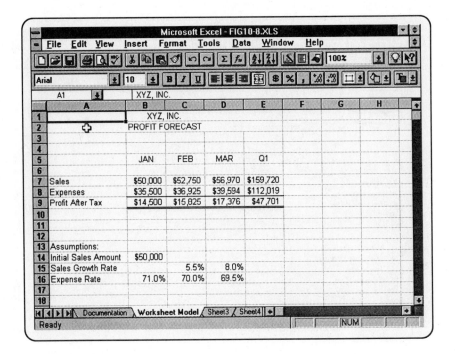

Print the results after you use the template workbook.

Close the PROFTEMP template workbook document. Do not save any changes.

CHAPTER ELEVEN

CREATING AND USING MULTIPLE WORKSHEETS AND FILES

OBJECTIVES

In this chapter, you will learn to:
- Copy information between worksheets
- Enter data and formulas in multiple worksheets
- Format multiple worksheets
- Print multiple worksheet data
- Use multiple files

■ CHAPTER OVERVIEW

In the previous chapters, you worked with workbooks that included a documentation sheet, worksheet model, and a chart. In this chapter, you are introduced to the process for using worksheet models that include more than one worksheet. You may also link workbooks together.

■ EXAMPLE PROBLEM

Suppose ABC Company has three divisions and sells two products in each division. Data for projected sales in the three divisions are explained on the following page.

Division 1:	Q1	Q2	Q3	Q4
Mowers	5,000	12,000	14,000	10,000
Edgers	3,000	5,000	8,000	4,000

Division 2:	Q1	Q2	Q3	Q4
Mowers	7,000	14,000	16,000	11,000
Edgers	2,000	4,000	7,000	5,000

Division 3:	Q1	Q2	Q3	Q4
Mowers	6,000	12,000	15,000	8,000
Edgers	1,000	7,000	8,000	3,000

You need to create a workbook that includes the data for the division on individual worksheets. Also, you need to compute division totals for each quarter and for annual sales.

■ CREATING THE INITIAL WORKSHEET

Since you already have completed many worksheets as you have progressed through the earlier chapters, the instructions for creating the worksheet for Division 1 are abbreviated and do not include all of the steps. Also, the documentation for proper worksheet design has been omitted.

Figure 11-1 includes the worksheet for Division 1. Create the worksheet and enter all of the data for each of the quarters. Use the SUM function to compute the quarterly and annual totals. Do not format the data.

Figure 11-1

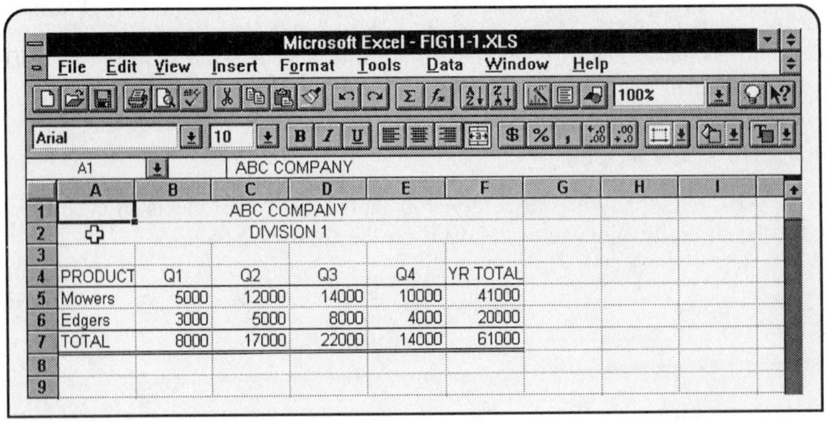

Save the workbook to a file using the name DIVSALES.

■ COPYING INFORMATION BETWEEN WORKSHEETS

To copy the worksheet titles and column titles from the Division 1 worksheet to another worksheet:

Select	cells A1:F4
Click	the Copy 🗐 button
Click	the Sheet2 tab
Click	on cell A1
Hold down	the Shift key
Click	the Sheet3 tab

Notice that the Sheet2 and Sheet3 tab names are selected. This selection is indicated by both tabs having the same white color and [Group] appears on the title bar.

Click	the Paste 🗐 button

User Tip

If you want to select sheets that are nonadjacent, hold down the CTRL key and click on the appropriate tab names.

To ungroup the sheets:

Move	the mouse pointer to one of the selected tabs
Click	the alternate mouse button to activate the shortcut menu
Choose	Ungroup Sheets

It is important to ungroup the two worksheets before you enter information. Otherwise, if you enter information into the Division 2 worksheet, it will automatically be copied to the Division 3 worksheet.

Edit the Division titles so that DIVISION 2 appears in cell A2 on Sheet2 and DIVISION 3 appears in cell A2 on Sheet3. Change the name of the Sheet2 and Sheet3 tabs to "Division 2" and "Division 3", respectively. After making cell A1 of the Division 3 worksheet the active cell, your screen should look like Figure 11-2.

Figure 11-2

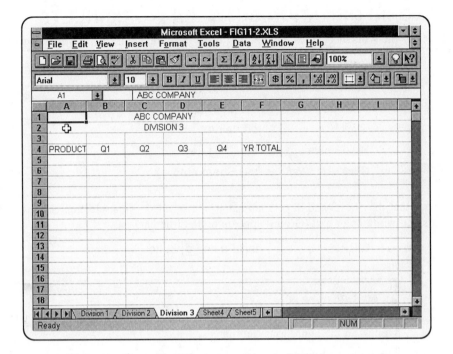

■ ENTERING DATA AND FORMULAS IN MULTIPLE WORKSHEETS

Enter the row labels Mowers, Edgers, and TOTAL in cells A5, A6, and A7, respectively, in the Division 2 and Division 3 worksheets. Make the bottom of cells A4 through F4 and cells A6 through F6 appear as a solid line, and make the bottom of cells A7 through F7 appear as solid double underlines in the Division 2 and Division 3 worksheets. You may copy the row labels to further practice the process of copying information from one worksheet to other worksheets.

Enter the quarterly information shown in Figure 11-3, Parts 1 and 2 in the Division 2 and Division 3 worksheets.

Figure 11-3
Part 1

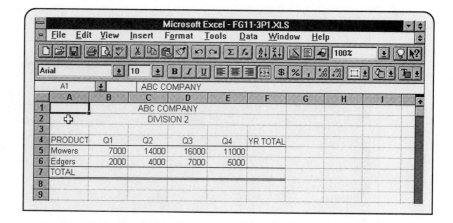

Figure 11-3
Part 2

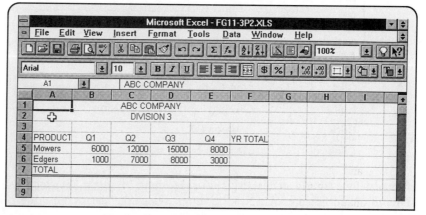

To examine the formulas for determining annual sales for each of the products:

Click   on cell F5 in the Division 1 worksheet

The formula for computing the annual total sales for Mowers, =SUM(B5:E5), appears in the formula bar. A similar formula appears in cell F6 for Edgers.

To copy the formulas for computing the annual sales for both products in the Division 1 worksheet to the Division 2 and Division 3 worksheets:

Select   cells F5:F6

Click   the Copy 🗎 button

Select   the Division 2 and Division 3 tabs

Click   on cell F5

Click   the Paste 🗎 button

The formulas for computing annual sales have been copied to the Division 2 and Division 3 worksheets and the appropriate values appear in these worksheets. After you have ungrouped the sheets and made cell F5 on the Division 2 worksheet the active cell, your screen should look like Figure 11-4.

Figure 11-4

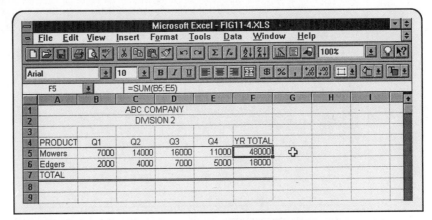

To place the formulas for determining the total sales for each quarter on the Division 1 worksheet to the other division worksheets:

Select	cells B7:F7 on the Division 1 worksheet
Click	the Copy 📋 button
Select	the Division 2 and Division 3 tabs
Click	on cell B7
Click	the Paste 📋 button

The formulas for quarterly product totals have been copied from the Division 1 worksheet to the Division 2 and Division 3 worksheets. After you have ungrouped the sheets and made cell B7 on the Division 2 worksheet the active cell, your screen should look like Figure 11-5.

Figure 11-5

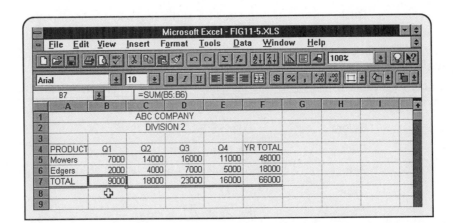

Click on the Division 3 tab. After making cell B7 the active cell, your screen should look like Figure 11-6.

Figure 11-6

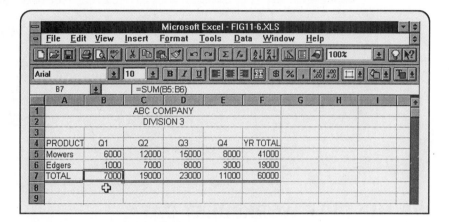

■ FORMATTING MULTIPLE WORKSHEETS

For this example problem, the format specifications need to be the same for all of the worksheets. Rather than format each worksheet individually, you can format all numeric cells at the same time. First, you must select the cells needing formatting on the Division 1 worksheet. Then select the three division tab names. When you use the Cells command on the Format menu, the selected cells will be formatted in all the division worksheets.

To illustrate the process for formatting cells in multiple worksheets:

Select	cells B5:F7 in the Division 1 worksheet
Select	the Division 2 and Division 3 tabs
Choose	Format
Choose	Cells
Click	the Number tab (if necessary)
Click	the Number choice in the Category list box
Click	the #,##0 option in the Format Codes list box
Click	the OK command button

The cells on all the division worksheets are formatted. After you have ungrouped the sheets and made cell A1 on the Division 1 worksheet the active cell, your screen should look like Figure 11-7.

Figure 11-7

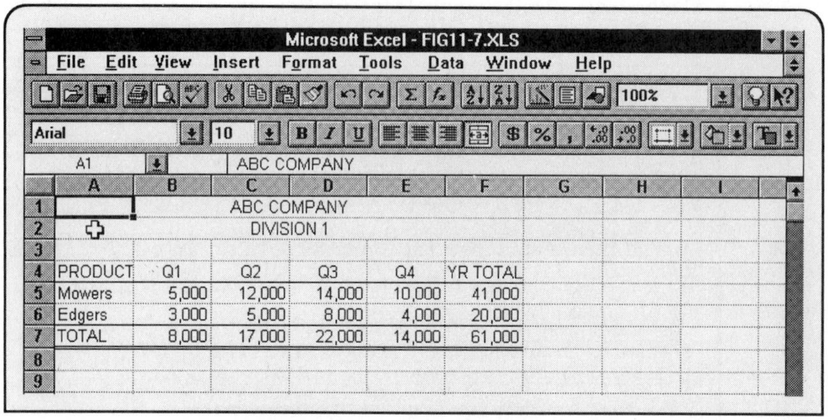

■ PRINTING MULTIPLE WORKSHEET DATA

Just as it is convenient to format all worksheets at one time, you may want to print several worksheets at one time. To print the information appearing in the Division 1, Division 2, and Division 3 worksheets:

Choose	File
Choose	Print
Click	the Entire Workbook option button in the Print What group box
Click	the OK command button

Your printout should look similar to Figure 11-8, Parts 1 through 3.

Figure 11-8
Part 1

ABC COMPANY					
DIVISION 1					
PRODUCT	Q1	Q2	Q3	Q4	YR TOTAL
Mowers	5,000	12,000	14,000	10,000	41,000
Edgers	3,000	5,000	8,000	4,000	20,000
TOTAL	8,000	17,000	22,000	14,000	61,000

Figure 11-8
Part 2

ABC COMPANY					
DIVISION 2					
PRODUCT	Q1	Q2	Q3	Q4	YR TOTAL
Mowers	7,000	14,000	16,000	11,000	48,000
Edgers	2,000	4,000	7,000	5,000	18,000
TOTAL	9,000	18,000	23,000	16,000	66,000

Figure 11-8
Part 3

ABC COMPANY					
DIVISION 3					
PRODUCT	Q1	Q2	Q3	Q4	YR TOTAL
Mowers	6,000	12,000	15,000	8,000	41,000
Edgers	1,000	7,000	8,000	3,000	19,000
TOTAL	7,000	19,000	23,000	11,000	60,000

Save the DIVSALES workbook document. Close the workbook document.

■ USING MULTIPLE FILES

In Excel, you can have several workbook files open at the same time. Each workbook file appears in a separate window on your screen. When more than one workbook window is open, you can copy data between the workbooks.

SUMMARY

Using multiple worksheets provides you flexibility in creating worksheet applications that have similar structures and formats. The capability of having multiple files open in memory at the same time gives you more options for worksheet applications.

KEY CONCEPTS

Copying information between worksheets
Formatting multiple worksheets
Printing data from multiple worksheets
Selecting sheets
Ungrouping sheets

EXERCISE 1

INSTRUCTIONS: Circle T if the statement is true and F if the statement is false.

T	F	1.	At most, you can place three worksheets in an Excel file.
T	F	2.	You can copy information from one worksheet to another.
T	F	3.	It is important to ungroup the worksheets before entering information.
T	F	4.	You cannot copy data from one worksheet to another.
T	F	5.	You can open more than one file at one time.
T	F	6.	To select sheets that are nonadjacent, hold down the SHIFT key and click on the appropriate tab names.
T	F	7.	To select adjacent sheets, hold down the CTRL key and click on the appropriate tab names.

EXERCISE 2

INSTRUCTIONS: Explain a typical situation when you use the following items in Excel:

Problem 1:   Shift +Click on a tab name

Problem 2:   Click the alternate mouse button with the mouse pointer on a tab name

Problem 3:   Format Cells Number

Problem 4:   File Print

EXERCISE 3

INSTRUCTIONS: XYZ Consulting Company provides computer training, computer consulting, and system documentation services. The company has offices in New York, Chicago, Houston, and Los Angeles. Data on sales for the months of June, July, and August for each of the locations follows:

New York	June	July	August
Training	15,000	19,000	17,000
Consulting	9,000	8,000	10,000
Documentation	5,000	7,000	9,000

Chicago	June	July	August
Training	12,000	15,000	14,000
Consulting	12,000	18,000	11,000
Documentation	3,000	5,000	7,000

Houston	June	July	August
Training	20,000	15,000	22,000
Consulting	17,000	18,000	19,000
Documentation	8,000	6,000	4,000

Los Angeles	June	July	August
Training	13,000	12,000	15,000
Consulting	11,000	9,000	14,000
Documentation	10,000	10,000	12,000

Create a workbook that has the data for each of the locations on a separate worksheet.

Calculate the total sales by month and type of service for each of the locations.

Format the cells appropriately, and include subtotal lines as well as double underlines to indicate the end of each worksheet.

Save the workbook to a file using the name XYZCONS.

Print the four worksheets.

Close the XYZCONS workbook document.

EXERCISE 4 -- Adding a Worksheet to an Existing File

INSTRUCTIONS: Open the DIVSALES workbook file.

ABC Company forgot to reveal that it has acquired another company that sells mowers and edgers. The newly acquired organization has been designated as Division 4. The data on sales for the new division follows:

Division 4:	Q1	Q2	Q3	Q4
Mowers	3,000	2,000	9,000	2,000
Edgers	2,000	3,000	6,000	1,000

Place the data on Sheet4. Then change the name of the sheet tab to "Division 4".

Print the worksheets.

Save the DIVSALES workbook file and include the new sheet.

Close the DIVSALES workbook document.

EXERCISE 5 -- Creating a Workbook File with Multiple Worksheets

---

INSTRUCTIONS: Create a workbook file with multiple worksheets that will be helpful to you.

Print the worksheets.

Save the workbook to a file using the name of your choice.

Close the workbook document.

CHAPTER TWELVE

CONSOLIDATING WORKSHEETS AND LINKING WORKBOOK FILES

OBJECTIVES

In this chapter, you will learn to:
- Create several worksheets quickly with a template worksheet
- Combine data from several worksheets in a workbook into a summary worksheet
- Move information between worksheets by linking workbook files

■ CHAPTER OVERVIEW

Sometimes you want to combine information from several worksheets into one summary worksheet. An example of such a situation occurs when organizations need to consolidate worksheets for several operating divisions during the budgeting process.

In this chapter, you will use the template you constructed for salaries in Chapter 10 to create a worksheet for each division in the ABC Company. Then you will create a summary worksheet and combine the total salaries data from the three worksheets into the summary worksheet. At this point, you will have the total salaries for ABC Company. Finally, you will link the total salary cells in the summary worksheet to the cells associated with salaries in the BUDGET workbook to copy the salary totals.

■ USE A TEMPLATE WORKBOOK TO CREATE SEVERAL WORKSHEETS

In the following exercise, you will use the DIVTEMP worksheet template you constructed in Chapter 10 to create worksheets for computing total salaries in ABC Company's three operating divisions. Then you will construct a summary worksheet that calculates the total salaries for the three divisions.

To start the exercise, open the DIVTEMP template workbook file. Make sure your screen looks like Figure 12-1.

Figure 12-1

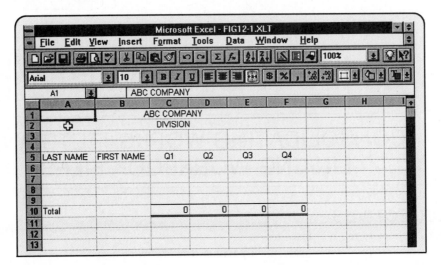

For the purposes of this exercise, you need to create three worksheets using the template worksheet. Change the names of the sheet tabs as follows:

Current Sheet Tab Name	New Sheet Tab Name
Worksheet Model	Division 1
Sheet3	Division 2
Sheet4	Division 3

To place the template information in the Worksheet Model on the next two worksheets:

Select	cells A1:F10 on the Division 1 worksheet
Click	the Copy 📋 button
Select	cell A1 on the Division 2 worksheet
Click	the Paste 📋 button
Select	cell A1 on the Division 3 worksheet
Click	the Paste 📋 button

Notice that the width of columns A and B did not change. Change the width of columns A and B to 12 characters on the Division 2 and Division 3 worksheets.

To enter the data for the Division 1, Division 2, and Division 3 worksheets, use the information shown in Figure 12-2, Parts 1 through 3.

Figure 12-2
Part 1

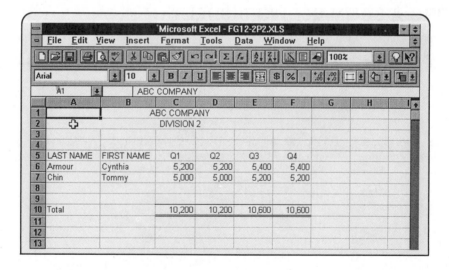

Figure 12-2
Part 2

Figure 12-2
Part 3

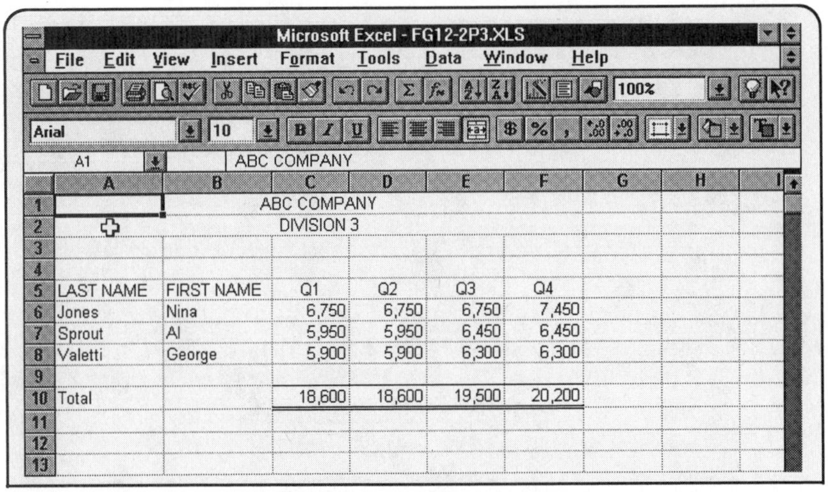

Save the workbook to a file using the name DIVISION.

■ CREATING A SUMMARY WORKSHEET

To insert a summary worksheet:

Click	the Division 1 tab
Choose	Insert
Choose	Worksheet

The new worksheet appears to the left of the Division 1 worksheet. After you have changed the Sheet1 tab name to "Summary", your screen should look like Figure 12-3.

Figure 12-3

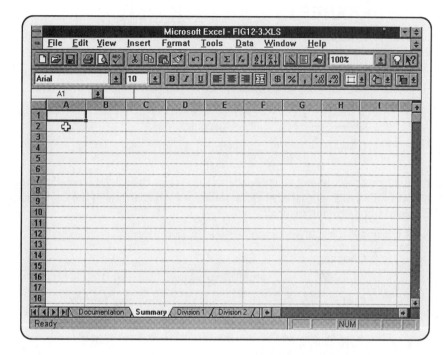

Enter the information shown in Figure 12-4 to place the worksheet titles, row titles, column titles, underlines, double underlines, and the SUM function to calculate totals. When you have finished, your screen should look like Figure 12-4.

Figure 12-4

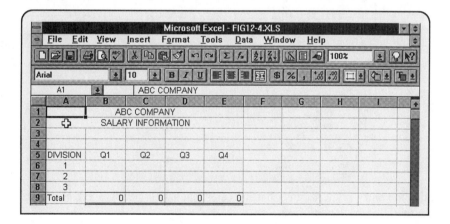

■ LINKING WORKSHEETS TOGETHER

To link the total salary cells in the Division 1 worksheet to the Summary worksheet:

Click	the Division 1 tab
Select	cells C10:F10
Click	the Copy 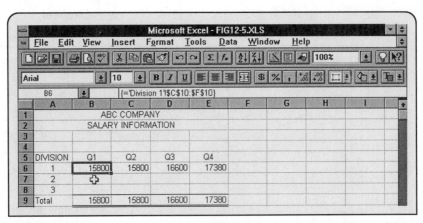 button
Click	the Summary tab
Click	on cell B6

Rather than paste the values, you need to include a link between the Division 1 worksheet and the Summary worksheet. With this approach, when a number is changed in one of the Division worksheets, the Summary worksheet is updated automatically.

To link a line between the Summary and Division worksheets:

Choose	Edit
Choose	Paste Special
Click	the Paste Link command button

The values for total salaries in the Division 1 worksheet now appear in the Summary worksheet. Notice that the formats were not pasted.

After making cell B6 the active cell, your screen should look like Figure 12-5.

Figure 12-5

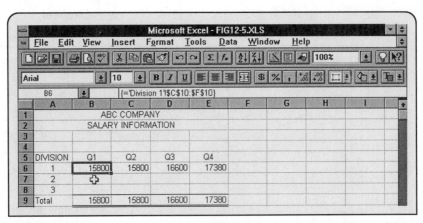

Notice the entry in the formula bar indicates that a link has been established to the Summary worksheet from the Division 1 worksheet.

Apply the process again to establish similar links to the Summary worksheet from the Division 2 and Division 3 worksheets. Format the cells with numeric values using the #,##0 format option. After making cell A1 on the Summary worksheet the active cell, your screen should look like Figure 12-6.

Figure 12-6

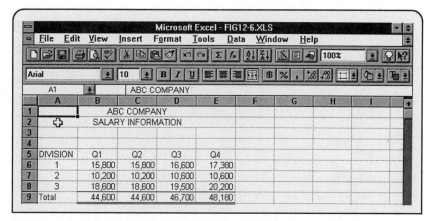

Save the DIVISION workbook document. Do not close the DIVISION workbook document.

■ LINKING WORKBOOK FILES TOGETHER

Excel allows you to link workbook files. Suppose you would like to use the total salary information appearing on the Summary worksheet in the DIVISION workbook file to the Salaries item on the BUDGET workbook file.

To illustrate the process of linking two workbook files:

Open	the BUDGET workbook file
Clear	the quarterly Salaries values in cells B10:E10 on the Worksheet Model worksheet
Select	cells B9:E9 on the Summary worksheet on the DIVISION file
Click	the Copy 🖺 button
Select	cell B10 on the Worksheet Model worksheet on the BUDGET file
Choose	Edit
Choose	Paste Special
Click	the Paste Link command button

The values from the Summary worksheet on the DIVISION workbook now appear on the Worksheet Model worksheet on the BUDGET workbook.

After making cell B10 the active cell, your screen should look like Figure 12-7.

Figure 12-7

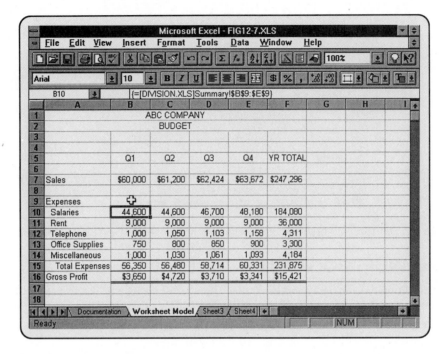

Notice the link that appears in the formula bar.

Close the BUDGET workbook document. Do not save any changes. Close the DIVISION workbook document.

SUMMARY

You can use a template workbook to create several identical worksheets. Appropriate data can be entered into the worksheets. You can use a summary worksheet to summarize the data in the individual worksheets. Excel gives you the capability to link worksheets in different workbook files.

KEY CONCEPTS

Consolidating information between worksheets
Linking worksheets in different workbook files

EXERCISE 1

INSTRUCTIONS: Circle T if the statement is true and F if the statement is false.

T   F   1.   You can use a template workbook to create several worksheets very rapidly.

T   F   2.   You can link worksheets in a workbook.

T   F   3.   Although you can link worksheets, you cannot link workbook files.

T   F   4.   Only two files can be open at one time, but many worksheets can appear within one workbook file.

EXERCISE 2 -- Consolidating Worksheets

INSTRUCTIONS: Open the XYZCONS workbook file that you created as an exercise in Chapter 11.

Add a summary worksheet that contains the total monthly revenues for the New York, Chicago, Houston, and Los Angeles locations.

Include a total line on the summary sheet that computes the total revenues for XYZ Consulting Company.

Print the summary worksheet.

Save and close the XYZCONS workbook document.

EXERCISE 3 -- Linking Workbook Files

INSTRUCTIONS: Open the DIVSALES workbook file that you completed as an exercise in Chapter 11.

Rather than include an additional worksheet in the DIVSALES workbook, open a new workbook file named ABCSUMRY.

Create a summary worksheet in the ABCSUMRY workbook that includes cells for the quarterly sales of each division of the ABC Company and calculates the total revenue by quarter and for the year.

Link the appropriate cells containing the data from the worksheets in the DIVSALES workbook file to the proper cells in the ABCSUMRY workbook file.

Print the ABCSUMRY workbook.

Save and close the ABCSUMRY workbook document. Close the DIVSALES workbook document.

EXERCISE 4 -- Consolidating Multiple Worksheets in a File

INSTRUCTIONS: Create a workbook file with multiple worksheets and include a summary worksheet that will be helpful to you in some way. Link some of the data in the worksheets to the summary worksheet.

Print your worksheets.

Save and close the workbook document.

EXERCISE 5 -- Linking Workbook Files

INSTRUCTIONS: Create an application of Excel that uses the concept of linking workbook files that will be helpful to you.

Print the worksheets associated with the workbook files.

Save and close the workbook document.

CHAPTER THIRTEEN

INTRODUCTION TO LISTS, DATABASES, SORTING, AND FILTERING

OBJECTIVES

In this chapter, you will learn to:
- Create a list
- Identify basic database terms
- Enter data for a list
- Sort data in a list
- Use a data entry form
- Filter data in a list
- Find data using the Form command
- Use complex criteria to filter a list
- Filter only unique records contained in a list

■ CHAPTER OVERVIEW

You can use worksheets in Excel workbooks to store information. Such worksheets are called **lists**. An example of a list that can be stored on a worksheet might be the names and salaries for employees in a small company or department of a large organization. Sometimes, such lists are referred to as **databases**.

Once you have prepared a list, you can sort the information in the list by a particular category such as an identification number, total salary, or last name. You may find a specific item in a list such as a particular invoice or a certain individual's salary in a list that satisfy a particular condition. For example, you can determine all those individuals in a particular division of a company who have a total annual salary in excess of $25,000.

■ CREATING A LIST

In Excel, you can create a list for a variety of applications, including invoices, salary information, grade sheets, and personal budgets.

Some suggestions to use when you create a list follow:

Include only one list on a worksheet.

If other information is included on a worksheet, leave at least one blank row and one blank column between the list and the other parts of the worksheet.

Place column labels in the initial row in your list. Each of the column labels should be unique.

Make the column labels appear different from other text by using a different font, capitalizing the text, underlining the text, or making the text appear as boldface type.

Do not include any blank rows below the column labels or between rows in the list.

Make sure the rows all have similar data under each column.

If your worksheet includes other data, you may want to specify a name for your list using the Name command on the Insert menu.

Format all data in a specific column consistently.

■ SOME BASIC DATABASE TERMS

Excel recognizes a list as a **database**. You can use Excel to sort information in a list or database or to find information in your database.

Some of the basic terms used in database management are field, record, and key.

A **field** is a collection of characters that are grouped together. In Excel, each field is contained in a separate column within the list or database. An example would be a person's last name. A **field name** is the term used to describe each field. You include a field name on a list by specifying a unique **column label**. For example, you can use the column label LAST NAME as a field name. In Excel, each field name is in the cell immediately above the column containing the data for the field.

A **record** is a group of data fields that are combined in some logical pattern. For example, the personnel record for individuals in a company might include the individual's social security number, last name, first name, middle initial, or department in which the individual works. When you combine a set of records together, you have a database. Excel refers to such a database simply as a list.

A **key** is a specific field that you can use for distinguishing between records. For example, you could use an identification number or the social security number for an employee as a key for a human resources list.

■ ENTERING DATA FOR A LIST

To illustrate the process for completing a list, you will first need to enter the documentation information in Figure 13-1, Parts 1 and 2. Then you will use the Form command on the Data menu to prepare the worksheet shown in Figure 13-1, Part 3.

Figure 13-1
Part 1

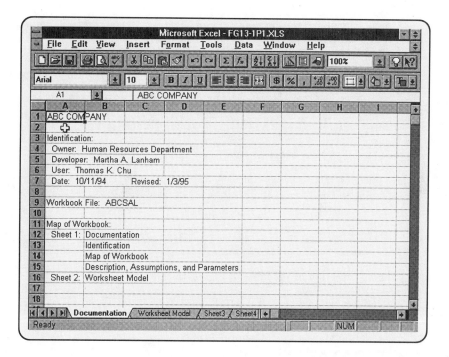

Figure 13-1
Part 2

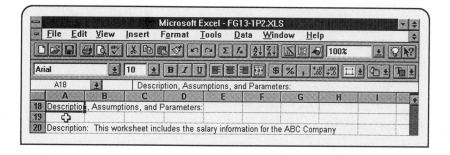

Figure 13-1
Part 3

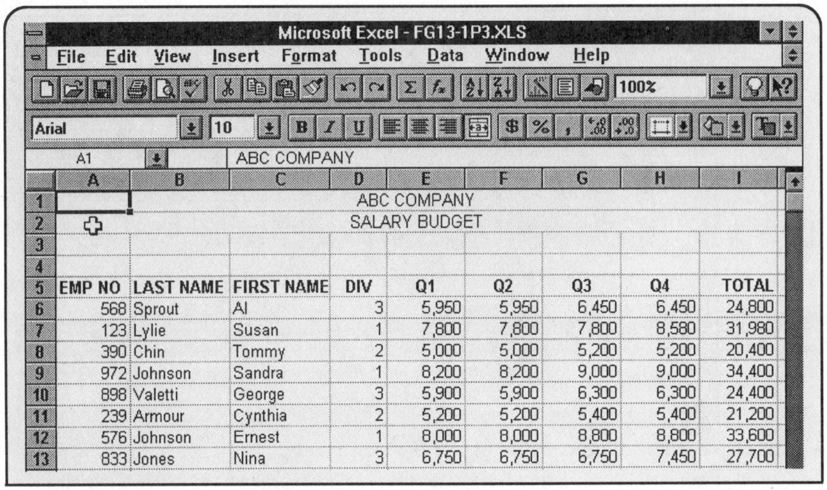

To initiate the construction of the table in Figure 13-1, Part 3:

> **Enter**   the information in cells A1:I5

Column	Column Width
A	8
B	11
C	11
D	6

Change the Sheet2 tab name to Worksheet Model.

To place the entries in the list, you must select the row of headers:

> **Select**   cells A5:I5

To initiate the use of the Form command:

> **Choose**   Data
>
> **Choose**   Form

A message dialog box appears on your screen asking if you want to use the selected cells as the header row for the list.

> **Click**   the OK command button

A dialog box appears and your screen should look like Figure 13-2. Note that the name of the dialog box is the name of the current worksheet. In this case, the dialog box name is "Worksheet Model".

Figure 13-2

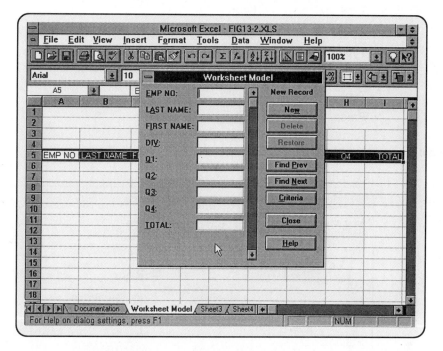

The column headings, or headers, appear and there is a text box to enter the information for each item on a record. Recall that Excel considers a list a database. After you have entered each of the items for a record in the various text boxes, press the ENTER key to place the information in the worksheet.

To enter the data for the first employee:

Click	the EMP NO text box (if necessary)
Type	568
Press	Tab
Type	Sprout
Press	Tab
Type	Al
Press	Tab
Type	3
Press	Tab
Type	5950
Press	Tab
Type	5950
Press	Tab

Type	6450
Press	[Tab⇆]
Type	6450
Press	[Tab⇆]
Type	24800
Press	[←Enter]

Your screen should look like Figure 13-3.

Figure 13-3

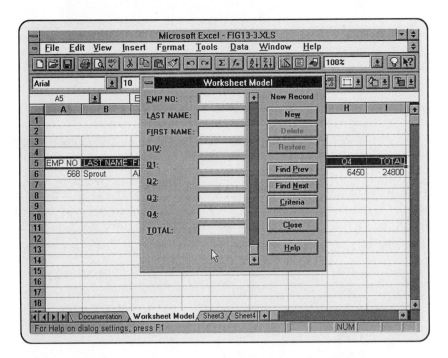

Notice that the data for the first employee appears in the list. The dialog box remains on your screen so you can enter additional employee records.

To enter the data record for the second employee into the list:

Click	the EMP NO text box (if necessary)
Type	123
Press	[Tab⇆]
Type	Lylie
Press	[Tab⇆]
Type	Susan

Press	Tab⇆
Type	1
Press	Tab⇆
Type	7800
Press	Tab⇆
Type	7800
Press	Tab⇆
Type	7800
Press	Tab⇆
Type	8580
Press	Tab⇆
Type	31980
Press	↵Enter

The second record now appears in the list.

Enter the remaining data until your screen looks like Figure 13-4. After you have input the data, click the Close command button to remove the dialog box from your screen. Note that you will need to format the cells containing the salary values to include commas and no decimal places. Be sure to bold the column labels.

Figure 13-4

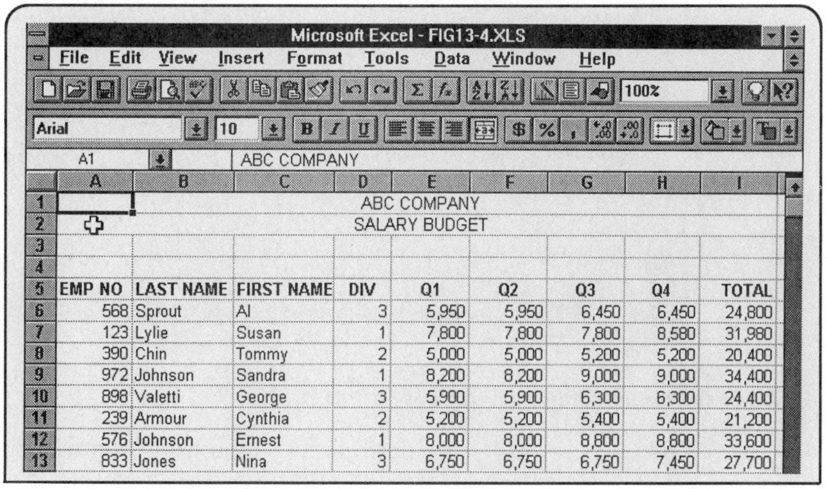

Save the workbook document to a file using the name ABCSAL.

■ SORTING DATA IN A LIST

Sometimes you may need to sort list data in a particular order. For example, you may want to sort some sales transactions in order by type of transaction such as cash or credit sale. Excel allows you to sort by three sort keys.

Suppose you need to sort the employee salary data in the salary list contained in the ABCSAL workbook by division number.

To sort the data:

Select	cells A5:I13
Choose	Data
Choose	Sort

The Sort dialog box appears. Your screen should look like Figure 13-5.

Figure 13-5

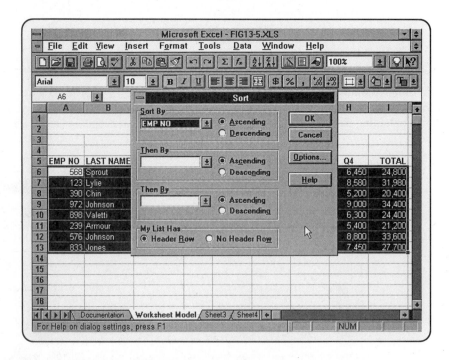

To specify the initial column or sort key to sort by:

Click	the down arrow in the Sort By group box to display the Sort By drop-down list
Click	the DIV header
Click	the Ascending option button in the Sort By group box

The two options for sorting are Ascending and Descending. **Ascending order** can refer to alphabetical order (from A to Z) or numerical order (from the smallest number to the largest number). **Descending order** can refer to reverse alphabetical order (from Z to A) or to numerical order (from largest number to the smallest number).

Sorting the Data

To complete the sort procedure:

Click the OK command button

The employee records in the list are sorted by division number. After making cell A1 the active cell, your screen should look like Figure 13-6.

Figure 13-6

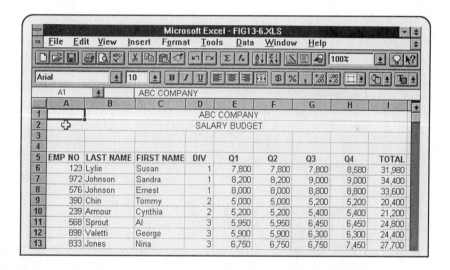

User Tip

If you sort by only one column (sort key), an alternative is to click on the cell containing the appropriate column label. Then click the Sort Ascending or Sort Descending button on the Standard toolbar. This approach is not appropriate if you sort by more than one column.

Sorting by Two Keys

Please note that employees' names in Figure 13-6 are not in alphabetical order. If you had a large number of employees in each division, you would need to place the data in alphabetical order.

To sort the information in Figure 13-6 in alphabetical order by last name:

Select	cells A5:I13
Choose	Data
Choose	Sort
Click	the down arrow in the first Then By group box to display the drop-down list
Click	the LAST NAME header
Click	the Ascending option button in the first Then By group box
Click	the OK command button

The data is now sorted by division and in alphabetical order by last name within each division. After making cell A1 the active cell, your screen should look like Figure 13-7.

Figure 13-7

Microsoft Excel - FIG13-7.XLS

	EMP NO	LAST NAME	FIRST NAME	DIV	Q1	Q2	Q3	Q4	TOTAL
1			ABC COMPANY						
2			SALARY BUDGET						
6	972	Johnson	Sandra	1	8,200	8,200	9,000	9,000	34,400
7	576	Johnson	Ernest	1	8,000	8,000	8,800	8,800	33,600
8	123	Lylie	Susan	1	7,800	7,800	7,800	8,580	31,980
9	239	Armour	Cynthia	2	5,200	5,200	5,400	5,400	21,200
10	390	Chin	Tommy	2	5,000	5,000	5,200	5,200	20,400
11	833	Jones	Nina	3	6,750	6,750	6,750	7,450	27,700
12	568	Sprout	Al	3	5,950	5,950	6,450	6,450	24,800
13	898	Valetti	George	3	5,900	5,900	6,300	6,300	24,400

Sorting by Three Keys

The example in the previous section sorted the last names in alphabetical order within each division. Notice that the records are not in alphabetical order. The information for Sandra Johnson is listed before Ernest Johnson's. Fortunately Excel allows you to use an additional sort key.

Continuing with the example from the previous section, you need to include the FIRST NAME as the third key to sort the employee names in alphabetical order within each division.

To include FIRST NAME as the third sort key:

Select	cells A5:I13
Choose	Data

Choose	Sort
Click	the down arrow in the second Then By group box to display the drop-down list
Click	the FIRST NAME header
Click	the Ascending option button in the second Then By group box
Click	the OK command button

The data is now sorted by division and in proper alphabetical order within each division. After making cell A1 the active cell, your screen should look like Figure 13-8.

Figure 13-8

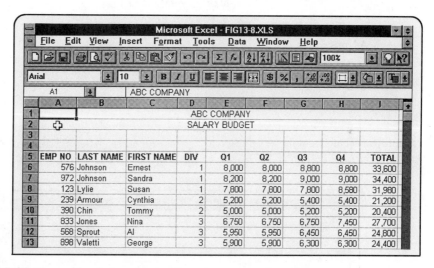

Close the ABCSAL workbook document. Do not save any changes.

■ USING A DATA ENTRY FORM

You can use the Form command on the Data menu to enter additional data or edit data that already exists in a list.

Inserting a New Record in a List

Suppose you need to include an additional person in the ABCSAL workbook file. The information to add is shown below:

EMP NO	LAST NAME	FIRST NAME	DIV	Q1	Q2	Q3	Q4	Total
759	Smith	Kathy	2	5,300	5,300	5,500	5,500	21,600

To place the new data in the ABCSAL workbook:

Open	the ABCSAL workbook file
Select	cells A5:I14
Choose	Data
Choose	Form

A dialog box appears. Notice that the first record is selected and the field names and data appear for this record. A character is underlined in each field name. Excel has determined a unique character to use so that you can select the text box for each field name by pressing the ALT key and the appropriate underlined character.

Click	the New command button
Enter	the data for Kathy Smith
Press	⏎Enter

To stop entering additional information:

Click	the Close command button

The record for the new employee appears at the end of the list. After making cell A1 the active cell, your screen should look like Figure 13-9.

Figure 13-9

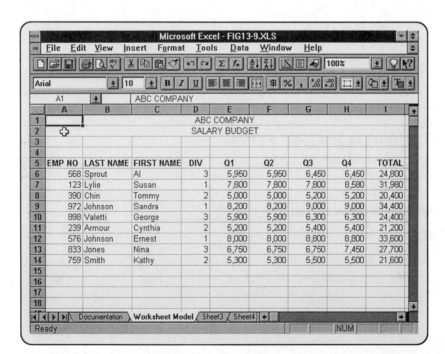

Deleting a Record from a List

You can delete a record from a list by deleting the row in which it appears or by using the Form command on the Data menu.

To remove the record you just entered using the Form command on the Data menu:

Select	cells A5:I14
Choose	Data
Choose	Form
Click	the Find Next command button until the information for Kathy Smith appears

Notice that the record number indicator is "9 of 9." To remove the record:

Click	the Delete command button

A message indicating that the record displayed in the dialog box will be permanently deleted appears. To complete the process:

Click	the OK command button
Click	the Close command button

The record disappears from the list and the original ABCSAL workbook document appears on your screen. Close the ABCSAL workbook document. Do not save any changes.

■ FILTERING DATA IN A LIST

Excel allows you to find and work with only a subset of the data in a list. This process is called **filtering**. Whenever you filter a list, you must specify a set of search conditions called a **criteria**. Excel displays those rows that satisfy the criteria conditions.

Excel provides two ways to filter a list. You can use the **AutoFilter** to match cell contents using a simple criteria. For example, using the ABCSAL workbook file, you could use the AutoFilter to examine all rows containing total salaries greater than $25,000 or those rows containing employees in Division 2. For more complex criteria or computed criteria, you can use the Advanced Filter capability of Excel.

If you use the Excel filtering features, your worksheet is placed in Filter mode. In this situation, you can format, edit, chart, and print your subset list without moving or rearranging it.

Using AutoFilter to Filter a List

You can filter a list by selecting AutoFilter after you choose the Filter command on the Data menu. After you initialize the use of AutoFilter, you can specify a subset of your list by selecting a column and selecting a particular item. The subset of your list will then appear on your screen.

Suppose you want to work with only the individual employees in Division 2 of the ABCSAL workbook file. To use AutoFilter to view the rows associated with these employees:

Open	the ABCSAL workbook file
Select	cells A5:I13
Choose	Data
Choose	Filter
Choose	AutoFilter

A drop-down arrow is placed on each of the column labels in the list. Your screen should look like Figure 13-10.

Figure 13-10

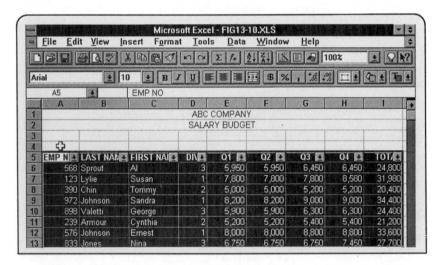

When you click one of the drop-down arrows, a list of the unique items in the column appears. If you click an item in the list of items, all rows containing the item are listed. All other rows disappear.

To display only the Division 2 employees:

Click	the drop-down arrow on the DIV column label
Click	the 2 option

Only the Division 2 employees are now listed. After making cell A1 the active cell, your screen should look like Figure 13-11.

Figure 13-11

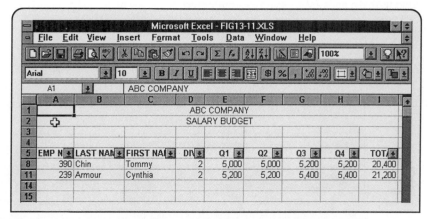

Notice that some row headings are missing, which indicates that those rows not associated with a Division 2 employee have been removed from the screen.

You can now sort, edit, print, or format the data in any manner you wish.

You may display all rows in the list again by selecting Show All after you choose the Filter command on the Data menu. To place the entire list on your screen again:

Choose	Data
Choose	Filter
Choose	Show All

The complete employee list appears. You can continue with other selections if you wish.

To stop using AutoFilter and to remove the drop-down arrows from the column labels:

Choose	Data
Choose	Filter
Choose	AutoFilter

The original ABCSAL workbook document appears again.

When you use AutoFilter, you can customize the selection of rows. For example, suppose you want to examine the list of employees who have a total salary greater than $25,000.

To initiate the use of AutoFilter:

Select	cells A5:I13
Choose	Data
Choose	Filter
Choose	AutoFilter

To indicate that you want to use a custom criterion:

Click	the drop-down arrow on the TOTAL column label
Click	the (Custom...) option

The Custom AutoFilter dialog box appears. Your screen should look like Figure 13-12.

Figure 13-12

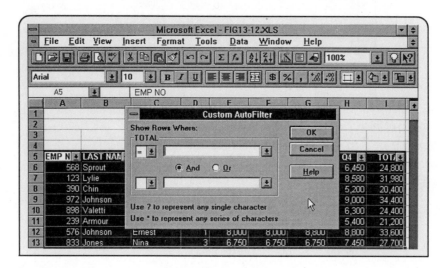

You can enter a criterion to determine what rows in the list to display. Note that the text TOTAL appears, because you selected it.

To indicate that you want to use the ">" operator instead of "=":

Click	the drop-down arrow next to the = operator
Click	the > operator

To specify the value to use in the criteria:

Click	the text box in the first criteria line
Type	25,000

If you want to use one of the values in the TOTAL column, you can click the drop-down arrow on the text box and choose one of the values.

To complete the process:

Click	the OK command button

Only the employees who have a total annual salary greater than $25,000 are displayed. After making cell A1 the active cell, your screen should look like Figure 13-13.

Figure 13-13

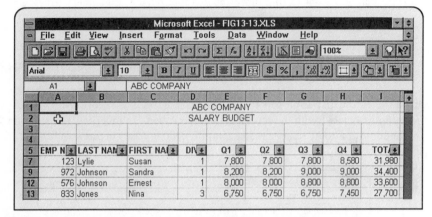

To display all rows in the list and stop using the AutoFilter:

Choose	Data
Choose	Filter
Choose	Show All
Choose	Data
Choose	Filter
Choose	AutoFilter

Close the ABCSAL workbook document. Do not save any changes.

■ FINDING DATA USING THE FORM COMMAND

An alternative method for locating data in a list is to use the Form command on the Data menu.

Suppose you want to examine the records in the ABCSAL workbook file that have a salary greater than $25,000.

To initiate the process:

Open	the ABCSAL workbook file
Select	cells A5:I13

To find the records containing employees who have a salary greater than $25,000:

Choose	Data
Choose	Form
Click	the Criteria command button

Note that a blank record appears.

To indicate that you want to find those records that have a total salary greater than $25,000:

Click   the TOTAL text box

Type   >25,000

Click   the Find Next command button

Excel searches the list from top to bottom until it finds a record with a total salary >$25,000.   The information associated with the record is then displayed. In this case, the second record is the first record encountered with a total salary greater than $25,000. Your screen should look like Figure 13-14.

Figure 13-14

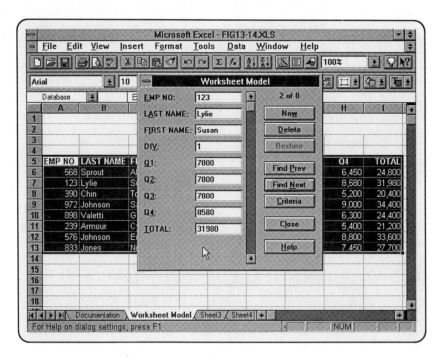

To find the next record matching the criteria:

Click   the Find Next command button

The fourth record is displayed. Continue clicking the Find Next command button until the last record containing a total salary greater than $25,000 appears. In this case, the eighth record is both the last record in the list and the last record containing a total salary greater than $25,000.

To stop the process and remove the dialog box from your screen:

Click   the Close command button

Close the ABCSAL workbook document. Do not save any changes.

■ USING COMPLEX CRITERIA TO FILTER A LIST

Excel allows you to use two type of criteria: comparison criteria and computed criteria. You should use a **comparison criteria** to display rows that fall within a range of values. A comparison criteria could be a series of characters to match or a logical comparison. For the ABCSAL workbook example, you might specify a "3" for Division 3.

You can also use **computed criteria**. For this type of criteria, you can evaluate items in a selected column in a list against values that do not appear in the list. For example, you might want to select the personnel in the ABCSAL workbook file who have a salary greater than the average salary for all employees.

If you only have one or two comparison criteria, you should use the Custom option available when you use AutoFilter. When you have more than two comparisons, you can use comparison criteria in a criteria range.

Filtering a List Containing Multiple Criteria Using AutoFilter

In this exercise, you will use AutoFilter to search the ABCSAL employee list to display the records for individuals who have a total salary less than $25,000 and who are in Division 3.

To initiate the process:

Open	the ABCSAL workbook file
Select	cells A5:I13

To show the rows containing employees with a total salary less than $25,000:

Choose	Data
Choose	Filter
Choose	AutoFilter
Click	the drop-down arrow on the TOTAL column label
Click	the (Custom...) option
Click	the drop-down arrow next to the = operator
Click	the < operator
Click	the text box in the first criteria line
Type	25,000
Click	the OK command button

The rows containing a total salary less than $25,000 appear on your screen.

To show only the rows having a total salary less than $25,000 and in Division 3:

Click	the drop-down arrow on the DIV column label
Click	the 3 option

The appropriate rows appear on your screen. After making cell A1 the active cell, your screen should look like Figure 13-15.

Figure 13-15

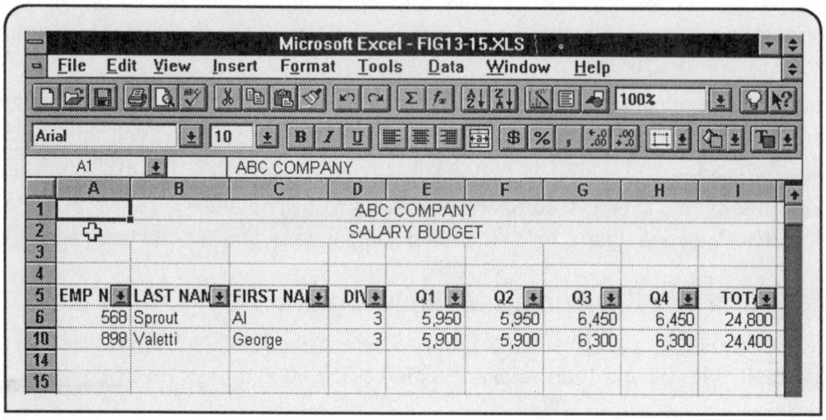

Close the ABCSAL workbook document. Do not save any changes.

In some cases, you may want to specify a criteria with a range. For example, suppose you want to display the rows for individuals who have a salary of less than or equal to $22,000 or greater than $30,000.

To initiate the process:

Open	the ABCSAL workbook file
Select	cells A5:I13

To show the rows for those individuals with total salaries satisfying the criteria:

Choose	Data
Choose	Filter
Choose	AutoFilter
Click	the drop-down arrow on the TOTAL column label
Click	the (Custom...) option
Click	the drop-down arrow next to the = operator
Click	the <= operator
Click	the text box in the first criteria line
Type	22,000
Click	the Or option button
Click	the drop-down arrow in the second operator box
Click	the > operator

| **Click** | the text box in the second criteria line |
| **Type** | 30,000 |

Your screen should look like Figure 13-16.

Figure 13-16

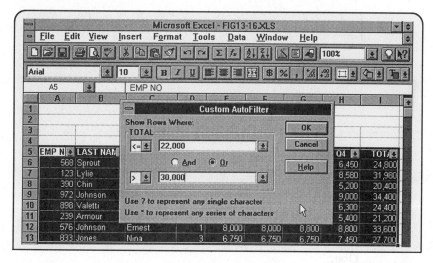

To complete the process:

| **Click** | the OK command button |

The appropriate rows in the list are displayed. After making cell A1 the active cell, your screen should look like Figure 13-17.

Figure 13-17

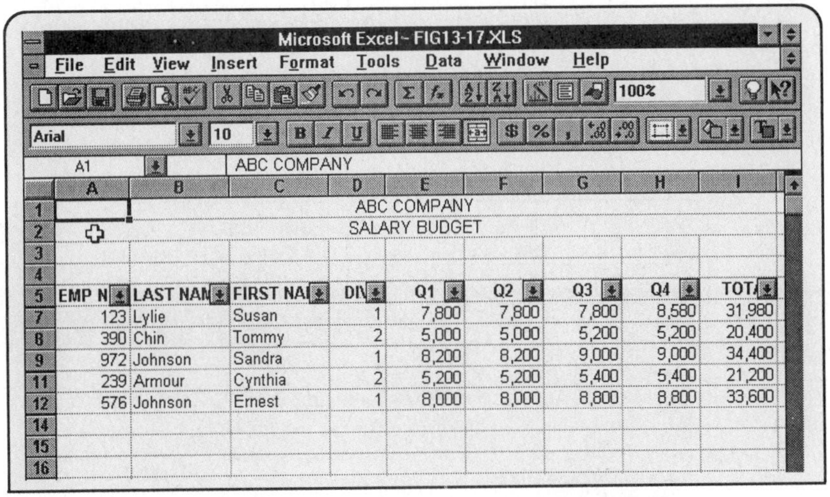

Close the ABCSAL workbook document. Do not save any changes.

Filtering a List Using a Criteria Range

As noted earlier, if you have more than one or two criteria, you can filter a list using a **criteria range**. In such a situation, you can filter a list by selecting Advanced Filter after you choose the Filter command on the Data menu.

You should use some guidelines when you enter comparison criteria on your worksheet:

Place all criteria in the same row to determine the records that satisfy all the criteria in that row: for example, if you want to determine all individuals who have a salary in excess of $25,000 and are in Division 3.

Enter a column more than once if there are multiple criteria associated with one column: for example, if you need to ascertain those individuals who have a salary greater than $20,000 and less than or equal to $30,000.

Input criteria in different rows when you need to determine those rows that meet all criteria in the first row or the second row: for example, if you want to find those rows that contain salary information for those individuals who are in Division 2 or who have a total salary greater than $28,000.

A good location for the criteria range is above the columns in the list.

Suppose you want to find those individuals in the ABCSAL workbook file who have a salary greater than $27,000 or less than or equal to $34,000. In such a situation, you will enter the TOTAL column twice in the criteria range.

To initiate the process:

Open   the ABCSAL workbook file

To place the criteria range on the worksheet:

Insert   three rows at row 4

Enter the criteria range information in rows 4 and 5 in Figure 13-18.

Figure 13-18

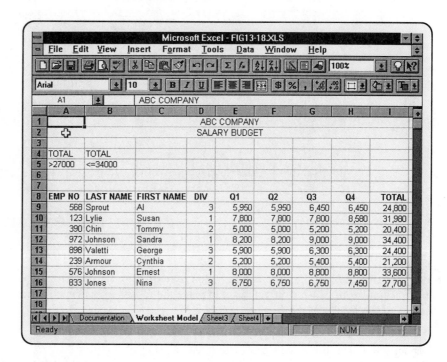

To continue the process:

Select   cells A8:I16

Choose   Data

Choose   Filter

Choose   Advanced Filter

The Advanced Filter dialog box appears. Your screen should look like Figure 13-19.

Figure 13-19

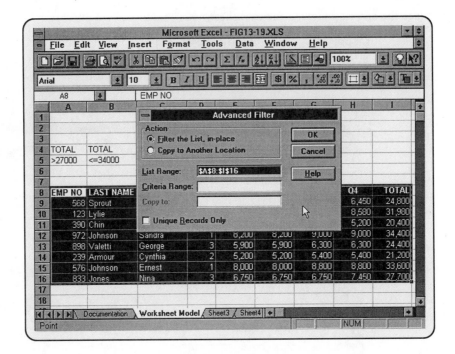

Since the Filter the List, in-place option button is selected in the Action group box, the resulting list will appear beginning in cell A9. If you want to place the results in a different location, you must specify the location of the results in the Copy to text box.

Since you already selected the List Range, it is not necessary to enter it.

To specify the location of the Criteria Range:

| **Click** | the Criteria Range text box |
| **Select** | cells A4:B5 |

Notice that the sheet tab name and the absolute location are included in the Criteria Range.

To complete the process:

| **Click** | the OK command button |

After making cell A1 the active cell, your screen should look like Figure 13-20.

Figure 13-20

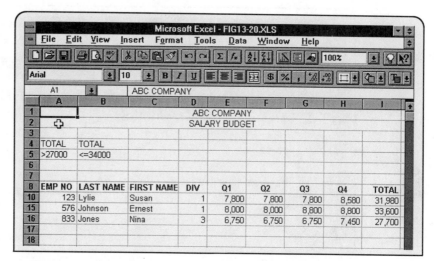

Notice that two individuals are in Division 1 and one is in Division 3.

Suppose you now decide to find only individuals in Division 1 that satisfy the criteria specified for salaries. You can complete the process again or add the additional criteria to the results on your screen.

Enter	DIV in cell C4
Enter	1 in cell C5
Choose	Data
Choose	Filter
Choose	Advanced Filter

Notice that the original List Range and Criteria Range appear in the Advanced Filter dialog box. To modify the Criteria Range:

Select	the text in the Criteria Range text box
Select	cells A4:C5

Notice that the Criteria Range changes to include the additional criteria.

To complete the process:

Click	the OK command button

Only the individuals in Division 1 who also satisfy the salary criteria are shown in the resulting list. After making cell A1 the active cell, your screen should look like Figure 13-21.

Figure 13-21

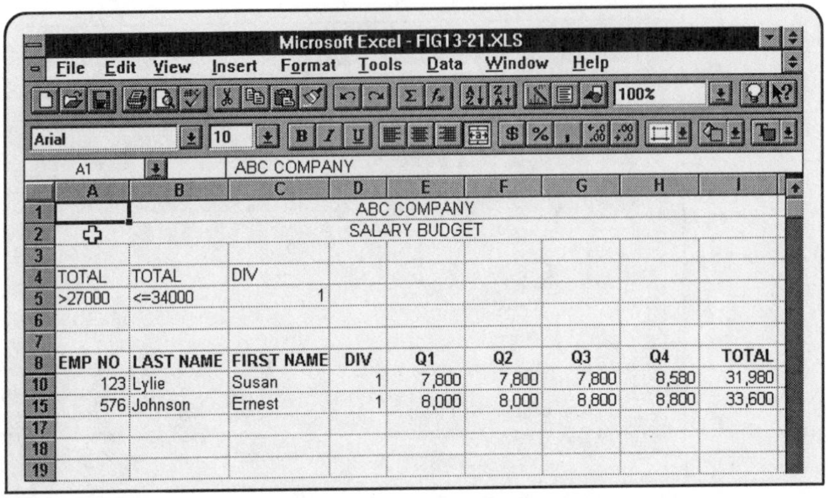

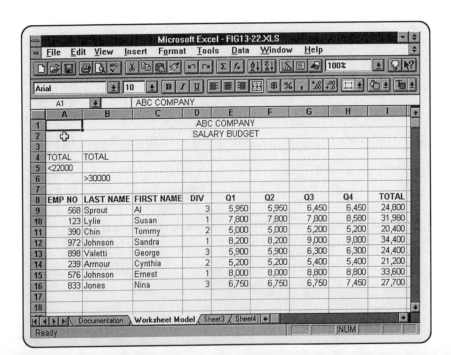

Close the ABCSAL workbook document. Do not save any changes.

Suppose you need to ascertain those individuals in the ABCSAL workbook file who have a total salary less than $22,000 or greater than $30,000. You also want to place the results at a different location on the worksheet.

To initiate the process:

Open   the ABCSAL workbook file

Modify the worksheet to include the appropriate criteria range. Use Figure 13-22 to change your worksheet.

Figure 13-22

To specify the location for the results and the criteria range:

Select	cells A8:I16
Choose	Data
Choose	Filter
Choose	Advanced Filter
Click	the Criteria Range text box
Select	cells A4:B6
Click	the Copy to Another Location in the Action group box
Click	the Copy to text box
Select	cell A20

To complete the process:

Click	the OK command button

After making row 20 the first row appearing on your screen and cell A20 the active cell, your screen should look like Figure 13-23.

Figure 13-23

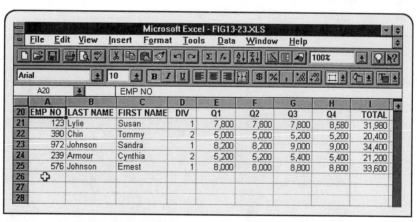

Close the ABCSAL workbook document. Do not save any changes.

Using Wildcard Characters to Filter a List

In some situations, you may need to find all individuals in a list that start with the same first letter or obtain a list based on a single character in the same position. To create such a list, use wildcard characters. Use an asterisk (*) to find any number of characters in the exact same position as the asterisk. You can use a question mark (?) to find any single character in the same position as the question mark. Employ a tilde (~) to find a question mark, asterisk, or a tilde.

Suppose you would like a list of all individuals in the ABCSAL workbook file who have a last name beginning with the letter J.

To initiate the process:

Open	the ABCSAL workbook file
Select	cells A5:I13
Choose	Data
Choose	Filter
Choose	AutoFilter

To specify the criteria:

Click	the drop-down arrow on the LAST NAME column label
Click	the (Custom...) option

To input the criteria for finding all last names that start with a "J":

Type	J∗

To complete the process:

Click	the OK command button

Only the employees having a last name beginning with "J" appear on your screen.

After making cell A1 the active cell, your screen should look like Figure 13-24.

Figure 13-24

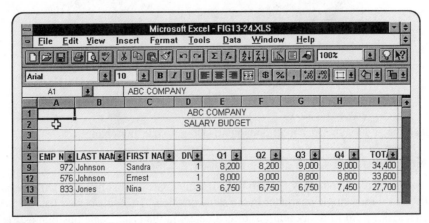

Close the ABCSAL workbook document. Do not save any changes.

■ FILTERING ONLY UNIQUE RECORDS CONTAINED IN A LIST

In some situations, you may have duplicate records or rows in your database. When you look at the filtered list, you may only want to have a resulting list that contains unique records or rows.

For this exercise, you will need to place an additional record in the ABCSAL workbook file.

Open	the ABCSAL workbook file
Click	on cell A9
Insert	a row
Copy	the contents of cells A6:I6 to cells A9:I9

The row of information for Al Sprout now appears twice in your workbook.

To illustrate the process for finding only unique records, assume that you want to prepare a list of employees only in Division 3. Since Al Sprout is in Division 3, you must specify to filter only unique records to avoid having Al Sprout appear in the desired list twice.

To create the list of employees in Division 3:

Insert	3 rows at row 4
Click	on cell A4
Enter	DIV
Click	on cell A5
Enter	3
Select	cells A8:I17
Choose	Data
Choose	Filter
Choose	Advanced Filter

The List Range is now defined. To specify the Criteria Range:

Click	the Criteria Range text box
Select	cells A4:A5

To indicate that only unique records are to be considered:

Click	the Unique Records Only check box to insert an X

To complete the process:

Click	the OK command button

The resulting list includes only one record for Al Sprout. After making cell A1 the active cell, your screen should look like Figure 13-25.

Figure 13-25

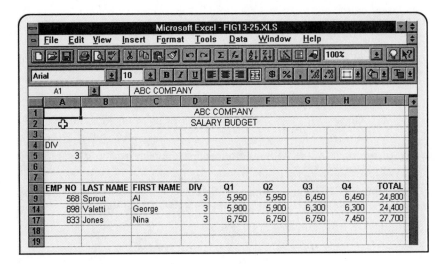

Close the ABCSAL workbook document. Do not save any changes.

SUMMARY

In Excel, you can group data together into a list. A list should always have column labels or row headers. Sometimes, a list is referred to as a database and the rows are called records. You can create or modify a list using the Form command on the Data menu. After you have created a list, you can sort it. You can determine specific entries in a list using criteria and either AutoFilter or Advanced AutoFilter.

KEY CONCEPTS

Ascending order
AutoFilter
Column label
Comparison criteria
Computed criteria
Criteria
Criteria range
Database
Data Filter Advanced Filter
Data Filter AutoFilter
Data Filter Show All

Data Form
Data Sort
Descending order
Field
Field name
Filtering
Key
List
Record
Row header

EXERCISE 1

INSTRUCTIONS: Circle T if the statement is true and F if the statement is false.

T   F   1.   When sorting a list in Excel, the range of rows selected must include the column labels.

T   F   2.   The column names must be located in the row immediately above the first row in a list for AutoFilter to work properly.

T   F   3.   It is appropriate to have more than one row consisting of column labels.

T   F   4.   Each criteria in a complex criteria must have at least two cells in the same column.

T   F   5.   You must specify the criteria range prior to using AutoFilter.

T   F   6.   You must select the list range prior to using AutoFilter.

T   F   7.   When you filter a list, you must copy the resulting list to another location on the worksheet.

T   F   8.   When duplicate records are present in a list, you can filter the list and exclude the duplicate records.

EXERCISE 2 -- Sorting a List Using One Column Label

INSTRUCTIONS: Create the worksheet shown in Figure 13-26. Save the workbook document to a file using the name PERSON.

Column A has a width of 16.

Column B has a width of 15.

Column C has a width of 14.

Column D has a width of 7.

Figure 13-26

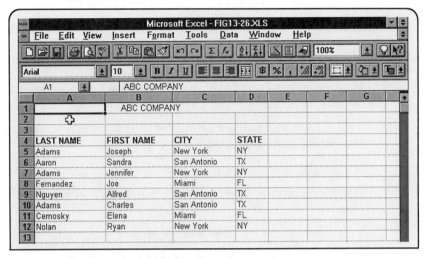

Sort the data in the PERSON worksheet alphabetically by city.

Print the worksheet with the properly sorted data.

Save the workbook document to a file using the name PERSONCT.

Close the PERSONCT workbook document.

EXERCISE 3 -- Sorting Records Using Two Column Labels

INSTRUCTIONS: Open the PERSONCT workbook file.

Sort the last name in the PERSONCT workbook in alphabetical order by city. (In Exercise 4, you will place Joseph Adams and Jennifer Adams in the proper order by first name.)

Print the worksheet with the properly sorted data.

Save the PERSONCT workbook document with the changes.

Close the PERSONCT workbook document.

EXERCISE 4 -- Sorting Records Using Three Column Labels

INSTRUCTIONS: Assuming that you have just completed Exercise 3, notice that Joseph Adams and Jennifer Adams from New York city are not in the proper order. To place these names in correct order:

Open the PERSONCT workbook file.

Sort the data using FIRST NAME as a third sort key.

Print the worksheet with the appropriately sorted data.

Save the PERSONCT workbook document with the changes.

Close the PERSONCT workbook document.

EXERCISE 5 -- Filtering Data in a List Using AutoFilter

INSTRUCTIONS: Open the PERSON workbook file.

Use AutoFilter to create a list of individuals living in Miami, FL.

Print the list of individuals living in Miami, FL.

Close the PERSON workbook document. Do not save any changes.

EXERCISE 6 -- Filtering Data in a List Using AutoFilter

INSTRUCTIONS: Open the PERSON workbook file.

Use AutoFilter to create a list of individuals living in San Antonio, TX.

Print the worksheet.

Sort the individuals in San Antonio in alphabetical order by LAST NAME.

Print the worksheet.

Close the PERSON workbook document. Do not save any changes.

EXERCISE 7 -- Filtering Data in a List Containing Multiple Criteria Using AutoFilter

INSTRUCTIONS: Open the PERSON workbook file.

Use AutoFilter to create a list of individuals living in New York, NY or San Antonio, TX.

Print the resulting list.

Sort the resulting list by LAST NAME alphabetically within each city.

Print the worksheet.

Close the PERSON workbook document. Do not save any changes.

EXERCISE 8 -- Filtering Data in a List Using Advanced AutoFilter and Complex Criteria

---

INSTRUCTIONS: Open the PERSON workbook file.

Create a criteria range to determine only those individuals living in New York who have a last name beginning with the letter "A."

Print the resulting list.

Close the PERSON workbook document. Do not save any changes.

EXERCISE 9 -- Using a Data Entry Form

INSTRUCTIONS: Open the PERSON workbook file.

Insert the following record into the PERSON workbook:

LAST NAME	FIRST NAME	CITY	STATE
Osgood	Maria	San Francisco	CA

Print the new list.

Delete the record for Joseph Adams.

Print the new list.

Close the PERSON workbook document. Do not save any changes.

CHAPTER FOURTEEN

ADVANCED DATABASE CAPABILITIES

OBJECTIVES

In this chapter, you will learn to:
- Fill cells with sequences of data
- Create data tables
- Create subtotals

■ CHAPTER OVERVIEW

In Chapter 13, you learned some of the basic list and database capabilities available in Excel. Here, you will expand your knowledge in these areas. You will learn to fill cells with specific sequences of data, create data tables for use in decision-making situations, and prepare subtotals.

■ FILLING CELLS WITH SEQUENCES OF DATA

In some situations, you may need to enter a sequence of numbers, dates, times, or text in a worksheet. Excel facilitates the input of such data using AutoFill or the Series command on the Edit menu.

Using AutoFill to Enter a Series of Numbers

You can use AutoFill to create series of values. For example, you may need to enter the set of numbers 1 through 10 or the months of the year. Use the fill handle in such situations.

To place the numbers 1 through 10 in cells B6 through B15:

Select	cells B6:B7
Enter	1 in cell B6
Enter	2 in cell B7
Drag	the fill handle to cell B15

The numbers 1 through 10 appear in cells B6 through B15. After making cell A1 the active cell, your screen should look like Figure 14-1.

Figure 14-1

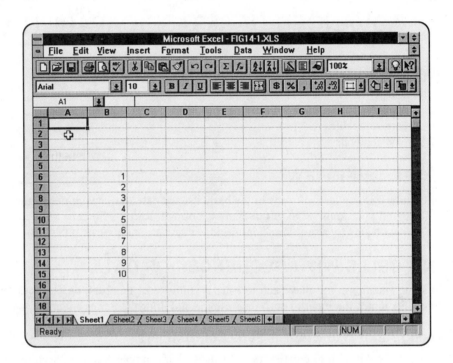

Using the Fill Command to Enter a Series of Numbers

Now suppose you are asked to enter a sequence of even numbers beginning with the number 2 in cells A3 through H3.

To enter the numbers in cells A3 through H3:

Click	on cell A3
Enter	2
Select	cells A3:H3
Choose	Edit

Choose	Fill
Choose	Series

The Series dialog box appears. To complete the process for entering the even numbers:

Double-click	the Step Value text box (if necessary)
Type	2
Click	the Stop Value text box
Type	16
Click	the OK command button

The even numbers appear in cells A3 through H3. After making cell A1 the active cell, your screen should look like Figure 14-2.

Figure 14-2

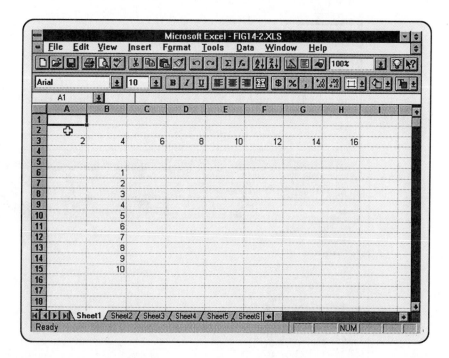

We included the steps for entering the stop value for completeness. Since the range of cells is selected, you could have omitted the steps and clicked the OK command button.

Close the workbook document. Do not save any changes.

In This Chapter

Rather than show the use of AutoFill and the Fill command on the Edit menu, AutoFill is used here for placing various series on a worksheet.

Entering a Sequence of Dates

At times, you may wish to place a series of dates on a worksheet. For example, you may want to place the dates for 10 days in a column, or you may want to enter a series of dates that are a specified amount of time apart such as a week, month, or quarter.

Make sure you have a blank workbook document on your screen.

To illustrate the process for entering a sequence of 10 consecutive dates in cells B3 through B12 on a worksheet:

Select	cells B3:B4
Enter	7/1/95 in cell B3
Enter	7/2/95 in cell B4
Drag	the fill handle to cell B12

The dates appear in cells B3 through B12. After making cell A1 the active cell, your screen should look like Figure 14-3.

Figure 14-3

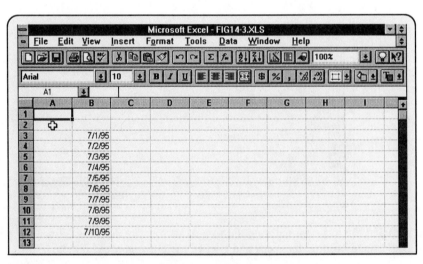

Close the workbook document. Do not save any changes.

Suppose you are asked to create a worksheet in which the column titles are a series of six dates in cells B2 through G2. Each date should be a week apart with the initial date being 2-Aug.

Make sure you have a blank workbook document on your screen.

To place the series of dates on a worksheet:

Select	cells B2:C2
Enter	8/2 in cell B2
Enter	8/9 in cell C2
Drag	the fill handle to cell G2

The dates appear in cells B2 through G2. After making cell A1 the active cell, your screen should look like Figure 14-4.

Figure 14-4

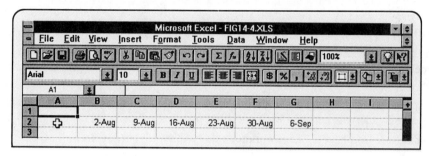

Since you did not enter a year, Excel automatically changes the format of the date so the day and month appear.

Suppose you want to format the date so the month appears before the day.

Select	cells B2:G2
Choose	Format
Choose	Cells
Click	the Number tab (if necessary)
Click	the Date choice in the Category list box

Since the appropriate code does not appear in the Format Codes list box, you will need to create a custom format.

Select	the contents of the Code text box
Type	mmm-d
Click	the OK command button

The dates are now properly formatted. After making cell A1 the active cell, your screen should look like Figure 14-5.

Figure 14-5

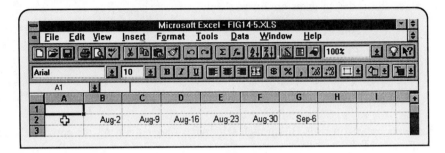

Close the workbook document. Do not save any changes.

Entering Sequences of Times

In the last section, you placed sequences of dates on a worksheet. Sometimes you may want to enter specific sequences of times. For example, it might be necessary to prepare a schedule with times separated by a specific time increment.

Suppose you need to prepare a daily calendar that has the sequence of times from 8:00 AM to 5:00 PM with one-hour intervals between each specified time.

Make sure you have a blank workbook document on your screen.

To place the time sequence in cells A4 through A13 of a worksheet:

Select	cells A4:A5
Enter	8:00 AM in cell A4
Enter	9:00 AM in cell A5
Drag	the fill handle to cell A13

The proper times appear in the cells. After making cell A1 the active cell, your screen should look like Figure 14-6.

Figure 14-6

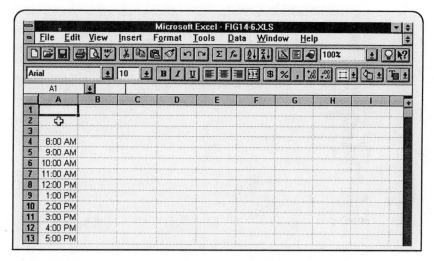

Close the workbook document. Do not save any changes.

■ USING DATA TABLES FOR WHAT-IF ANALYSIS

One of the most important features of Excel is that it allows you to complete a what-if analysis by changing the values of key variables and immediately recalculating the results. You can then see the impact of the changes on your worksheet. Excel permits you to create data tables to complete a what-if analysis effectively and efficiently.

A classic example of the need for completing a what-if analysis occurs when a person tries to evaluate the monthly payment amount for a loan for various interest rates, principal amounts, and time periods. Another example occurs when a sales manager desires to examine the impact on an employee's compensation of proposed changes in quotas and commission rates.

Suppose you are considering the purchase of a new luxury automobile by borrowing the money from a bank. Given a specific purchase value, the variables that can change are interest rate and time period.

Before using the data table feature available in Excel, you need to have a blank workbook document on your screen and then create the worksheet shown in Figure 14-7, Parts 1 and 2 on the Documentation sheet.

Figure 14-7
Part 1

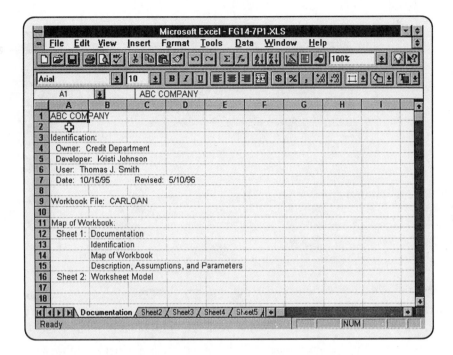

Figure 14-7
Part 2

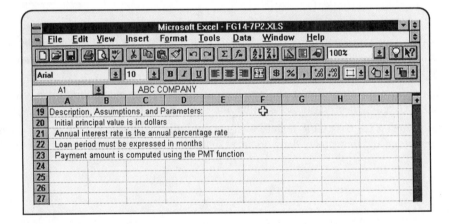

Then enter the information in Figure 14-7, Part 3 on the Worksheet Model sheet. Compute the payment amount by using the payment function, PMT, available in Excel. Cell A7 should have the formula =A5/12 as its contents and the formula computes the monthly interest rate. Notice that since you want a monthly payment value, the annual interest rate must be converted to a monthly rate by dividing by 12.

Figure 14-7
Part 3

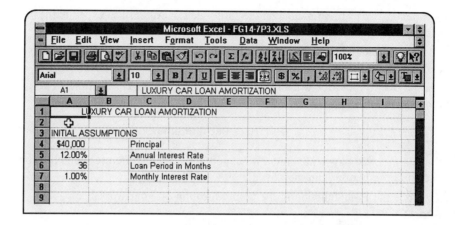

Changing the Values of One Variable

You can use the Table command on the Data menu to change one of the variables used in computing the payment amount. Suppose you want to determine the impact of changing the loan period while holding the principal amount and interest rate constant.

To construct the data table for varying the loan period, enter the information shown in Figure 14-8.

Figure 14-8

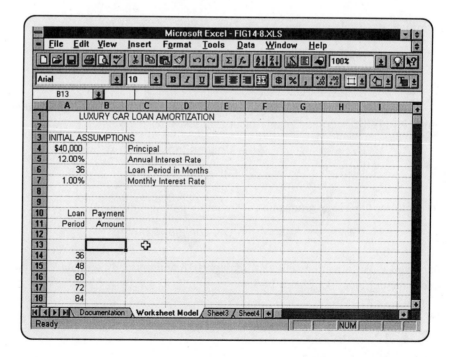

You may use the Fill command on the Edit menu or AutoFill to expedite the process for entering the loan period values that represent three- through seven-year loan periods.

The use of data tables requires the use of input cells. In this case, the input cell is cell A6, which is the loan period variable.

The payment value for a loan is computed using the PMT function. The general format of the PMT function is:

=PMT(interest rate,time period,principal amount)

Since a monthly payment amount is desired, the monthly interest rate is the annual interest divided by 12 and the time period is in months.

To place the PMT function in the proper location on your worksheet:

Click	on cell B13
Enter	=PMT(A7,A6,A4)

Change the width of column B to 10.

Notice that the payment value is in parentheses to indicate a cash outflow for you.

To specify the data table range:

Select	cells A13:B18

To initiate the Table command on the Data menu:

Choose	Data
Choose	Table

The Table dialog box appears. Since the data to use as the input cell is in a column, you need to enter the input cell identifier in the Column Input Cell text box.

Click	the Column Input Cell text box
Click	on cell A6

To complete the Table command:

Click	the OK command button

Once you have formatted cells B14 through B18 appropriately and made cell A13 the active cell, your screen should look like Figure 14-9.

Figure 14-9

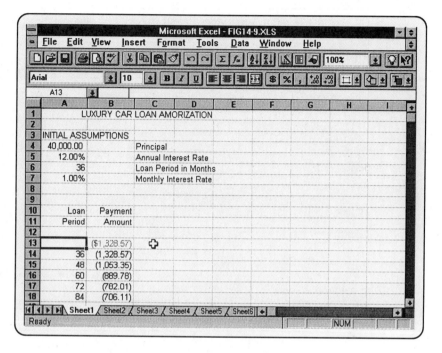

As expected, the payment amount decreases as the loan time period increases.

Using the Table Command with Several Formulas

Excel permits you to substitute the value of the input cell in more than one formula. For example, you may want to set up a data table that allows you to examine simultaneously a change in the principal amount and interest rate for the various loan periods.

Suppose you need to evaluate the following sensitivity cases for the car purchase decision discussed in the last section.

1. What is the payment amount for the various loan period options if the principal is $45,000 instead of $40,000?

2. What is the payment amount for the various loan options if the annual interest rate is 10% instead of 12%?

Before starting this exercise, make sure that your screen looks like Figure 14-9. Prior to issuing the Table command on the Data menu, include the additional information shown in Figure 14-10 on your worksheet. Make sure columns C and D have a width of 10.

Figure 14-10

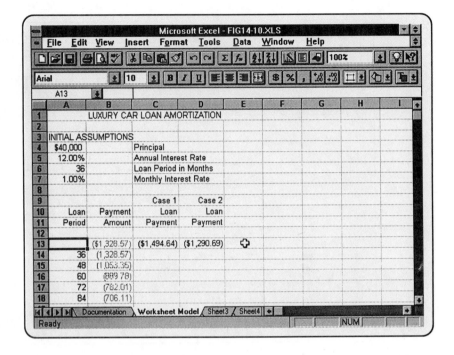

The PMT function entry for cell C13 is =PMT(A7,A6,45000). This function is used for sensitivity case 1. The PMT function in cell D13, =PMT(0.1/12,A6,A4), is for sensitivity case 2.

To initiate the Table command:

Select	cells A13:D18
Choose	Data
Choose	Table

When the Table dialog box appears:

Click	the Column Input Cell text box
Click	on cell A6

To complete the Table command:

Click	the OK command button

The values for the sensitivity cases are computed and displayed on your screen. Once you have formatted cells C14 through D18 appropriately and made cell A13 the active cell, your screen should look like Figure 14-11.

Figure 14-11

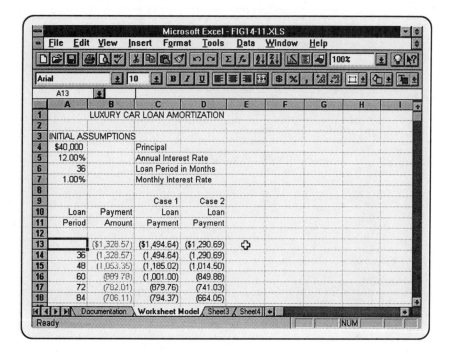

Close the workbook document. Do not save any changes.

Changing the Values of Two Variables

At times, you may want to change two of the variables in a formula. Excel permits you to simultaneously modify two input cells using the Table command on the Data menu.

Suppose for the luxury car loan decision introduced in an earlier section of this chapter, you want to vary the loan period and interest rates in the loan payment calculation. Specifically, you want to determine the loan payment amount for 36, 48, 60, 72, and 84 months using 9%, 10%, 11%, 12%, 13%, and 14% interest rates, respectively.

Before initiating the use of the Table command on the Data menu, create the worksheet shown in Figure 14-12. Columns A through G must have a width of 10.

Figure 14-12

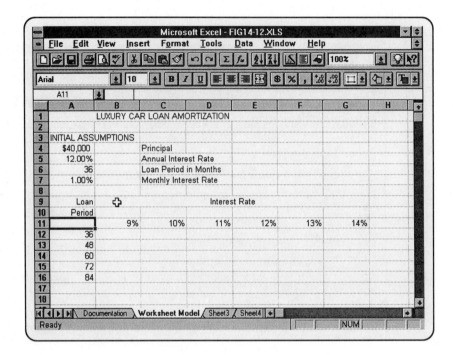

When you create a data table that allows you to modify the values of two input cells, the formula that uses the input cells must be placed in the top-left corner cell of the data table. In this case, you need to place the payment function in cell A11.

Click	on cell A11
Enter	=PMT(A5/12,A6,A4)

To initiate the Table command on the Data menu:

Select	cells A11:G16
Choose	Data
Choose	Table

When the Table dialog box appears:

Click	the Row Input Cell text box (if necessary)
Click	on cell A5
Click	the Column Input Cell text box
Click	on cell A6

The values for loan period and interest rate are substituted into the loan-payment calculation formula. Within a few seconds, the values for the various combinations of loan periods and interest rates will appear on the worksheet. The values in the left column of the data table (column A) are substituted into the row input cell (loan period). The values in the top row of the data table (row 11) are substituted into the column input cell (interest rate).

Once you have formatted cells B12 through G16 appropriately and made cell A11 the active cell, your screen should look like Figure 14-13.

Figure 14-13

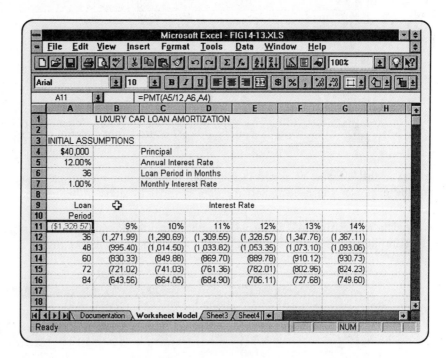

Close the workbook document. Do not save any changes.

■ CREATING SUBTOTALS IN A LIST

Sometimes you may need to calculate subtotals in a list. For example, you may need to compute the subtotals of sales for products.

Excel can insert automatic subtotals to assist you in summarizing data that appear in the list. Grand totals are also computed. Use the Subtotals command on the Data menu to determine subtotals and grand totals.

In the last chapter, you created the ABCSAL workbook. On the Worksheet Model sheet, you prepared a list of the salaries for ABC Company employees. Suppose now you need to compute the subtotals for salaries and a grand total of all salaries.

Open the ABCSAL workbook file. Your screen should look like Figure 14-14.

Figure 14-14

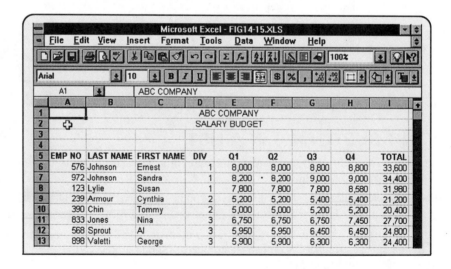

The data in the list must be sorted in the order in which you want to calculate subtotals. In the ABC Company example, you need to sort the data in order by division before you use Excel to determine subtotals.

Sort the data in the ABCSAL workbook in alphabetical order within each division. When you complete the sort and make cell A1 the active cell, your screen should look like Figure 14-15.

Figure 14-15

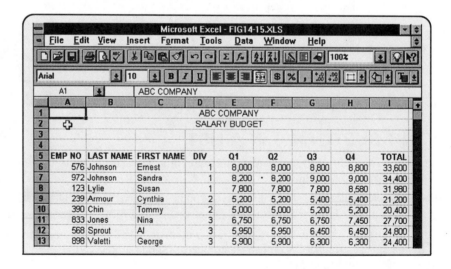

To calculate the subtotals for the salaries by division and the grand total for salaries:

Select	cells A5:I13
Choose	Data
Choose	Subtotals

The Subtotal dialog box appears.

Click	the down arrow on the At Each Change in the list box
Click	the DIV choice
Click	the OK command button

The subtotals and grand total are calculated. After making cell A1 the active cell and scrolling to display column I, your screen should look like Figure 14-16.

Figure 14-16

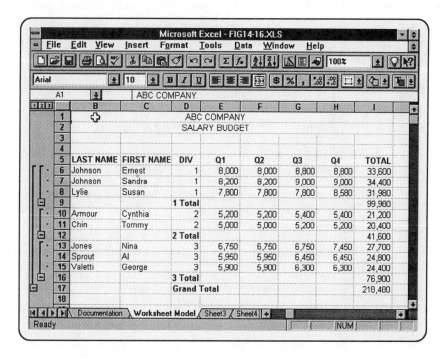

Close the ABCSAL workbook document. Do not save any changes.

SUMMARY

AutoFill provides an easy process to place sequences of values and dates on a worksheet. The Table command on the Data menu lets you create tables that illustrate the impact of changing values for a variable in a decision-making situation. With the Subtotals command on the Data menu, you can automatically calculate subtotals and a grand total for a worksheet.

KEY CONCEPTS

AutoFill	Edit Fill
Column Input Cell	Row Input Cell
Data Subtotals	Step Value
Data Table	Stop Value

EXERCISE 1

INSTRUCTIONS: Circle T if the statement is true and F if the statement is false.

T   F   1.   You cannot place a sequence of numbers or dates on different worksheets in a workbook.

T   F   2.   The Data Subtotals command only calculates subtotals.

T   F   3.   The stop value does not have to be specified if a range of cells is selected prior to using the Fill command on the Edit menu.

T   F   4.   You can specify a maximum of three input cells each time you use the Table command on the Data menu.

T   F   5.   The Table command on the Data menu allows an individual to determine the impact of changes for a variable in a decision-making situation.

EXERCISE 2 -- Filling Cells with Numbers

INSTRUCTIONS: Make sure you have a blank workbook document on your screen.

Using AutoFill, place the sequence of numbers 11, 14, 17, 20, 23, 26, and 29 in cells A2 through G2.

Using the Fill command on the Edit menu, place the sequence of numbers 0.11, 0.12, 0.13, 0.14, 0.15, and 0.16 in cells A6 through A11.

Place the numbers -10, 20, 50, 80 in cells A13 through D13.

Print the completed worksheet.

Close the workbook document. Do not save any changes.

EXERCISE 3 -- Filling Cells with Dates

INSTRUCTIONS: Make sure you have a blank workbook document on your screen.

Place the sequence of dates June 3, June 7, June 11, and June 15 for the year 1996 in cells B2 through E2.

Place the sequence of dates June 1, July 1, August 1, September 1, October 1, November 1, and December 1 for the year 1996 in cells B6 through H6.

Place the sequence of dates January 15, April 15, July 15, and October 15 for the year 1996 in cells B10 through E10

Place the sequence of dates for January 1 of the years 1994, 1996, 1998, 2000, 2002, and 2004 in cells B15 through G15.

Print the worksheet.

Close the workbook document. Do not save any changes.

EXERCISE 4 -- Filling Cells with Times

INSTRUCTIONS: Make sure you have a blank workbook document on your screen.

Place the times 10:00 AM, 10:02 AM, 10:04 AM, 10:06 AM, and 10:08 AM in cells A1 through A5.

Place the times 7:00 AM through 7:00 PM where the interval between each time on the worksheet is 2 hours. Place the time 7:00 AM in cell B7. The remaining times should appear in column B below cell B7.

Print the completed worksheet.

Close the workbook document. Do not save any changes.

EXERCISE 5 -- Changing the Values of One Variable in a Data Table

---

INSTRUCTIONS: Make sure you have a blank workbook document on your screen.

Suppose you are considering the purchase of a house. The current interest rate is 9.5% for a 15-year fixed-rate loan.

Create a data table that contains the monthly payments for a house if the price of the house is $95,000, $100,000, $105,000, $110,000, or $115,000 using an interest rate of 9.5% and assuming a 15-year fixed-rate loan.

Print the data table.

Close the workbook document. Do not save any changes.

EXERCISE 6 -- Changing the Values of Two Variables in a Data Table

---

INSTRUCTIONS: Make sure you have a blank workbook document on your screen.

Suppose you are considering the purchase of some property in the $60,000 to $80,000 price range. Assume that you can obtain a 30-year fixed-rate loan from several financial institutions with an interest rate varying between 8% and 11%.

Create a data table that contains the monthly payment amounts after varying the purchase price from $60,000 to $80,000 in increments of $5,000. You also need to use an initial interest rate of 8% and increase it to a maximum of 11% using one-half percent increments.

Use a 30-year loan period for all calculations.

Print the data table.

Close the workbook document. Do not save any changes.

EXERCISE 7 -- Calculating Subtotals and a Grand Total

INSTRUCTIONS: Make sure you have a blank workbook document on your screen.

Create the worksheet shown in Figure 14-17, Parts 1 through 3.

Figure 14-17
Part 1

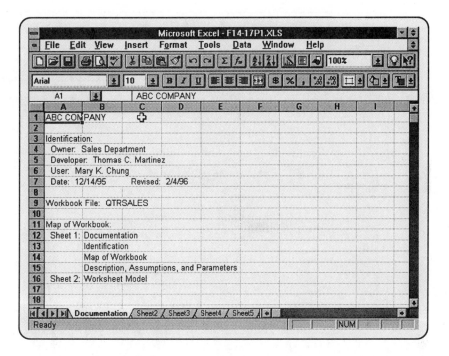

Figure 14-17
Part 2

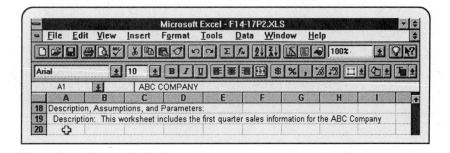

Figure 14-17
Part 3

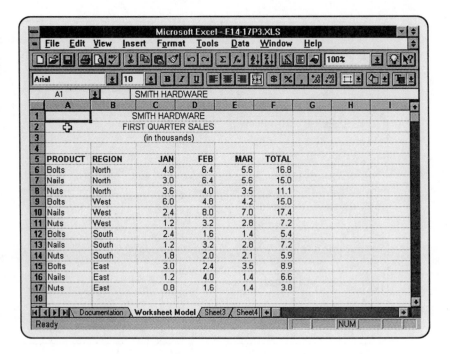

Save the workbook document to a file using the name QTRSALES.

Create subtotals and a grand total for sales by product.

Print the worksheet.

Close the workbook document. Do not save any changes.

Open the QTRSALES workbook file.

Create subtotals and a grand total for sales by region.

Print the worksheet.

Close the workbook document. Do not save any changes.

CHAPTER FIFTEEN

WORKSHEET FUNCTIONS IN MICROSOFT EXCEL

OBJECTIVES

In this chapter, you will learn to use and apply the following types of worksheet functions available in Excel:

- Statistical
- Financial
- Date and Time
- Logical
- Database
- Math and Trig
- Lookup and Reference
- Text

■ CHAPTER OVERVIEW

There are hundreds of functions available for use on worksheets. This chapter covers many, but not all, of the worksheet functions. If you need to use a function not discussed, see the Microsoft Excel User's Guide that comes with the Microsoft Excel software or use the Help feature.

Suppose you want to compute the monthly payment for a 30-year, $100,000 bank loan with an 11% interest rate. Excel has the PMT function that allows you to compute the payment amount. In earlier chapters, you have used some of the other functions such as SUM and ROUND.

In this chapter, you will learn to apply many of the worksheet functions available for the following categories: statistical analysis, financial analysis, date and time, logical, database, math and trig, lookup and reference, and text. Each of the functions has a specific structure that you must use. The general format of a function is:

=function name(argument1,argument2,...,argumentn)

If you do not enter the function on your worksheet using the correct syntax, errors will occur. In some cases, an argument may be optional. If an argument is optional, brackets will appear in the text, but these are not required when the function is used.

In Excel, you can enter a function in several ways. One method is to use the Function command on the Insert menu. The Function Wizard dialog box appears. Once you have chosen the appropriate category in the Function Category list box, select the desired function in the Function Name list box. Then click the Next command button. After you have entered the appropriate argument(s), click the Finish command button.

A second alternative for placing a function on a worksheet is to click the Function Wizard button on the Standard toolbar. After the Function Wizard dialog box appears, use the same process as when you use the Function command on the Insert menu. A third way to put a function on a worksheet is to press the "=" sign. Then click the Function Wizard button that appears in the formula bar. Then complete the process specified earlier. The fourth method is to simply type the function entry along with the argument(s) and press the ENTER key.

In this chapter, you may choose any of the methods. The instructions will ask you to simply enter the function name and the appropriate argument(s).

In This Chapter

This chapter includes examples of many of the worksheet functions available in Excel. Most of the examples require that you start with a blank workbook document. The text assumes that you will close the previous workbook and open a new workbook document.

For additional information on each function described in this chapter, refer to the Excel Help feature or the Microsoft Excel User's Guide.

■ STATISTICAL FUNCTIONS

The statistical functions covered in the chapter are:

COUNT	Counts the number of nonblank cells in a list of cell values.
AVERAGE	Computes the arithmetic mean for a list of cell values.
MIN	Identifies the minimum value for a list of cell values.
MAX	Identifies the maximum value for a list of cell values.
VARP	Computes the population variance for a list of cell values.

STDEVP	Computes the population standard deviation for a list of cell values.
VAR	Computes the sample variance for a list of cell values.
STDEV	Computes the sample standard deviation for a list of cell values.

The format used most often for these statistical functions is:

$$\text{=function name(value1,value 2,...)}$$

where each value can be a cell or range of cells.

For example, to compute the average of the numbers in cells A1 through G1 in a worksheet, use the function =AVERAGE(A1:G1). If you wanted to include cells K1 and M1 through P1, the function entry in your worksheet would appear as =AVERAGE(A1:G1,K1,M1:P1).

Using the Statistical Functions

In this section, you will learn to use each of the listed statistical functions. First, create a worksheet like the one shown in Figure 15-1.

Figure 15-1

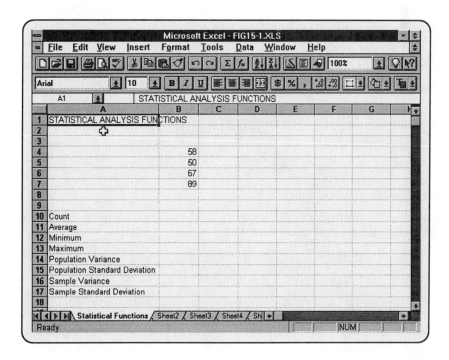

COUNT

To determine how many numbers are in the range of cells B4 through B7 using the COUNT function:

Click   on cell B10

Enter   =COUNT(B4:B7)

The formula =COUNT(B4:B7) appears in the formula bar and the number 4 appears in cell B10.

AVERAGE

To compute the average of the numbers in cells B4 through B7:

Click   on cell B11

Enter   =AVERAGE(B4:B7)

The formula =AVERAGE(B4:B7) appears in the formula bar. The number 66 appears in cell B11.

MIN

To determine the smallest value of the numbers in cells B4 through B7 using the MIN function:

Click   on cell B12

Enter   =MIN(B4:B7)

The formula =MIN(B4:B7) appears in the formula bar. The number 50 appears in cell B12.

MAX

To ascertain the largest value of the numbers in cells B4 through B7:

Click   on cell B13

Enter   =MAX(B4:B7)

The formula =MAX(B4:B7) appears in the formula bar. The number 89 appears in cell B13.

Variance for a Population

Assuming the numbers in cells B4 through B7 represent a population of values, you can calculate the variance of the numbers using the VARP function:

Click   on cell B14

Enter   =VARP(B4:B7)

The formula =VARP(B4:B7) appears in the formula bar. The number 212.5 appears in cell B14. It is assumed that you have all the values that need to be considered and the data is not a sample of values from a larger set of data.

Standard Deviation for a Population

Assuming the numbers in cells B4 through B7 represent a population, you can determine the standard deviation of the numbers using the STDEVP function:

Click	on cell B15
Enter	=STDEVP(B4:B7)

The formula =STDEVP(B4:B7) appears in the formula bar. The number 14.57738 appears in cell B15. The standard deviation is equal to the square root of the variance.

It is assumed that you have all of the values that need to be considered and the data is not a sample of values from a larger set of data.

Variance of a Sample

When you computed the population variance, you assumed that you had all of the data that you were considering. If instead, the data is only a sample of all the data that you want to examine, then the formula for calculating the variance is:

$$\sum_{i=1}^{n} (x_i - \overline{x})^2 / (n-1) \quad \text{rather than} \quad \sum_{i=1}^{n} (x_i - \mu)^2 / n$$

Assuming that the data in cells B4 through B7 is a sample, to calculate the sample variance:

Click	on cell B16
Enter	=VAR(B4:B7)

The formula =VAR(B4:B7) appears in the formula bar and the number 283.3333 is in cell B16.

Standard Deviation of a Sample

When you computed the population standard deviation, you assumed that you had all of the data that you were considering. If instead, the data is only a sample of all the data that you want to consider, then the formula for calculating the standard deviation is:

$$\sqrt{\frac{\sum_{i=1}^{n} (x_i - \overline{x})^2}{n-1}} \quad \text{rather than} \quad \sqrt{\frac{\sum_{i=1}^{n} (x_i - \mu)^2}{n}}$$

Assuming that the data in cells B4 through B7 is a sample, then you can compute the sample standard deviation as follows:

Click   on cell B17

Enter   =STDEV(B4:B7)

The formula =STDEV(B4:B7) appears in the formula bar and the value 16.83251 is in cell B17. Your screen should look like Figure 15-2.

Figure 15-2

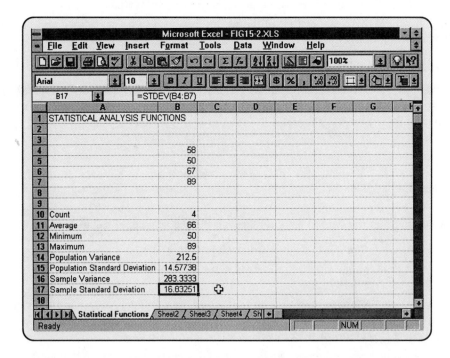

When you are using the statistical functions, note that only the cells containing numbers are used. In the following exercise, you will erase one of the numbers in the range B4 through B7 by pressing the DELETE key.

Click   on cell B6

Press   Delete

Notice that the values for most of the cells have changed. To return to the original situation:

Click   on cell B6

Enter   67

See the Excel Help feature for information on additional statistical functions available in Excel.

■ FINANCIAL FUNCTIONS

The financial functions covered in this chapter are:

CAPITAL BUDGETING

IRR   Internal rate of return.

NPV   Net present value.

ANNUITIES

FV   Future value.

PV   Present value.

NPER   Number of time periods needed in the term of an ordinary annuity to accumulate a future value earning a specific periodic interest rate.

PMT   Payment amount.

DEPRECIATION

SLN   Straight-line depreciation.

DB   Declining-balance depreciation.

DDB   Double-declining balance depreciation.

SYD   Sum-of-the-years' digits depreciation.

VDB   Variable declining balance.

Capital Budgeting

Two financial functions that can be used in capital budgeting and project evaluation are IRR and NPV.

IRR

The IRR function computes the internal rate of return for a series of cash flows that occur at regular periodic intervals. You must supply the cash flows and a guess rate for the internal rate of return. The format of the IRR function is as follows:

IRR(range of cash flows,guess rate)

You need two sets of information in the formula, the cash flows and the guess rate. Sets of information needed for a function to compute accurately are referred to as arguments. You must enter the arguments in the correct order and separate them by a comma. Notice that no space should be entered after the comma that separates the two arguments in the IRR function.

In this exercise, suppose that an investment is being considered that requires a cash investment of $2,100 the first year and the anticipated cash flows in years 2 through 5 are, respectively, $1,300, $700, $500, and $300.

Make sure a blank workbook document appears on your screen. Create a worksheet like the one appearing in Figure 15-3.

Figure 15-3

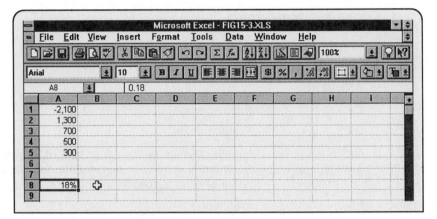

The initial investment, actually a cash outflow, is in cell A1. The negative number indicates the initial cash investment the investor made. The range of anticipated cash flows from the investment appear in cells A2 through A5. The guess at the internal rate of return of 18% appears in cell A8.

To find the internal rate of return for the investment on which you entered data:

Click	on cell B11
Enter	=IRR(A1:A5,A8)

The first argument in the IRR function identifies the cells containing the cash flows for the investment. The second argument identifies the cell containing the guess rate for the internal rate of return.

The function appears in the formula bar. The result, 17%, is displayed in cell A11. Your screen should look like Figure 15-4.

Figure 15-4

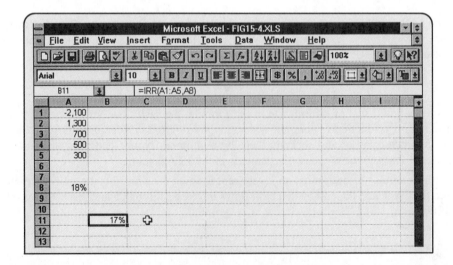

If you change the format for cell A11 so it contains two decimal places, the internal rate of return equals 16.83%.

Notice that you could have entered the guess rate directly into the function as IRR(A1:A5,.18). The advantage of entering the guess rate outside of the function is that you can change it more readily. The cash flows must be entered as a range that is located elsewhere on the worksheet. A single-cell item, however, either can be entered directly into the function or referenced with a cell address (e.g., .18 or A8 is acceptable in the IRR function you just used).

#NUM! may appear as a result of using the IRR function if convergence to within 0.00001 does not occur within 20 iterations. Change the guess rate to a higher or lower value until a value appears for the internal rate of return.

NPV

The net present value computes the present value for a set of cash flows using a specified discount rate. All cash flows are assumed to occur at the end of each year. The format of the NPV function is:

NPV(rate,range of cells)

In this exercise, consider an investment project that requires you to invest $2,000 initially and you receive payments of $900, $850, $600, $350, $200, and $50 at the end of the first through sixth years. Assume that 10% is an appropriate discount rate.

To solve this problem, create the worksheet shown in Figure 15-5.

Figure 15-5

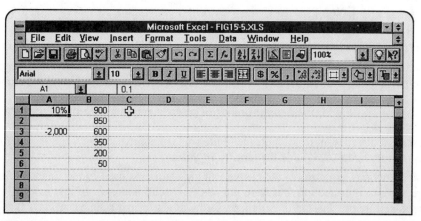

The discount rate is 10% and appears in cell A1. The initial investment of $2,000 is in cell A3. The cash flow payments are in cells B1 through B6.

To calculate the net present value of the cash flows and add it to the initial investment of $2,000 (in cell A3):

Click	on cell C1
Enter	=NPV(A1,B1:B6)+A3

The first argument identifies cell A1 as the discount rate. The second argument identifies cells B1 through B6 as the cash flows beginning with the first year of $900 and ending with the last year at $50. Notice that A3 (the initial investment) must be added to the net present value of the cash flows because, if it is included in the function, it will be discounted.

The function appears in the formula bar. The net present value, $362.91, is displayed in cell C1. Your screen should look like Figure 15-6.

Figure 15-6

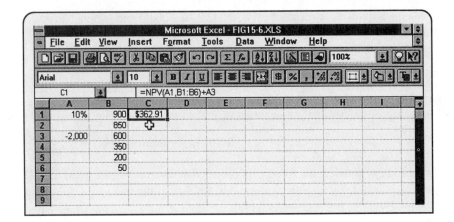

Annuities

The four functions illustrated in this chapter for annuities are FV, PV, NPER, and PMT.

FV

The future value function computes the future value of an investment given the payment per period, interest rate per period, and the number of periods. The general format of the FV function is as follows:

FV(interest rate,number of periods,payment amount,[present value],[type])

Assume that you want to compute the future value of an investment when the payment per period is $1,500, the interest rate is 13%, and the term is 10 years.

In the previous exercises in the chapter, single-cell items used in the financial functions were not placed directly into the function, but were referenced by cell address. In this example, all three arguments are single-cell items. Instead of entering a formula in a format such as =FV(C1,C2,C3), you can place all of the arguments directly into the formula =FV(13%,10,-1500).

To find the future value for the given data:

Click	on cell A1
Enter	=FV(13%,10,-1500)

The first argument specifies the interest rate. The second argument indicates the number of time periods. The third argument specifies the payment amount. The negative sign indicates the payment amount is a cash outflow for the individual.

The function appears in the formula bar. After you have changed the column width to 10, the result, $27,629.62, appears in cell A1. Your screen should look like Figure 15-7.

Figure 15-7

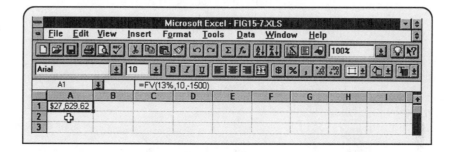

PV

The present value function computes the present value of an investment given a payment per period, interest rate per period, and the number of time periods. The general format of the PV function is:

PV(interest rate,number of periods,payment amount,[future value],[type])

In this exercise, you will determine the present value of an investment where payments are $1,500 per year, the interest rate is 13 percent, and the term is 10 years.

To determine the present value for the given data:

Click	on cell A1
Type	=PV(13%,10,-1500)

The first argument identifies the interest rate of 13%. The second argument identifies the term as 10 years. The third argument identifies the payment amount as $1,500.

The function appears in the formula bar. After you have changed the column width to 10, the result, $8,139.37, appears in cell A1. Your screen should look like Figure 15-8.

Figure 15-8

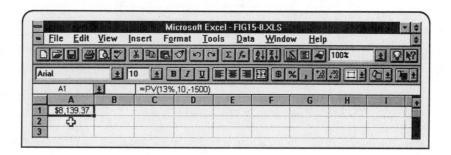

NPER

The NPER function calculates the number of payment periods in a term for an investment necessary to accumulate a future value earning a periodic interest rate. Each payment is equal to the given payment amount in the function. The general format for the NPER function is:

> NPER(interest rate,payment amount per period,present value of the investment,
> [future value of the investment],[type])

In this exercise, assume that $4,500 has been deposited each year on the same date into an account that pays 6%, compounded annually. You can use the NPER function to determine how long it will take for you to have $20,000 in the account.

Using the given data:

Click	on cell A1
Enter	=NPER(6%,-4500,0,20000)

The first argument identifies 6% as the periodic interest rate. The second argument specifies the payment amount of $4,500. The third argument indicates the present value is zero. The fourth argument specifies the desired future value of $20,000.

The function appears in the formula bar. The answer appears in cell A1. The answer of 4.05686 indicates that it will take a little over four years to accumulate the desired future value. Your screen should look like Figure 15-9.

Figure 15-9

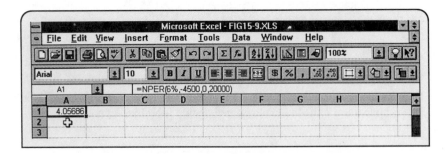

PMT

You can compute the payment per period if you have the interest rate, number of periods, and present value (principal amount). The general format of the PMT function is:

> PMT(interest rate,number of periods,present value (principal amount),
> [future value (usually 0)],[type])

Suppose the principal amount for a loan is $1,200, the interest rate is 15%, and the number of time periods is 10 years.

To determine the payment per year for the given data:

Click	on cell A1
Enter	=PMT(15%,10,-1200)

The function appears in the formula bar. The result, $239.10, appears in cell A1. Your screen should look like Figure 15-10.

Figure 15-10

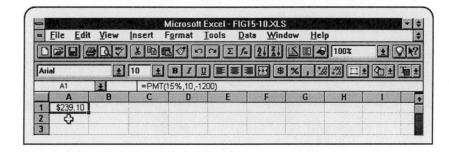

Depreciation

The five depreciation functions discussed in this section are SLN, DB, DDB, SYD, and VDB.

SLN

You can compute the straight-line depreciation of an asset for one period given the cost, salvage value, and estimated useful life of the asset. The general format for the SLN function is as follows:

SLN(cost,salvage value,estimated useful life)

In this exercise, you will determine the straight-line depreciation for equipment that is purchased for $13,000. The estimated useful life of the equipment is 6 years, and the salvage value is estimated at $1,000.

To complete the next four exercises, create the worksheet shown in Figure 15-11.

Figure 15-11

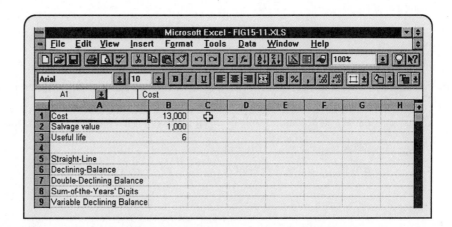

To determine the straight-line depreciation for the equipment data:

| **Click** | on cell B5 |
| **Enter** | =SLN(B1,B2,B3) |

The first argument identifies B1 as the cell containing the cost of $13,000. The second argument identifies B2 as the cell containing the salvage value of $1,000. The third argument identifies B3 as the cell containing the useful life of 6 years. You could have entered the formula =SLN(13000,1000,6) as an alternative to using cell addresses for the various arguments.

Widen column A to 10.

The function appears in the formula bar. The result, $2,000.00, is displayed on the worksheet. Your screen should look like Figure 15-12.

Figure 15-12

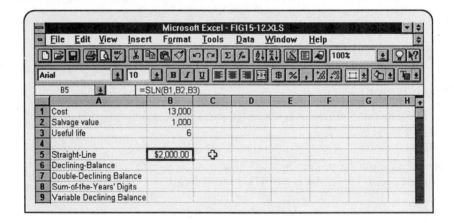

DB

This exercise assumes that you have just finished the previous exercise and the results are still displayed on your screen.

The depreciation of an asset using the declining-balance method can be computed for a specified period given the cost, salvage value, estimated useful life, and the desired time period. The general format for the DB function is:

DB(cost,salvage,estimated useful life,period,[month])

Month is the number of months in the first year. If the argument is omitted, it is assumed to be 12.

In this exercise, you will use the data given in the previous exercise to compute the depreciation for the equipment for the first year using the declining-balance method.

To document that the depreciation will be computed only for Year 1 in this example (an optional step):

| **Click** | on cell C6 |
| **Enter** | Year 1 |

To compute the depreciation using the declining-balance method:

Click	on cell B6
Enter	=DB(B1,B2,B3,1)

The first argument identifies B1 as the cell containing the cost at $13,000. The second argument identifies B2 as the cell containing the salvage value at $1,000. The third argument identifies B3 as the cell containing the useful life of the equipment as 6 years. The fourth argument indicates that this computation represents the depreciation for Year 1.

The function appears in the formula bar. The result, $4,524.00, appears in cell B6.

Your screen should look like Figure 15-13.

Figure 15-13

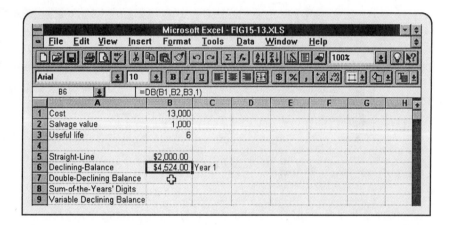

DDB

This exercise assumes you have just finished the previous exercise and the results are still displayed on your screen.

The depreciation of an asset using the double-declining balance method can be computed for a specified period given the cost, salvage value, estimated useful life, and the desired time period. The general format for the DDB function is as follows:

DDB(cost,salvage value,estimated useful life,period,[factor])

Factor is the rate at which the balance declines. If factor is omitted, it is assumed to be 2, which represents double-declining balance.

In this exercise, you will use the data given in the previous exercise to compute the depreciation for the equipment for the first year using the double-declining balance method.

To document that the depreciation will be computed only for Year 1 in this example (an optional step):

Click	on cell C7
Enter	Year 1

To compute the depreciation using the double-declining balance method:

Click	on cell B7
Enter	=DDB(B1,B2,B3,1)

The first argument identifies B1 as the cell containing the cost at $13,000. The second argument identifies B2 as the cell containing the salvage value of $1,000. The third argument identifies B3 as the cell containing the useful life of the equipment of 6 years. The fourth argument indicates that this computation represents the depreciation for Year 1.

The function appears in the formula bar. The result, $4,333.33, is displayed. Your screen should look like Figure 15-14.

Figure 15-14

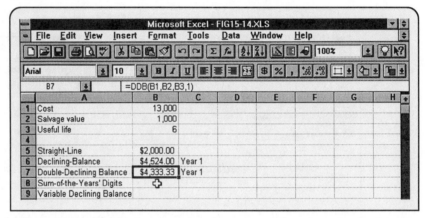

To compute the depreciation for the other time periods, you would have to enter the function again for each of the desired time periods.

SYD

This exercise assumes you have just finished the previous exercise and the results are still displayed on the screen.

The depreciation of an asset using the sum-of-the-years' digits method can be computed for a specified period given the cost, salvage value, estimated useful life, and the desired time period. The general format for the SYD function is as follows:

SYD(cost,salvage value,estimated useful life,period)

In this exercise, you will use the data given in the previous exercise to calculate the depreciation for the equipment for the third year using the sum-of-the-years' digits method.

To indicate that the depreciation will be computed only for Year 3 in this example:

Click	on cell C8
Enter	Year 3

To compute the depreciation using the sum-of-the-years' digits method:

Click	on cell B8
Enter	=SYD(B1,B2,B3,3)

The first argument identifies B1 as the cell containing the cost at $13,000. The second argument identifies B2 as the cell containing the salvage value of $1,000. The third argument identifies B3 as the cell containing the useful life of 6 years. The fourth argument indicates that this computation is for Year 3.

The function appears in the formula bar. The result, $2,285.71, is displayed in cell B8 on the worksheet. Your screen should look like Figure 15-15.

Figure 15-15

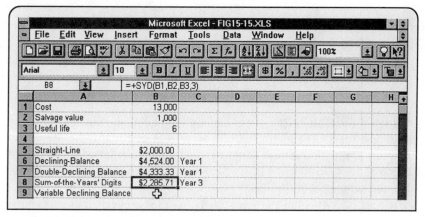

To compute the depreciation values for the other time periods, you would have to enter the function again for each of the desired time periods.

VDB

This exercise assumes that you have just completed the exercise in the previous section and the results are still displayed on your screen. The general format for the VDB (variable declining balance) function is:

VDB(cost,salvage,life,start_period,end_period,depreciation_factor,[no_switch])

This function calculates the depreciation allowance of an asset for a length of time specified by the start-period and the end-period using the double-declining balance method. You can use the optional depreciation-factor to allow the percentage of straight-line depreciation to vary so you calculate depreciation values other than those determined using the double-declining balance method. The optional no switch allows you to change the depreciation values in periods when the straight-line depreciation value is greater than that determined using the double-declining balance calculation.

The depreciation-factor can be any value greater than zero. If you do not specify a value for depreciation-factor, the VDB function will compute depreciation using the double-declining balance method.

You should only include a value for the switch option if you do not want @VDB to automatically switch from declining-balance to straight-line when the straight-line depreciation is greater than declining-balance. The values that can be used for the switch are TRUE and FALSE. If the value for the switch is FALSE or if it is omitted, which is the default value, VDB automatically changes from declining-balance to straight-line when straight-line values are greater. If the value assigned to the switch is TRUE, then VDB never switches from the declining-balance method.

In this exercise, you will use the data given in the previous exercise to compute the depreciation for Year 1 using 150 percent instead of 200 percent for the depreciation-factor. You will also assume that you want to automatically switch to straight-line depreciation when the values for straight-line depreciation are greater than the values for 150 percent declining-balance.

To document that the depreciation value will be computed only for Year 1 (an optional step):

Click	on cell C9
Enter	Year 1

Assuming you purchased the equipment on the first day of the year, to calculate the depreciation for the first year, use the variable-rate depreciation function as follows:

Click	on cell B9
Enter	=VDB(B1,B2,B3,0,1,1.5,FALSE)

The first three arguments indicate that the cost is $13,000, the salvage value is $1,000 and the estimated useful life is 6 years. The fourth and fifth arguments specify that the depreciation is to be computed for the first year. The sixth argument designates the depreciation-factor as 150 percent. The seventh argument indicates that the VDB function is to automatically switch to straight-line depreciation when it is greater than the declining-balance depreciation.

Notice that the FALSE value did not actually need to be included because no switch is optional and the default value is FALSE.

The function appears in the formula bar. The result, $3,250.00, is displayed in cell B9. Your screen should look like Figure 15-16.

Figure 15-16

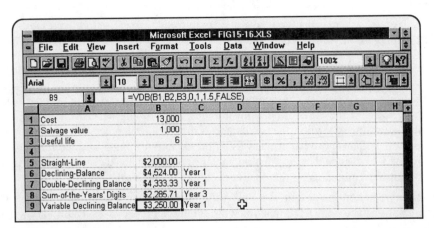

To compute the depreciation values for the other time periods, you would have to enter the function again for each of the desired time periods.

■ DATE AND TIME FUNCTIONS

This section covers 13 date and time functions in Excel. They can be grouped as follows:

DATE

DATE	Determines the serial number for a specific date.
DATEVALUE	Changes a string of characters that looks like a date to a serial number.
MONTH	Determines the month from a serial number.
DAY	Calculates the day of the month from a serial number.
YEAR	Computes the year from a serial number.
DAYS360	Calculates the number of days between two dates assuming there are 360 days in a year.

TIME

TIME	Computes a serial number for a particular time.
TIMEVALUE	Changes a string of characters that looks like a time to a serial number.
HOUR	Calculates the hour from a serial number.
MINUTE	Computes the minute from a serial number.
SECOND	Determines the second from a serial number.

CURRENT DATE AND TIME

TODAY	Computes the serial number for the current date.
NOW	Determines a serial number that corresponds to the current date and time.

Date

The six date functions available in Excel covered in this section are DATE, DATEVALUE, MONTH, DAY, YEAR, and DAYS360.

DATE

The format of the DATE function is:

$$DATE(year,month,day)$$

where year is any two-digits between 00 and 99, month is any integer between 1 and 12, and day is any integer between 1 and 31.

To enter the date June 24, 1995 with the DATE function in cell A1:

Click	on cell A1
Enter	=DATE(95,6,24)

Note that the date "6/24/95" appears in cell A1 rather than a serial number. To display the serial number in cell A1:

Choose	Format
Choose	Cells
Click	the Number tab (if necessary)
Click	the All option in the Category list box
Click	the General option in the Format Codes list box
Click	the OK command button

The serial number 34874 appears in cell A1. Your screen should look like Figure 15-17.

Figure 15-17

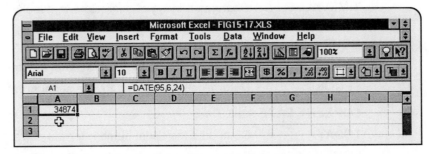

The number indicates that 34,874 days have passed since December 31, 1899. If the year number is 101, 102, and so forth, a date for the year 2000, 2001, and so forth will be displayed.

To format the date appropriately:

Choose	Format
Choose	Cells
Click	the Number tab (if necessary)
Click	the Date option in the Category list box
Click	the m/d/yy option in the Format Codes list box

Notice that five options appear in the Format Codes list box. The first four options are for displaying the date only. The fifth option displays the date and time.

Click	the OK command button

The date appears again.

Your screen should look like Figure 15-18.

Figure 15-18

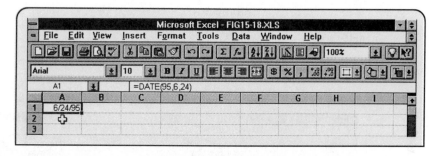

Depending on which option in the Format Codes list box is chosen, the date in cell A1 can be displayed in one of the following ways:

Format	Choice in the Format Codes list box
6/24/95	m/d/yy
24-Jun-95	d-mmm-yy
24-Jun	d-mmm
Jun-95	mmm-yy

DATEVALUE

The DATEVALUE function returns a serial number just as the DATE function does. However, you can enter a single string of characters for the argument in the parentheses. The date string used in the DATEVALUE function must be one of the acceptable Excel date formats. The format of the DATEVALUE function is:

DATEVALUE(string of characters)

Suppose you want to use the DATEVALUE function to place the serial number for June 24, 1995 on your worksheet.

Click	on cell A1
Enter	=DATEVALUE("24-Jun-95")

The serial number for June 24, 1995, 34874, appears in cell A1.

Suppose you then decide to determine the number of days between December 31, 1995 and June 24, 1995. To calculate the number of days between the two dates:

Click	on cell A2
Enter	=DATEVALUE("31-Dec-95")-DATEVALUE("24-Jun-95")

The number 190 appears in cell A2.

An alternative way to determine the number of days between June 24, 1995 and December 31, 1995 follows:

Click	on cell A3
Enter	=DATEVALUE("31-Dec-95")-A1

Your screen should look like Figure 15-19.

Figure 15-19

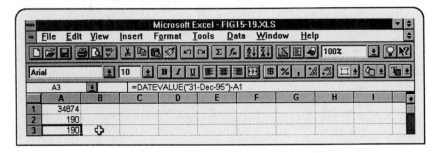

Notice that the values in cells A2 and A3 are the same because you used two different approaches for entering the formulas.

MONTH

At times, you may be given a serial number for which you need to determine the month, day, or year corresponding to the serial number. For example, suppose you need to determine the month, day, and year represented by the date serial number 34874.

The MONTH function determines the month in which a particular serial number appears. The value computed using the MONTH function will be an integer between 1 and 12 for the months January through December, respectively. The format of the MONTH function is:

MONTH(serial number)

To determine the month in which the serial number 34874 occurs:

Click	on cell A1
Enter	Month
Click	on cell B1
Enter	=MONTH(34874)

The number 6 appearing in cell B1 indicates the serial number occurs in the month of June.

DAY

The DAY function determines on what day of the month a date occurs for a serial number. An integer between 1 and 31 is entered into the cell in which the DAY function is used. The format of the DAY function is:

DAY(serial number)

For example, suppose you want to know the day of the month on which the date number 34874 occurs. To calculate the day of the month while leaving the results of the previous example in your worksheet:

Click	on cell A2
Enter	Day
Click	on cell B2
Enter	=DAY(34874)

The number 24 appears in cell B2, indicating that the day of the month is the 24th.

YEAR

The YEAR function determines the year in which a serial number occurs. The format for the YEAR function is:

YEAR(serial number)

For example, suppose you want to know the year in which the date number 34874 occurs. To determine the year while leaving the results of the previous example in your worksheet:

Click	on cell A3
Enter	Year
Click	on cell B3
Enter	=YEAR(34874)

The number 1995 appears in cell B3. Your screen should look like Figure 15-20.

Figure 15-20

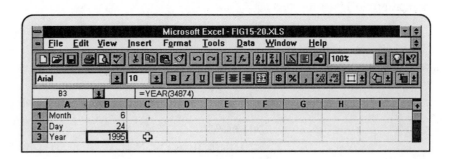

Combining the information in Figure 15-20, the serial number represents June 24, 1995. This result is consistent with the serial number you determined using the DATE function for June 24, 1995.

DAYS360

The DAYS360 function computes the number of days between two dates. This function uses a 360-day year and assumes there are 30 days in each month. The format of the DAYS360 function is:

DAYS360(start_date,end_date)

Suppose you need to know the number of days between January 1, 1995 and July 1, 1995. To calculate the number of days:

Click	on cell A1
Enter	=DAYS360(DATE(95,1,1),DATE(95,7,1))

Your screen should look like Figure 15-21.

Figure 15-21

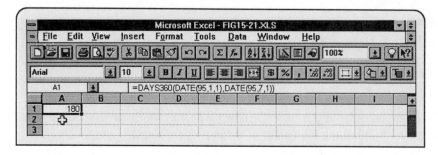

Notice that the time period represents six months and the calculated number of days is 180, indicating that the function assumes there are 30 days per month.

Time

The five time functions available in Excel include TIME, TIMEVALUE, HOUR, MINUTE, and SECOND.

TIME

The format of the TIME function is:

TIME(hour,minute,second)

where hour is any integer between 1 and 24, minute is any integer between 0 and 60, and second is any integer between 0 and 60.

Suppose you want to know the serial number for the time 7:10:59 PM. To obtain the serial number:

Click	on cell A1
Enter	=TIME(19,10,59)

Notice that the time 7:10 PM appears in cell A1 rather than a serial number. To display the seconds also:

Choose	Format
Choose	Cells
Click	the Number tab (if necessary)
Click	the h:mm:ss AM/PM option in the Format Codes list box
Click	the OK command button

Widen column A to 10 so the time is displayed. Your screen should look like Figure 15-22.

Figure 15-22

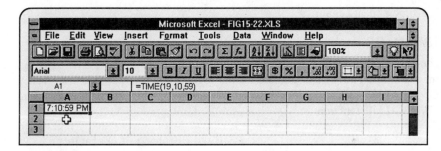

To display the serial number in cell A1:

Choose	Format
Choose	Cells
Click	the Number tab (if necessary)
Click	the All option in the Category list box
Click	the General option in the Format Codes list box
Click	the OK command button

The serial number .79929398 appears in cell A1. Your screen should look like Figure 15-23.

Figure 15-23

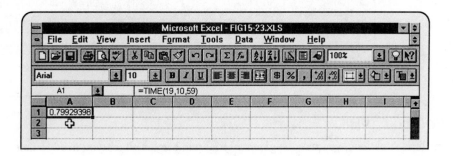

The serial number indicates that the time 7:10:59 PM is about 80% through the day.

To format the time appropriately:

Choose	Format
Choose	Cells
Click	the Number tab (if necessary)
Click	the Time option in the Category list box
Click	the h:mm:ss AM/PM option in the Format Codes list box
Click	the OK command button

The time appears again.

TIMEVALUE

The TIMEVALUE function returns a serial number just as the TIME function does. However, you can enter a single string of characters for the argument in the parentheses. The time string you use in the TIMEVALUE function must be one of the acceptable Excel TIME formats. The format of the TIMEVALUE function is:

TIMEVALUE(string of characters)

Suppose you want to use the TIMEVALUE function to place the serial number for 7:10:59 PM on your worksheet.

Click	on cell A1
Enter	=TIMEVALUE("7:10:59 PM")

The serial number 0.799294 representing 7:10:59 PM appears in cell A1. Your screen should look like Figure 15-24.

Figure 15-24

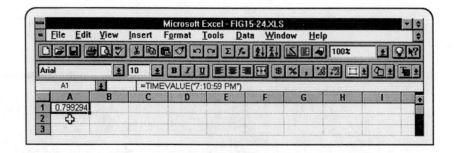

HOUR

In some situations, you may be given a serial number for which you need to determine the hour, minute, and second corresponding to the serial number.

The HOUR function determines the hour associated with a given serial number.

The format for the HOUR function is:

HOUR(serial number)

Suppose you are given the serial number 0.799294. To determine the hour of the day represented by this serial number:

Click	on cell A1
Enter	Hour
Click	on cell B1
Enter	=HOUR(0.799294)

The number 19 appears in cell B1 indicating the serial number represents a time between 7:00 P.M. and 8:00 P.M.

MINUTE

The MINUTE function calculates the minute of the hour represented by a serial number. The format of the MINUTE function is:

MINUTE(serial number)

Using the example serial number of 0.799294 again, you can compute the minute indicated by the serial number using this function.

To compute the minute number while leaving the results of the previous example in your worksheet:

Click	on cell A2
Enter	Minute
Click	on cell B2
Enter	=MINUTE(0.799294)

The number 10 in cell B2 specifies that the tenth minute is represented by the serial number.

SECOND

The SECOND function computes the second associated with a specific serial number. The format for the SECOND function is:

SECOND(serial number)

To determine the second associated with the serial number 0.799294 that was used in the last two examples:

Click	on cell A3
Enter	Second

| **Click** | on cell B3 |
| **Enter** | =SECOND(0.799294) |

Your screen should look like Figure 15-25.

Figure 15-25

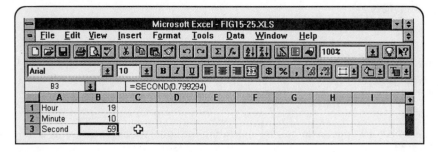

The value of 59 in cell B3 indicates the second represented by the time serial number is 59. Combining the information appearing in Figure 15-25, the serial number 0.799294 represents the time 7:10:59 PM. This result is consistent with the serial number you calculated using the TIME function for 7:10:59 PM.

Current Date and Time

The two functions available in Excel to specify the current date and time are TODAY and NOW. These functions are very useful in documenting when a worksheet was last calculated. It is a good idea to use one of these functions on all of your worksheets.

TODAY

The TODAY function determines the date based on the current system date used by your computer. The format for the TODAY function is:

TODAY()

To illustrate the use of the TODAY function:

Click	on cell A1
Enter	Today
Click	on cell B1
Enter	=TODAY()

The current date appears in cell A1.

NOW

The NOW function returns the current date and time. The format of the NOW function is:

NOW()

Suppose you want to place the current date and time in a cell on a worksheet.

Click	on cell A2
Enter	Now
Click	on cell B2
Enter	=NOW()

Widen column B to 16 so you can see the date and time in cell B2. Your screen should look similar to Figure 15-26.

Figure 15-26

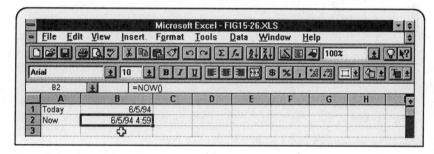

Notice that if you enter anything in the worksheet, the date and time will also be updated on the screen. The NOW function is particularly useful if you make changes to a worksheet several times in one day for "what-if" analysis purposes.

■ LOGICAL FUNCTIONS

The logical functions covered in this chapter are:

IF	Specifies a logical test to perform.
FALSE	Returns the logical value FALSE.
TRUE	Returns the logical value TRUE.

IF

The IF function allows you to test a condition and select one of two options depending on the results of the test.

The general format of the IF function for use on worksheets is:

IF(logical test,value if condition is true,value if condition is false)

To illustrate the use of the IF function, suppose the income before taxes for a company is $250,000 and the tax rate is 40%. Assume that you enter $250,000 in cell A1 of a worksheet and 40% in cell A2. To compute the taxes due, you could create the formula =A1∗A2 in cell A3.

In some situations, an organization may lose money. The formula, therefore, will not work properly because the company cannot pay a negative amount of taxes. In fact, the tax amount should be zero.

You can use the IF function so that the formula can work properly. To illustrate the use of the IF function:

Click	on cell A1
Enter	$250,000
Click	on cell A2
Enter	40%
Click	on cell A3
Enter	=IF(A1>0,A1*A2,0)

The first argument, A1>0, is the logical test. This logical test is used to determine if the number in cell A1 is greater than 0. The second argument, A1*A2, is the formula that will be used to place a number in cell A3 if the result of the logical test is true. The third argument, 0, indicates that a 0 will be entered in cell A3 if the logical test is false.

The function appears in the formula bar, and the number 100000 is displayed in cell A3. Since the result of the logical test is true, the formula A1*A2 is calculated and the number 100000 is placed in the cell.

Your screen should look like Figure 15-27.

Figure 15-27

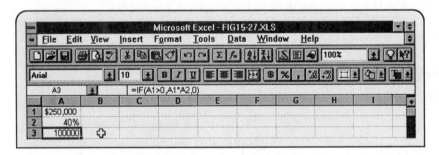

To test the false argument in the IF function:

Click	on cell A1
Enter	-10000

Notice that the number in cell A3 changes to 0.

The remaining portion of the IF function section includes illustrations of logical operators that you can use in an IF function and nested IF functions.

Logical Operators

Logical operators combine the numbers within conditional statements or formulas. The logical operators for simple logical statements are as follows:

Operator	Definition
=	equal
<	less than
<=	less than or equal
>	greater than
>=	greater than or equal
<>	not equal

Logical Operators for Compound Statements

You can use logical operators to combine multiple conditions. The AND, OR, and NOT logical operators are available in Excel.

AND

The AND function is used to combine multiple statements. For example, =IF(AND(A5=0,B5=0),Z5,C5) tests two conditions. That is, if both A5 and B5 equal zero, then the current content of cell Z5 is placed in the cell in which the IF function is located. If both conditions are not satisfied, then the current content of cell C5 is placed in the cell containing the IF function. When the AND function is used to link multiple conditions, *all* conditions must be true.

OR

Use the OR function to test if one condition or another condition is true. For example, IF(OR(A5=0,B5=0),Z5,C5) would result in the *true* result (Z5) if *either* A5=0 or B5=0.

NOT

Use the NOT function to indicate that a condition is not true. For example, IF(NOT(A5=0),Z5,C5) tests whether the contents of cell A5 is not equal to zero. If the contents of A5 are not equal to zero, then the content of cell Z5 is placed in the cell containing the IF function. Otherwise, the content of cell C5 is placed in the cell.

Nested IF

One IF function may be nested inside another, as the following example illustrates:

=IF(B1=25,B2*B1,IF(B1=35,B3*B1,IF(B1=45,B4*B1,0)))

The IF function is read from left to right. The first two IF functions have IF functions for the false response. The parentheses used to end the IF functions are at the end of the formula.

FALSE

When the FALSE function is used, it returns the logical value FALSE. The format of the FALSE function is:

FALSE

Suppose you want to pay someone a commission of 10% of the sales amount if their sales are at least $1,000 or nothing if their sales are less than $1,000. Instead of placing a value of zero, you want to have the word *FALSE* appear.

To illustrate the use of the FALSE function for this situation:

Click	on cell A1
Enter	Sales
Click	on cell A2
Enter	Commission
Click	on cell C1
Enter	900
Click	on cell C2
Enter	=IF(C1>=1000,C1*.1,FALSE)

In this IF function, the FALSE function will place a logical value of FALSE in cell C2 whenever the sales amount is less than $1,000.

Your screen should look like Figure 15-28.

Figure 15-28

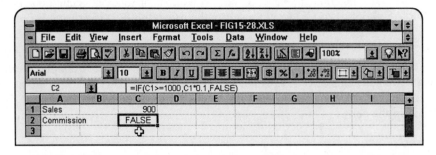

Notice that since the sales amount is less than $1,000, the logical value FALSE appears in cell C2. Change the value of sales to $1,000 and $1,500 to make sure the FALSE function works properly.

TRUE

When you use the TRUE function, it returns a logical value of TRUE. The format of the TRUE function is:

TRUE

Assume that you need to determine whether the value in a cell is less than 500. You can use the TRUE and FALSE functions together with an IF function to indicate whether the value is less than 500.

Click	on cell A1
Enter	450
Click	on cell A2
Enter	=IF(A1<500,TRUE,FALSE)

Your screen should look like Figure 15-29.

Figure 15-29

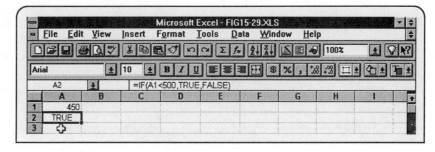

The logical value TRUE in cell A2 indicates that the condition tested is true. Change the value in cell A1 to 500 and then 750 to make sure the function works properly.

■ DATABASE FUNCTIONS

This book covers 10 database functions. The general format of a database function is:

$$Dfunction(database,field,criteria)$$

Database is the range of cells in a database. The field column names are included as the first row of the range. **Field** refers to which field in the database is used. The field column name identifies the field. **Criteria** is the set of cells containing the database criteria.

Most of the database functions are similar to the statistical functions covered earlier in this chapter. As mentioned in Chapter 13, a database is a collection of related data records. With the database functions, you can complete an analysis on the contents of the cells for a field column that satisfies a particular criteria.

For example, you may have a database of all employees for a company located in California, but you only want to know how many of the people live in Los Angeles. The COUNT function is used to determine how many employees are in the database. You can use the DCOUNT function to determine the number of employees living in Los Angeles.

The database functions covered in this book are summarized in the following table:

Function	Description
DSUM	Calculates the sum of values for a field column in a database that satisfy a specified criteria.
DCOUNT	Determines the number of cells containing numbers for a field column in a database that satisfy a specified criteria.
DAVERAGE	Computes the arithmetic mean for a field column in a database that satisfies a specified criteria.
DMIN	Determines the minimum value for a field column in a database that satisfies a specified criteria.
DMAX	Determines the maximum value for a field column in a database that satisfies a specified criteria.
DVARP	Calculates the population variance for a field column in a database that satisfies a specified criteria.
DSTDEVP	Calculates the population standard deviation for a field column in a database that satisfies a specified criteria.
DVAR	Computes the sample variance for a field column in a database that satisfies a specified criteria.
DSTDEV	Calculates the sample standard deviation for a field column in a database that satisfies a specified criteria.
DGET	Extracts from a database a single record for a field column in a database that satisfies a specified criteria.

You can specify the database by creating a range name that includes all cells in the database as its range. Excel assumes that the first row of the database includes the field names for the columns in the database. You can also define a name for the criteria that includes a set of cells that specify the criteria.

Before you use the database functions, you need to create the worksheet in Figure 15-30.

Figure 15-30

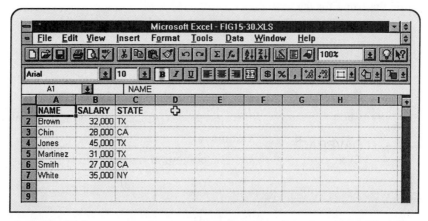

The database includes the last name, salary, and state location of employees working for an organization. Save the workbook document to a file using the name SALS.

Assume that you want to apply the database functions to those individuals earning more than $30,000. The persons satisfying this criteria are Brown, Jones, Martinez, and White.

Using the information in Figure 15-31, include the criteria and function names on the worksheet.

Figure 15-31

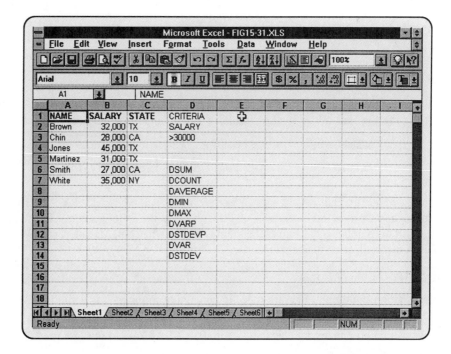

To define the name for the database:

Select	cells A1:C7
Choose	Insert
Choose	Name
Choose	Define
Click	the Names in Workbook text box (if necessary)
Type	Database
Click	the OK command button

To specify the name for the criteria:

Select	cells D2:D3
Choose	Insert
Choose	Name
Choose	Define
Click	the Names in Workbook text box (if necessary)
Type	Criteria
Click	the OK command button

DSUM

The DSUM function calculates the sum of values for a field in a database that satisfies a specified criteria.

To compute the sum of the salaries for those individuals having a salary greater than $30,000:

Click	on cell E6
Enter	=DSUM(Database,"SALARY",Criteria)

Database identifies cells A1 through C7 as the database range, "SALARY" specifies SALARY as the field location, and Criteria indicates cells D2 through D3 is the criteria range. The number 143000 appears in cell E6. This number is the sum of the salaries for Brown, Chin, Martinez, and White. Notice that the field column name must be inside quotes.

DCOUNT

This function counts the number of cells containing numbers for a field in a database that satisfies a specified criteria.

To determine how many numbers appear in the SALARY field that are greater than $30,000:

Click	on cell E7
Enter	=DCOUNT(Database,"SALARY",Criteria)

The number 4 appears in cell E7 indicating there are four individuals who have a salary greater than $30,000.

DAVERAGE

The DAVERAGE function calculates the arithmetic mean of the cells for a field in a database that satisfies a specified criteria.

To demonstrate the use of the DAVERAGE function for the SALS worksheet:

Click	on cell E8
Enter	=DAVERAGE(Database,"SALARY",Criteria)

The number 35750 appearing in cell E8 is the average salary of the four individuals who have a salary greater than $30,000.

DMIN

The DMIN function determines the minimum value for a field in a database that satisfies a specific criteria.

To illustrate the use of the DMIN function for the SALS worksheet:

Click	on cell E9
Enter	=DMIN(Database,"SALARY",Criteria)

The number 31000 that appears in cell E9 indicates that the lowest salary among the individuals having a salary greater than $30,000 is $31,000.

DMAX

The DMAX function determines the maximum value for a field in a database that satisfies a specified criteria.

To demonstrate the use of the DMAX function for the SALS worksheet:

Click	on cell E10
Enter	=DMAX(Database,"SALARY",Criteria)

The number 45000 appearing in cell E10 specifies that the highest salary among the employees having a salary greater than $30,000 is $45,000.

DVARP

The DVARP function calculates the population variance for a field in a database that satisfies a specified criteria. The use of the function assumes that the data included in the database represents all of the data that can be considered.

To illustrate the use of the DVARP function for the SALS worksheet:

Click	on cell E11
Enter	=DVARP(Database,"SALARY",Criteria)

The number 30687500 that appears in cell E11 is the population variance for the salaries of the persons having a salary greater than $30,000.

DSTDEVP

The DSTDEVP function computes the population standard deviation for a field in a database that satisfies a specified criteria.

To demonstrate the use of the DSTDEVP function for the SALS worksheet:

Click	on cell E12
Enter	=DSTDEVP(Database,"SALARY",Criteria)

The number 5539.62995 appearing in cell E12 is the population standard deviation for the salaries of the employees who have a salary greater than $30,000.

DVAR

The DVAR function computes the sample variance for a field in a database that satisfies a specified criteria. It is assumed that the database includes only a sample or portion of the data that can be considered.

To illustrate the use of the DVAR function for the SALS worksheet:

Click	on cell E13
Enter	=DVAR(Database,"SALARY",Criteria)

The number 40916666.7 appearing in cell E13 is the sample variance for the salaries of the personnel earning more than $30,000.

DSTDEV

The DSTDEV function calculates the sample standard deviation for a field in a database that satisfies a specified criteria. It is assumed that the database includes only a sample or portion of the data that can be considered.

To demonstrate the use of the DSTDEV function for the SALS worksheet:

Click	on cell E14
Enter	=DSTDEV(Database,"SALARY",Criteria)

The number 6396.61369 appearing in cell E14 is the sample standard deviation for the salaries of the employees having a salary greater than $30,000. Your screen should look like Figure 15-32.

Figure 15-32

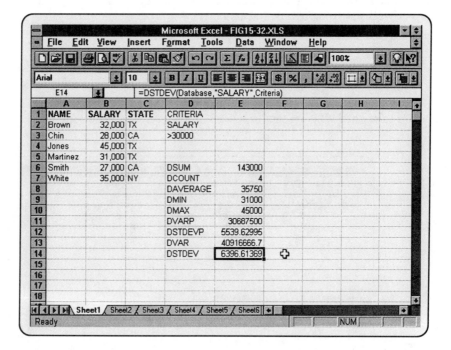

DGET

The DGET function allows you to search a database and find a particular value or text. The format of the DGET function is:

DGET(database,field,criteria)

where database is the database range, field is the name of the field within the database to be searched, and criteria is the criteria range. Before illustrating the use of the DGET function, you need to open the ABCSAL workbook file you created in Chapter 13.

Suppose you would like to know the total salary for the employee with the last name Armour. You can use the DGET function to search the TOTAL field column in the ABCSAL database to find the total salary.

Click	on cell B15
Enter	CRITERIA
Click	on cell B16
Enter	LAST NAME
Click	on cell B17
Enter	Armour

Define the name DATABASE and include cells A5 through I13 as its range. Define the name CRITERIA and specify cells B16 through B17 as its range.

To use the DGET function to determine Armour's total salary:

Click	on cell C17
Enter	=DGET(Database,"TOTAL",Criteria)

Armour's salary of 21200 appears in cell C17. Your screen should look like Figure 15-33.

Figure 15-33

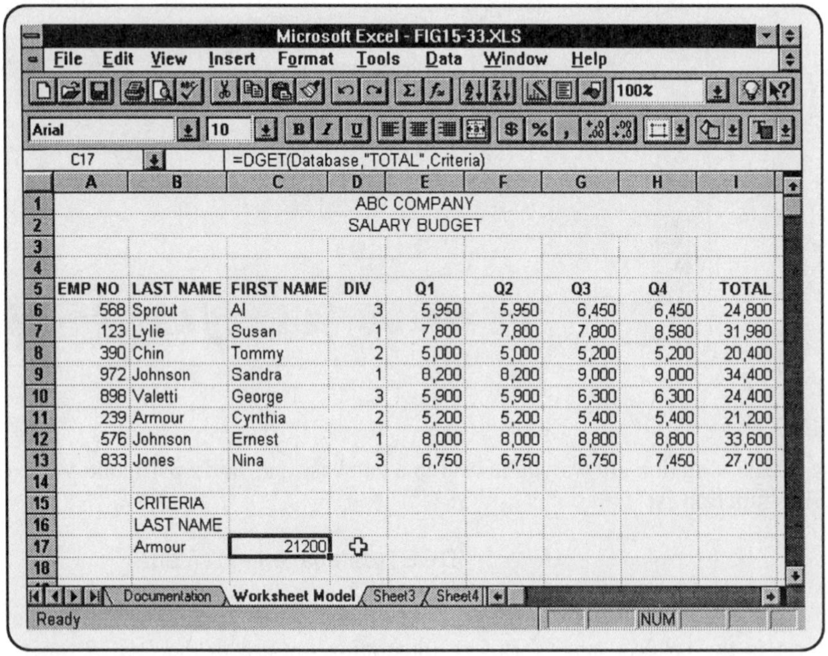

■ MATH AND TRIG FUNCTIONS

The 12 math and trig functions covered in this chapter are:

ABS	Computes the absolute value of a number in a cell.
CEILING	Rounds a number up to the nearest multiple of significance.
EVEN	Rounds a number to the nearest even number.
EXP	Computes the number e raised to a specific power.
INT	Rounds a number down to the nearest integer.

LN	Computes the natural logarithm (base *e*) of a number.
LOG10	Computes the common logarithm (base 10) of a number.
MOD	Computes the remainder (modulus) from a division calculation.
ODD	Rounds a number up to the nearest odd integer.
RAND	Generates a random number value between 0 and 1.
ROUND	Rounds a number to a specific number of decimal places.
SQRT	Computes the positive square root of a number.

If you need to use the trigonometric functions and other mathematical functions, see the Microsoft Excel User's Guide and the Help feature.

ABS

The ABS function determines the absolute value of a number. The number returned will always be positive. The format of the ABS function is:

ABS(number)

To illustrate the use of the ABS function:

Click	on cell A1
Enter	25
Click	on cell A2
Enter	-50
Click	on cell B1
Enter	=ABS(A1)
Click	on cell B2
Enter	=ABS(A2)

Your screen should look like Figure 15-34.

Figure 15-34

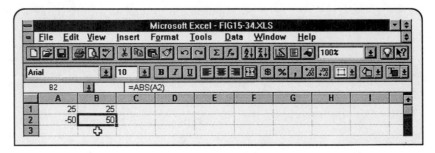

Notice that the absolute value of a positive number is the same positive number while the absolute value of a negative number is a positive number.

CEILING

The CEILING function rounds a number up to the nearest multiple level of significance. The format of the CEILING function is:

$$CEILING(number,significance)$$

Significance is the multiple to which to round.

Suppose you want a number to be rounded up to the nearest integer based on a multiple level of significance. To illustrate the use of the CEILING function in this case:

Click	on cell A1
Enter	12.14
Click	on cell A2
Enter	=CEILING(A1,1)
Click	on cell A3
Enter	=CEILING(A1,2)

Your screen should look like Figure 15-35.

Figure 15-35

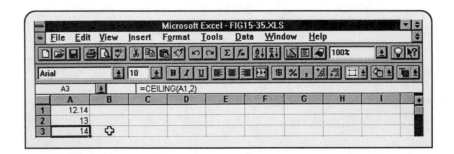

Notice that in cell A2 the number is rounded up to the next integer and in cell A3 the number is rounded up by two numbers.

EVEN

The EVEN function calculates a number rounded up to the nearest even integer. The format of the EVEN function is:

$$EVEN(number)$$

To illustrate the use of the EVEN function:

Click	on cell A1
Enter	22.34
Click	on cell A2
Enter	=EVEN(A1)

Your screen should look like Figure 15-36.

Figure 15-36

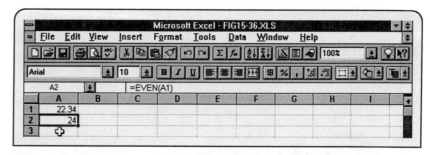

Notice that the number in cell A1 has been rounded to 24 because 24 is the next even integer greater than 22.34.

EXP

The EXP function computes the value of a number *e* raised to a specific power. The number *e* used in Excel has an approximate value of 2.718282. The format of the EXP function is:

$$EXP(number)$$

To demonstrate the use of the EXP function:

Click	on cell A1
Enter	=EXP(3)

Your screen should look like Figure 15-37.

Figure 15-37

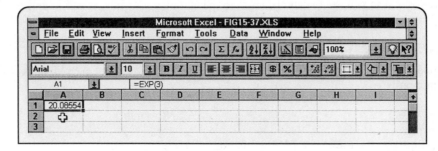

The value 20.08554 appearing in cell A1 is *e* (2.718282) raised to the power of 3.

INT

The INT function rounds a number down to the closest integer. The format of the INT function is:

$$INT(number)$$

To demonstrate the use of the INT function:

Click	on cell B1
Enter	33.1
Click	on cell B2
Enter	=INT(B1)

Your screen should look like Figure 15-38.

Figure 15-38

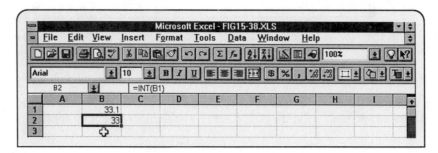

Notice that the value in cell B1 has been rounded down to the nearest integer.

LN

The LN function calculates the natural logarithm (base *e*) of a number. The format of the LN function is:

$$LN(number)$$

To illustrate the use of the LN function:

Click	on cell A1
Enter	2
Click	on cell A2
Enter	=LN(A1)

Your screen should look like Figure 15-39.

Figure 15-39

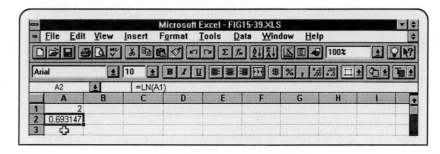

The value 0.693147 in cell A2 is the natural logarithm of the number 2.

LOG10

The LOG10 function computes the common logarithm (base 10) for a number. The format for the LOG10 function is:

$$LOG10(number)$$

To illustrate the use of the LOG10 function:

Click	on cell B1
Enter	20
Click	on cell B2
Enter	=LOG10(B1)

Your screen should look like Figure 15-40.

Figure 15-40

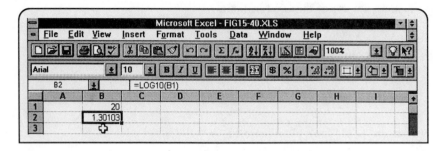

The number 1.30103 in cell B2 is the common logarithm for the number 20.

MOD

The MOD function computes the remainder (modulus) when you divide one number by another. The format for the MOD function is:

$$MOD(number, divisor)$$

The sign (+ or -) of the resulting value specifies the sign for result of the division.

To illustrate the use of the MOD function:

Click	on cell A1
Enter	X
Click	on cell B1
Enter	15
Click	on cell A2
Enter	Y
Click	on cell B2
Enter	6
Click	on cell C1
Enter	=MOD(B1,B2)

Your screen should look like Figure 15-41.

Figure 15-41

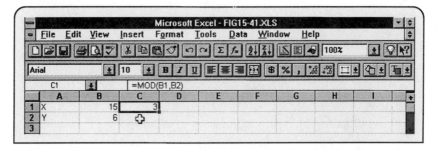

The number 3 in cell C1 is computed by dividing 15 by 6 and determining that the answer is 2 plus a remainder (modulus) of 3.

ODD

The ODD function calculates a number rounded up to the nearest odd integer. The format of the ODD function is:

ODD(number)

To illustrate the use of the ODD function:

Click	on cell A1
Enter	21.3
Click	on cell A2
Enter	=ODD(A1)

Your screen should look like Figure 15-42.

Figure 15-42

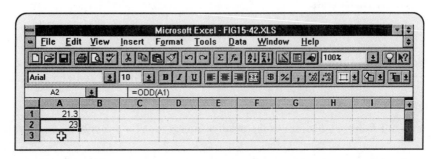

Notice that the number in cell A1 has been rounded up to 23 because 23 is the next odd integer greater than 21.3.

RAND

The RAND function calculates a random number between 0 and 1. The format of the RAND function is:

RAND()

A new value for the random number is computed each time the workbook document is calculated.
To illustrate the use of the RAND function:

Click	on cell A1
Enter	=RAND()

Your screen should look similar to Figure 15-43.

Figure 15-43

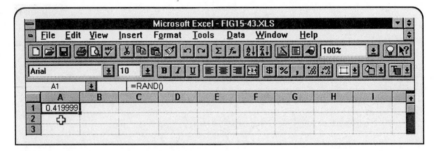

The value appearing in cell A1 is a random number between 0 and 1. If you want a random number between 0 and 100, you can multiply the RAND function by 100 or use the RANDBETWEEN function.

ROUND

The ROUND function is used to round a number to a specific number of decimal places. The format for the ROUND function is:

ROUND(x,y)

where x is any value or formula and y is the number of decimal places to the right of the decimal point.
Chapter 4 includes an extensive discussion of the ROUND function and several illustrations of its use.

SQRT

The SQRT function determines the positive square root for a number. The format of the SQRT function is:

SQRT(x)

where x is any positive value or formula that results in a positive number.

To demonstrate the use of the SQRT function:

Click	on cell A1
Enter	25
Click	on cell A2
Enter	=SQRT(A1)

Your screen should look like Figure 15-44.

Figure 15-44

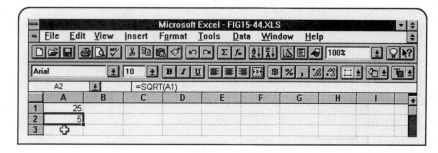

The number 5 shown in cell A2 is the square of 25. If you attempt to calculate the square root of a negative value, the characters #NUM! will appear in cell A2.

There are many other math functions available in Excel. For additional information, see the Microsoft Excel User's Guide or the Help feature.

Trig Functions

Excel includes a number of trig functions. These functions are used primarily by engineers and scientists. If you need to use these functions, you can obtain additional information in the Microsoft Excel User's Guide or the Help feature.

■ LOOKUP AND REFERENCE FUNCTIONS

This chapter covers five lookup and reference functions, categorized as follows:

REFERENCE

COLUMNS	Determines the number of columns in a reference.
ROWS	Determines the number of rows in a reference.

LOOKUP

CHOOSE	Finds a specific number in a list.

| HLOOKUP | Finds the contents of a cell in a specified row in a horizontal lookup table. |
| VLOOKUP | Finds the contents of a cell in a specified column in a vertical lookup table. |

Reference Functions

The two reference functions covered in this chapter are COLUMNS and ROWS.

COLUMNS

The COLUMNS function counts the number of columns in a specified reference or range of cells. The format of the COLUMNS function is:

COLUMNS(reference)

where reference is a range of cells, an array, or an array formula.

To demonstrate the use of the COLUMNS function:

| **Click** | on cell A1 |
| **Enter** | =COLUMNS(B1:M1) |

Your screen should look like Figure 15-45.

Figure 15-45

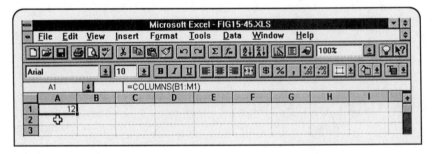

The number 12 in cell A1 indicates there are 12 columns in the specified range B1 through M1.

ROWS

The ROWS function counts the number of rows in a reference or range of cells. The format of the ROWS function is:

ROWS(reference)

where reference is a range of cells, an array, or an array formula.

To illustrate the use of the ROWS function:

Click   on cell A1

Enter   =ROWS(B32:B297)

Your screen should look like Figure 15-46.

Figure 15-46

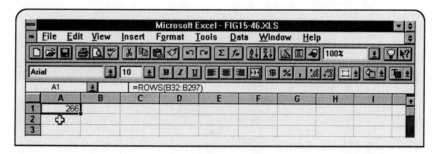

The number 266 in cell A1 indicates that there are 266 rows in the range of cells B32 through B297.

Excel has other reference functions available. See the Microsoft Excel User's Guide or the Help feature to obtain additional information on reference functions.

Lookup Functions

The three lookup functions covered in this chapter are CHOOSE, HLOOKUP, and VLOOKUP.

CHOOSE

The CHOOSE function finds a value in a specified list. The format of the CHOOSE function is:

CHOOSE(index_num,value1,value2,...)

where index_num is the position in a list. Index_num must have a value between 1 and 29. Index_num can be a reference to a cell or number. You can use a maximum of 29 values between 1 and 29. The value arguments are used to select a value or an action to complete based on index_num. You can use a number, cell reference, and range names for any of the value arguments.

Before using the CHOOSE function, you need to create the worksheet shown in Figure 15-47.

Figure 15-47

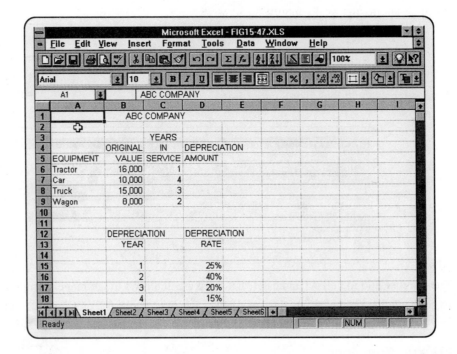

Suppose you need to compute the annual depreciation for the four pieces of equipment listed in cells A6 through A9. Assume that each of the properties has an economic useful life of four years. The depreciation used for the properties depends on how long the property has been in service. For example, the depreciation rate for the tractor is 25% because it has been in service for only one year. The depreciation amount for the tractor is $4,000 (0.25 times 16,000) in Year 1.

To demonstrate the use of the CHOOSE function to compute the depreciation amount for the tractor:

Click	on cell D6
Enter	=B6*CHOOSE(C6,$D$14,$D$15,$D$16,$D$17)

The number 4000 in cell D6 is the depreciation amount based on the depreciation rate of 25%. Cell C6 is the cell containing the index_num. Since the YEARS IN SERVICE number in cell C6 is 1, the first item in the list of values is used. If index_num is less than one or greater than the number of the last value in the list, the CHOOSE function displays #VALUE!.

Verify that the CHOOSE function works for the other equipment by copying the formula in cell D6 to cells D7 through D9.

Your screen should look like Figure 15-48.

Figure 15-48

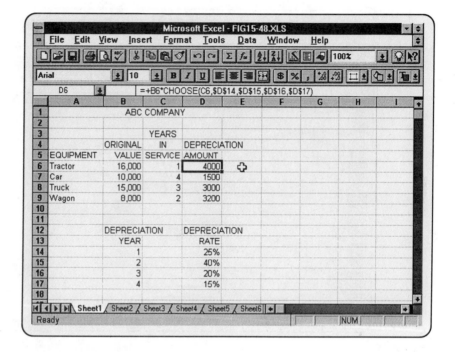

HLOOKUP

The HLOOKUP function searches across the top row of a table array until a particular value is found or condition is satisfied. Then the function looks down that column for the row specified in the function and returns the value in the specified cell. Such a table is sometimes referred to as a horizontal lookup table.

The format of the HLOOKUP function is:

HLOOKUP(lookup_value,table_array,row_index_num,[range_lookup])

The lookup_value is the number to be found in the first row of the table. Table_array is the table of information containing the lookup data. You specify the table_array by including a reference or a defined name. Row_index_num is the row containing the matching value.

Range_lookup, a logical value of TRUE or FALSE, is used to specify whether an exact match or approximate match is found. If the value TRUE is used or omitted, HLOOKUP will return an approximate match. When FALSE is used, HLOOKUP will return an exact match or #NA if no match is found.

Before illustrating the use of the HLOOKUP function, you need to create the worksheet shown in Figure 15-49.

Figure 15-49

The horizontal lookup table contains the cells B4 through E9. The information in cells A5 through A9 is for documentation purposes only. The table is used to determine the amount of withholding tax an employee must pay depending on the salary and number of exemptions declared. For example, an individual earning at least $1,840 and less than $1,880 who has two withholding allowances must have $228 withheld from his or her paycheck.

To demonstrate the use of the HLOOKUP function for this situation:

Click	on cell D14
Enter	=HLOOKUP(B14,$B$4:$E$9,C14+2)

Make sure you include $ signs to specify the absolute references. The value 228 in cell D14 is the amount of withholding for an individual who has two withholding allowances, earning greater than or equal to $1,840 and less than $1,880. Notice that the value 1,850 in cell B14 is greater than or equal to $1,840 and less than $1,880. The row_index_num is the value of cell C14 plus 2 because the row_index_num is two more than the corresponding number of allowances.

To verify that the HLOOKUP function works properly for the remaining employees, copy the formula in cell D14 to cells D15 through D18. When you are finished, your screen should look like Figure 15-50.

Figure 15-50

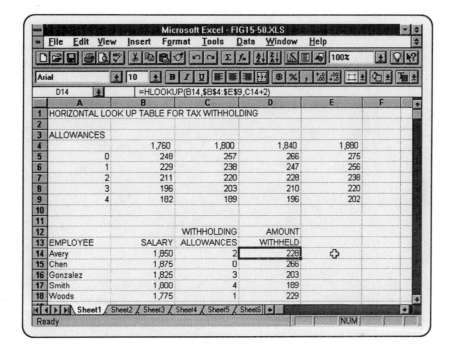

VLOOKUP

The VLOOKUP function searches down the left column of a table array until a particular value is found or condition is satisfied. Then the function looks across that row for the column specified in the function and returns the value in the specified cell. Such a table is sometimes referred to as a vertical lookup table.

The format of the VLOOKUP function is:

VLOOKUP(lookup_value,table_array,col_index_num,[range_lookup])

The lookup_value is the number to be found in the first column of the table. Table_array is the table of information containing the lookup data. You specify the table_array by including a reference or a defined name. Col_index_num is the column containing the matching value.

Range_lookup, a logical value of TRUE or FALSE, is used to specify whether an exact match or approximate match is found. If the value TRUE is used or omitted, VLOOKUP will return an approximate match. When FALSE is used, VLOOKUP will return an exact match or #NA if no match is found.

Before illustrating the use of the VLOOKUP function, you need to create the worksheet in Figure 15-51.

Figure 15-51

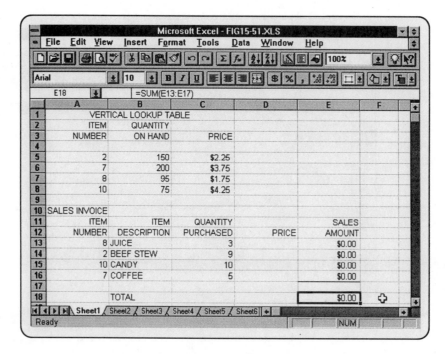

The amount cells are calculated by multiplying QUANTITY times PRICE, and the total AMOUNT is determined by summing the individual item sales amounts.

The vertical lookup table is in cells A5 through C8. This table includes information on the prices for four items sold by a distributor. The table is used to specify the proper sales price for items on a sales invoice.

To demonstrate the use of the VLOOKUP function for this situation:

Click   on cell D13

Enter   =VLOOKUP(A13,$A$5:$C$8,3)

Make sure you include the $ signs to specify the absolute references. The value of 1.75 in cell D13 is the price for juice (ITEM NUMBER 8). Notice that the col_index_num is 3 because the prices for the items are in the third column of the vertical lookup table.

To verify that the VLOOKUP function works properly for the other sales items, copy the contents of cell D13 to cells D14 through D16.

When you are finished, your screen should look like Figure 15-52.

Figure 15-52

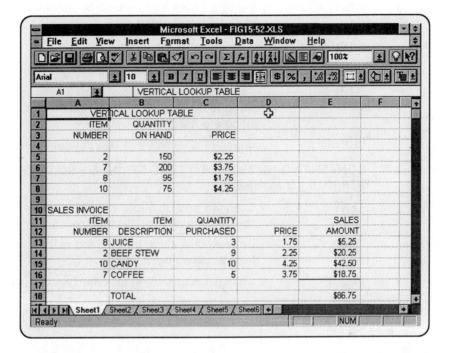

■ TEXT FUNCTIONS

This book covers 13 text functions. The term *text* refers to any set of characters. The text functions can be categorized as follows:

CREATING CHARACTERS

REPT   Duplicates text a specified number of times.

EXTRACTING PORTIONS OF TEXT

FIND   Determines the position of the first character or
                    string of text within another string of text.

LEFT   Returns a specified number of characters
                    beginning with the first character in a text
                    string.

LEN   Determines the number of characters in a text
                    string.

MID   Returns an indicated number of characters
                    beginning with a specific character.

REPLACE   Replaces some characters within a text string
                    with another specified text string.

RIGHT	Returns a specified number of characters at the end of the text string.

CHANGING THE CASE OF A TEXT STRING

LOWER	Changes all letters in a text string to lowercase.
PROPER	Changes the first letter of each word in a text string to uppercase; all other letters in the text string are lowercase.
UPPER	Changes all letters in a text string to uppercase.

CONVERTING NUMBERS TO TEXT STRINGS AND TEXT STRINGS TO NUMBERS

TEXT	Changes a value into a text string with a specified number of decimal places.
TRIM	Deletes all leading, trailing, and extra spaces from a text string.
VALUE	Changes a text string to a number.

Creating Characters

The function for creating text covered in this chapter is the REPT function.

REPT

The REPT function is used to duplicate a text string a specific number of times. The format of the REPT function is:

REPT(text,number_times)

where text is a set of characters you want to repeat and number_times is the number of times to repeat the text. Number_times must be a positive number.

To illustrate the use of the REPT function:

Click	on cell A1
Enter	=REPT("Worksheet ",3)

Your screen should look like Figure 15-53.

Figure 15-53

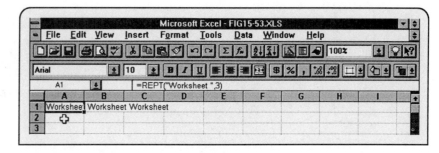

The set of characters "Worksheet " is repeated three times in cell A1. Notice that a space occurs between the words because you placed a space before the second " in the text definition.

Extracting Portions of Text

The six text functions in Excel for extracting text from a text string covered in this chapter are FIND, LEFT, LEN, MID, REPLACE, and RIGHT.

FIND

The FIND function determines the position within a text string where another text string starts. The format of the FIND function is:

$$FIND(find\_text,within\_text,start\_num)$$

where find_text is the set of characters you want to find. Within_text is the text containing the text you wish to find, and start_num is the character at which the search begins. If no start_num is specified, it is assumed to be a one.

To illustrate the use of the FIND function:

Click	on cell A1
Enter	Spreadsheet Analysis
Click	on cell A3
Enter	=FIND("sheet",A1,1)

Your screen should look like Figure 15-54.

Figure 15-54

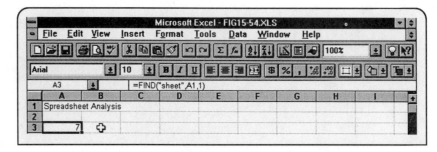

The number 7 is the position of the first character of the find_text string. FIND is case sensitive. For example, if "Sheet" had been used in the example, #VALUE! would have appeared in cell A3.

LEFT

The LEFT function returns a specified number of characters from a text string beginning with the first character in the text string. The format of the LEFT function is:

LEFT(text,num_char)

where text is any string of characters and num_char indicates the number of characters to return.

To demonstrate the use of the LEFT function:

Click	on cell B1
Enter	Mastering and Using Microsoft Excel

Suppose you want to return the characters "Mastering" and place them in cell B3.

Click	on cell B3
Enter	=LEFT(B1,9)

Your screen should look like Figure 15-55.

Figure 15-55

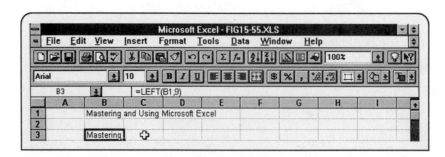

The text string "Mastering" appears in cell B3.

LEN

The LEN function counts the number of characters in a text string. The format of the LEN function is:

LEN(text)

where text is any string of characters. If a space is included in the text string, it is counted as a character. To illustrate the use of the LEN function:

Click	on cell A1
Enter	boyd & fraser publishing company
Click	on cell A4
Enter	=LEN(A1)

Your screen should look like Figure 15-56.

Figure 15-56

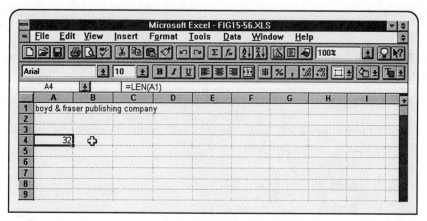

The number 32 appears in cell A4 indicating there are 32 characters in the text string contained in cell A1.

MID

The MID function is used to return a specific number of characters beginning at a particular point in a string. The format of the MID function is:

MID(text,start_num,num_char)

Text is a text string, start_num is the character number where you want to start extracting characters, and num_char is the number of characters to extract. Start_num must be a positive integer.

To demonstrate the use of the MID function:

Click	on cell B1
Enter	Mastering and Using Microsoft Excel

Click	on cell B3
Enter	=MID(B1,15,5)

Your screen should look like Figure 15-57.

Figure 15-57

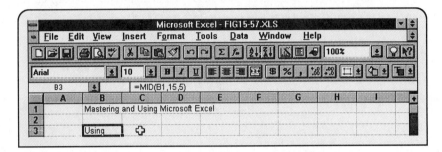

The word "Using" appears in cell B3 as a result of using the MID function.

REPLACE

The REPLACE function finds a set of characters in a text string and replaces the characters with another set of characters. The format of the REPLACE function is:

REPLACE(old_text,start_num,num_chars,new_text)

Old_text is the text in which some characters need to be changed, start_num is the position of the first character to change, num_chars is the number of characters to replace, and new_text is the new text string to include in old_text.

To illustrate the use of the REPLACE function:

Click	on cell A1
Enter	Softball and Feetball are popular sports

To replace the "ee" in Feetball with "oo":

Click	on cell A3
Enter	=REPLACE(A1,15,2,"oo")

Your screen should look like Figure 15-58.

Figure 15-58

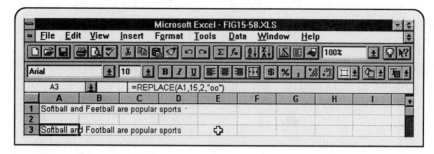

The spelling error in cell A1 is now corrected in cell A3.

RIGHT

The RIGHT function returns characters from the rightmost end of a text string. The format of the RIGHT function is:

$$RIGHT(text,num\_chars)$$

Text is the text string and num_chars is the number of characters to return beginning at the rightmost character in the text string. Num_chars must be a positive integer.

To demonstrate the use of the RIGHT function:

Click	on cell B1
Enter	Software Package
Click	on cell B3
Enter	=RIGHT(B1,7)

Your screen should look like Figure 15-59.

Figure 15-59

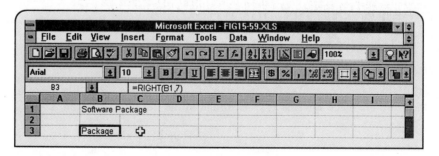

The word "Package" now appears in cell B3 because it represents the last seven characters of the text string in cell B1.

Changing the Case of a Text String

The three functions available in Excel to change the case of a text string are LOWER, PROPER, and UPPER.

LOWER

The LOWER function changes all letters in a text string to lowercase. The format of the LOWER function is:

LOWER(text)

Text is any text string. Text can be a string of characters inside quotes or a cell reference containing a text string.

To illustrate the use of the LOWER function:

Click	on cell A1
Enter	SOUTHWEST
Click	on cell A3
Enter	=LOWER(A1)

Your screen should look like Figure 15-60.

Figure 15-60

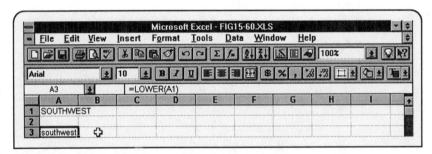

The letters in cell A3 are all lowercase.

PROPER

The PROPER function makes the first letter of each word in a text string uppercase. The remaining letters in the word are made lowercase. The format of the PROPER function is:

PROPER(text)

where text is any text string. Text can be a string of characters inside quotes or a cell reference containing a text string.

To illustrate the use of the PROPER function:

Click	on cell B1
Enter	mastering and using microsoft excel
Click	on cell B3
Enter	=PROPER(B1)

Your screen should look like Figure 15-61.

Figure 15-61

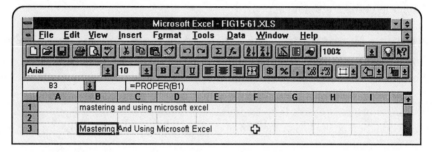

The first letter of each word in cell B3 is uppercase, and all other letters are lowercase.

UPPER

The UPPER function converts all lowercase letters in a text string to uppercase letters. The format of the UPPER function is:

$$UPPER(text)$$

where text is any text string. Text can be a string of characters inside quotes or a cell reference containing a text string.

To illustrate the use of the UPPER function:

Click	on cell A1
Enter	California
Click	on cell A3
Enter	=UPPER(A1)

Your screen should look like Figure 15-62.

Figure 15-62

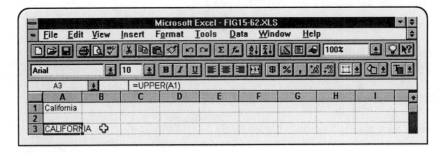

All letters in cell A3 are now uppercase.

Converting Numbers to Text Strings and Text Strings to Numbers

The three functions covered in this chapter that relate to converting numbers to text strings and text strings to numbers are TEXT, TRIM, and VALUE.

TEXT

The Text function changes a value to a text string with a specific number of decimal places. The format of the TEXT function is:

$$TEXT(value, format\_text)$$

Value is a number, a reference to a cell containing a number or a formula that evaluates to a number. Format_text is an acceptable number format.

To illustrate the use of the TEXT function:

Click	on cell B1
Enter	1123.457
Click	on cell B3
Enter	=TEXT(B1,"#,##0.00")

Your screen should look like Figure 15-63.

Figure 15-63

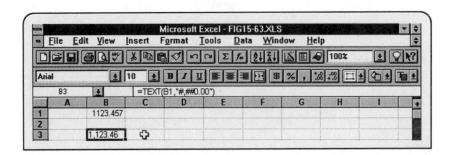

Notice that the characters in cell B3 are left-aligned to indicate the data is considered as text and not a value.

TRIM

The TRIM function deletes all leading, trailing, and extra spaces between words in a text string. Single spaces between words in the text string are preserved. The format of the TRIM function is:

TRIM(text)

Text can be a string of characters inside quotes or a cell reference containing a text string.

To illustrate the use of the TRIM function:

Click	on cell A1
Enter	Worksheets are fun to create

Notice that there are two spaces before Worksheets and between the words Worksheets, are, fun, and to.

Click	on cell A3
Enter	=TRIM(A1)

Your screen should look like Figure 15-64.

Figure 15-64

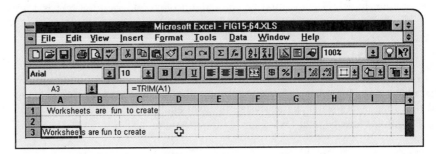

The leading spaces and extra spaces between the words in the text string have been deleted. Notice that the space between "to" and "create" remains because there was only one space originally.

VALUE

The VALUE function changes a text string that looks like a number into a value. The format of the VALUE function is:

VALUE(text)

Text can be a string of characters inside quotes or a cell reference containing a text string. The text string must appear as a number.

To illustrate the use of the VALUE function:

Click	on cell B1
Enter	97.5
Click	on cell B2
Enter	=TEXT(B1,"00.0")
Click	on cell B3
Enter	=VALUE(B2)

Your screen should look like Figure 15-65.

Figure 15-65

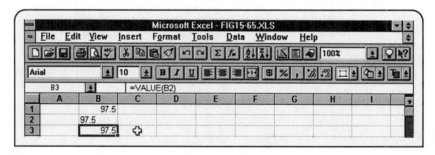

The number in cell B1 must first be converted to text and then the text is converted to a value.

SUMMARY

Excel has many functions that can perform standard calculations. The eight categories of functions covered in this chapter are statistical analysis, financial analysis, date and time, logical, database, math and trig, lookup and reference, and text.

KEY CONCEPTS

Database functions
Date and time functions
Financial analysis functions
Logical functions

Lookup and reference functions
Math and trig functions
Statistical analysis functions
Text functions

EXERCISE 1

INSTRUCTIONS: Circle T if the statement is true and F if the statement is false.

T   F   1.   The MINUTE function determines the minute of the hour represented by a serial number.

T   F   2.   Multiple items in a range may be listed individually (e.g., the syntax in the function =COUNT(B1,B3,B4) is correct).

T   F   3.   You may place arguments within a function in any order.

T   F   4.   Extra spaces are not acceptable within functions.

T   F   5.   You can alter a function with arithmetic operations to get the desired result (e.g., the function =PMT(B1,B2/12,B3∗12) is syntactically correct).

T   F   6.   The NOW function displays the current date and time in a cell on a worksheet.

T   F   7.   You may use more than one function in a formula.

T   F   8.   The IF function allows you to test one or more conditions in a worksheet and provide appropriate responses (either a true result or a false result).

T   F   9.   Date and time functions are available in Excel.

T   F   10.   VLOOKUP searches across the top row of a table until a particular value is found or condition is satisfied.

EXERCISE 2 -- Using the Statistical Functions

INSTRUCTIONS: Using the data 111, 125, 116, 130, and 127, apply the statistical functions available in Excel to:

1.   Determine the sum of the numbers.
2.   Count the number of values.
3.   Compute the arithmetic mean of the values.
4.   Determine the minimum value.
5.   Calculate the maximum value.
6.   Compute the population variance.
7.   Determine the population standard deviation.
8.   Compute the sample variance.
9.   Calculate the sample standard deviation.

Print the worksheet after completing the calculations.

Close the worksheet document. Do not save any changes.

EXERCISE 3 -- Using the Financial Functions

INSTRUCTIONS: Use the financial analysis functions available in Excel to solve the following problems:

1. Compute the internal rate of return for the following cash flow stream, using .15 as the guess rate:
    -1000, -500, 900, 800, 700, 600, 400, 200, and 100.

2. Compute the net present value for the following cash flow stream, using .10 as the discount rate:
    -1500, 900, 800, 700, 600, 400, 200, and 100.

3. Compute the future value if the payment per period is 500, the interest rate is 10%, and the term is 15 years. .

4. Compute the present value, using the arguments given in problem 3.

5. Compute the payment amount for a $100,000 loan that has an interest rate of 10% and is to be paid on an annual basis for a period of 12 years.

6. Compute the *monthly* payment amount assuming all arguments in problem 5 stay the same, except that the time period is 30 years.

7. Compute the straight-line depreciation for an office machine having an initial cost of $13,000, an estimated useful life of 8 years, and a salvage value of $200.

8. Using the data in problem 7, compute the depreciation of the office machine for the sixth year using the double-declining balance method.

9. Using the data in problem 7, compute the depreciation of the office machine for the sixth year using the sum-of-the-years' digits method.

10. Using the data in problem 7, compute the depreciation of the office machine for the fourth year using the variable declining balance method. Use 150% as the depreciation-factor.

Print the worksheet(s) showing your answers.

Close the workbook document. Do not save any changes.

EXERCISE 4 -- Using the Date and Time Functions

INSTRUCTIONS: Use the date and time functions available in Excel to solve the following problems:

1. Using the DATE function, enter the date January 19, 1996 in cell A1.

2. Using the TIME function, enter the time 9:49 PM in cell A2.

3. Calculate the number of days between January 3, 1996 and June 27, 1997 in cell A3.

4. Determine the number of days between January 3, 1996 and June 27, 1997, assuming there are 360 days in a year, in cell A4.

5. Use the TODAY function to place the current date in cell A5.

6. For the time 8:14:10 AM, place the hour in cell B1, the minute in cell B2, and the second in cell B3.

7. Determine the hour of the day represented by the serial number .481234.

Print the worksheet after completing all parts of the exercise.

Close the workbook document. Do not save any changes.

EXERCISE 5 -- Using the Logical Functions

INSTRUCTIONS: First, make sure you have a blank workbook document on your screen. Then enter the following data on the worksheet:

Cell	Data
A1	20
A2	30
A3	50

1. In cell B1, determine whether the value in A1 is within the range from 30 to 40. If the value is in the range, place the word *True* in cell B1; otherwise, place the word *False* in cell B1.

2. In cell B2, determine whether the value in A2 is greater than 25. If the value in cell A2 is greater than 25, enter a value of 1 in cell B2. If the value is less than or equal to 25, enter a value of zero in cell B2.

3. In cell B3, determine whether the value in A3 is greater than 60. If the value in cell A3 is greater than 60, enter a value of 1 in cell B3. If the value is less than or equal to 60, enter a value of zero in cell B3.

Print the worksheet with the results of the first three problems.

4. Change the values entered in cells A1, A2, A3 to the following:

Cell	Data
A1	35
A2	10
A3	75

Print the worksheet with the results after entering the new values.

Close the workbook document. Do not save any changes.

EXERCISE 6 -- Using the Database Functions

INSTRUCTIONS: Create the worksheet shown in Figure 15-66.

Figure 15-66

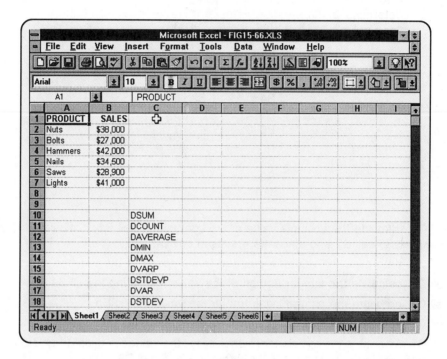

1. Construct criteria that will determine if a product included in the database has sales of more than $35,000.

2. Place the appropriate database functions in cells D10 through D18 to compute the indicated items for the information in the database that satisfies the criteria.

Print the worksheet after answering problems 1 and 2.

Close the workbook document. Do not save any changes.

EXERCISE 7 -- Using the Math Functions

INSTRUCTIONS: First, make sure you have a blank workbook document on your screen. Then enter the following data on the worksheet:

Cell	Data
B1	-45
B2	45
B3	2
B4	52.9876
B5	1.5
B6	10
B7	20
B8	12
B9	67.3468
B10	225

1. In cell C1, compute the absolute value of the contents of cell B1. Calculate the absolute value of the contents of cell B2 and place the results in cell C2.

2. In cell C3, determine the value for *e* raised to the power of the number included in cell B3.

3. In cell C4, calculate the integer portion of the value appearing in cell B4.

4. In cell C5, compute the natural logarithm for the value in cell B5.

5. In cell C6, specify the common logarithm for the value in cell B6.

6. In cell C7, determine the remainder (modulus) for the values in cells B7 and B8. In computing the remainder, divide the value in cell B7 by the value in cell B8.

7. In cell C8, enter a random number between 0 and 1.

8. In cell C9, round the value appearing in cell B9 to three decimal places.

9. In cell C10, compute the square root of the value in cell B10.

Print the worksheet with the answers to problems 1 through 9.

Close the workbook document. Do not save any changes.

EXERCISE 8 -- Using the Lookup Functions

INSTRUCTIONS: Create the worksheet shown in Figure 15-67.

Figure 15-67

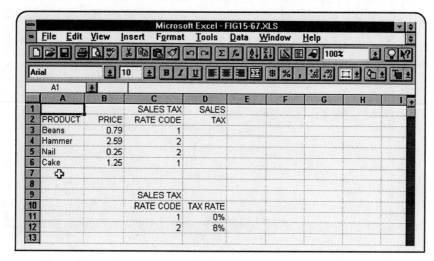

You need to compute the sales tax amount for the four products based on the sales tax rate code. Use the CHOOSE function to assist you in computing the proper sales tax amount for the four items.

Print the worksheet after you have completed the calculation of the sales tax amounts.

Create the worksheet shown in Figure 15-68.

Figure 15-68

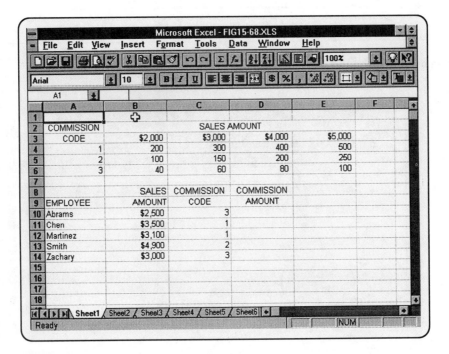

You need to calculate the commission owed to each of the salespersons. The amount of commission is based on a commission code assigned to each individual and the sales amount for the individuals. For example, a person who has a sales amount of $2,800 and a commission code of 2 is owed a commission of $100. Use the HLOOKUP function to help calculate the proper commission amounts.

Print the worksheet after computing the commission amounts.

Create the worksheet shown in Figure 15-69.

Figure 15-69

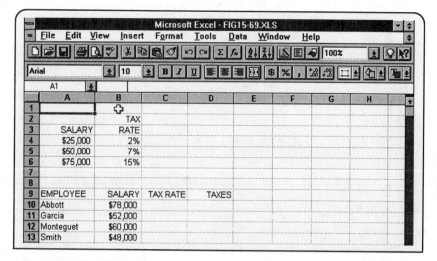

You must compute the state income taxes owed by the individuals. Compute the tax amount owed by each employee by multiplying the salary amount times the appropriate tax rate. For example, if a person has a salary equal to $50,000, then the amount of state income tax due is $3,500. Use the VLOOKUP function to determine the proper tax rate for each employee.

Print the worksheet after calculating the tax amount due for each of the employees.

Close the workbook document. Do not save any changes.

EXERCISE 9 -- Using the Text Functions

INSTRUCTIONS: First, make sure you have a blank workbook document on your screen.

1. Repeat the set of characters "Chart" six times in cell A1. Do not include the quotes.

2. Enter the label "Excel is a great software package" in cell A3. Do not include the quotes. Find the position of the word *great* in the label and place the answer in cell B4.

3. Using the label in cell A3, place the characters *Excel* in cell D4.

4. Using the label in cell A3, determine the number of characters in the label and place the answer in cell F4.

5. Using the label in cell A3, place the word *software* in cell B6.

6. Copy the label in cell A3 to cell A8. Using the label in cell A8, replace the word *great* with *wonderful*.

7. Using the label in cell A8, place the words *software package* in cell B9.

8. Enter the label "Fall is a beautiful time of year" in cell A11. Do not include the quotes.

9. Using the label in cell A11, change all of the letters to lowercase and place the results in cell A12.

10. Using the label in cell A11, change all of the letters to uppercase and place the results in cell A13.

11. Using the label in cell A11, capitalize the first letter in each word and make all other letters lowercase and place the results in cell A14.

Print the worksheet with the answers to problems 1 through 11.

Close the workbook document. Do not save any changes.

EXERCISE 10 -- Using the Text Functions

INSTRUCTIONS: First, make sure you have a blank workbook document on your screen.

1.   Enter the number 592.783 in cell A1. Using the value in cell A1, change the value into a text string with three decimal places and place the results in cell B1.

2.   Enter the label "Excel   is   fun   to   use" in cell A3. Do not include the quotes. Remove the leading spaces and extra spaces between the words. Place the results in cell A4.

3.   Enter 123.456 as a label in cell A6. Change the label in cell A6 to a number and place the results in cell B6.

Print the worksheet after completing problems 1 through 5.

Close the workbook document. Do not save any changes.

CHAPTER SIXTEEN

INTRODUCTION TO MACROS

OBJECTIVES

In this chapter, you will learn to:
- Create a macro on a separate workbook
- Execute a macro
- Edit a macro
- Add instructions to an existing macro
- Use the Personal Macro Workbook to store a macro
- Remove a macro from the Personal Macro Workbook
- Place a macro in the same workbook that uses the macro
- Use a shortcut key to execute a macro

■ CHAPTER OVERVIEW

A **macro** is a set of instructions used to automatically execute a series of Excel commands. Macros are especially useful when performing detailed, repetitive routines. You can create macros that consolidate worksheets, perform special edit routines, or print reports and charts.

The Visual Basic programming system is used to create macros in Excel 5.0. Macros created using Visual Basic are very different from macros prepared in earlier versions of Excel. Microsoft Corporation has announced that Visual Basic will be the programming language for completing macros for major application packages such as Excel.

The simplest way to create a macro in Excel is to record your activities. For example, you might record the steps for opening some files, consolidating information between the files, and printing the results. By placing the Excel commands in a macro, you can automate the process rather than repeat the commands each time the operations are completed.

You can save macros in a separate workbook, in the Personal Macro Workbook, or in the same workbook in which it will be used.

■ CREATING AND EXECUTING A MACRO

In Chapter 12, you consolidated salary information for three divisions of the ABC Company into a summary worksheet. You then linked the total salary data in the DIVISION workbook file to the Salaries row in the BUDGET workbook file.

In this section, you will create a macro to complete the consolidation and print the results. Initially, you will create a macro to link the total salary data in the DIVISION workbook file to the Salaries row in the BUDGET workbook file. After executing the macro, you will then add the steps for printing the results to your macro.

Creating a Macro

In this example, you will create a macro and place it in a separate workbook.

To initiate the process for creating a macro:

Open	a new workbook document
Choose	Tools
Choose	Record Macro
Choose	Record New Macro

The Record New Macro dialog box appears on your screen.

To specify a name and describe the macro:

Type	CONSOLIDATE in the Macro Name text box
Click	at the end of the entry in the Description text box
Enter	. This macro links the total salary data in the DIVISION workbook to the Salaries row in the BUDGET workbook.

Your screen should look like Figure 16-1.

Figure 16-1

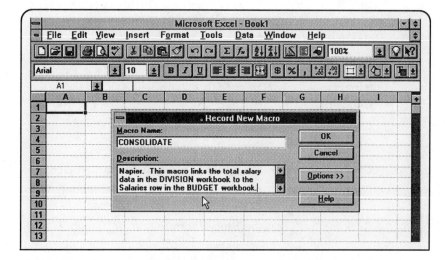

Click	the Options command button
Click	the This Workbook option button in the Store in box
Click	the OK command button

You are now in Record mode. Notice that the word Recording appears in the status bar. A button for stopping the record process appears on the screen. When you are finished recording the Excel commands, click the Stop Macro button.

Complete the following Excel commands:

Choose	File
Choose	Open
Click	on the DIViSION workbook file name
Click	the OK command button
Choose	File
Choose	Open
Click	on the BUDGET workbook file name
Click	the OK command button
Select	cells B10:E10 in the Worksheet Model of the BUDGET workbook document
Press	Delete
Choose	Window
Choose	DIVISION.XLS

Select	cells B9:E9 in the Summary worksheet of the DIVISION workbook document
Choose	Edit
Choose	Copy
Choose	Window
Choose	BUDGET.XLS
Choose	Edit
Choose	Paste Special
Click	the Paste Link command button
Click	on cell A1 in the Worksheet Model of the BUDGET workbook document
Click	the Stop Macro button

The macro recording process has been completed. It is assumed that the macro is placed on the BookX workbook document where X is the current new book number.

Your screen should look like Figure 16-2.

Figure 16-2

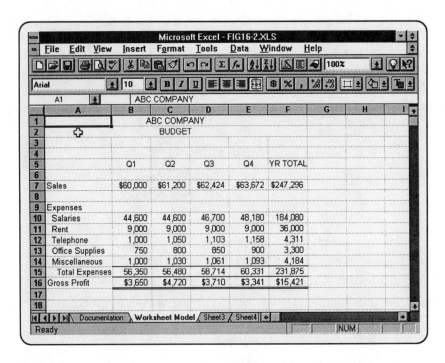

Notice that the original values for Salaries in the BUDGET workbook have been changed to the total salaries values in the DIVISION workbook.

Close the BUDGET and DIVISION workbook documents. Do not save any changes.

To view the macro:

Click   on the Module1 tab name to the right of the
                   Sheet16 tab name

Your screen should look like Figure 16-3.

Figure 16-3

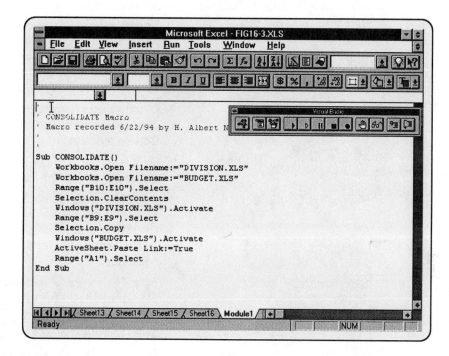

Notice that the macro and the Visual Basic toolbar appear on your screen. Save the macro to a file using the name CONSOL.

The first six lines of the macro contain the macro name and the description of the macro that you entered in the Record New Macro dialog box.

The information below describes the various lines in the macro:

Sub CONSOLIDATE()	Initial line of the macro. Sub marks the beginning of a macro.
Workbooks.Open Filename:="DIVISION.XLS"	Directs Excel to open the DIVISION workbook file.
Workbooks.Open Filename:="BUDGET.XLS"	Directs Excel to open the BUDGET workbook file.
Range("B10:E10").Select	Specifies selection of the range of cells B10:E10 on the current worksheet. Since BUDGET is the active window, cells B10:E10 on the Worksheet Model worksheet are selected.
Selection.ClearContents	Directs Excel to execute the Clear command on the Edit menu and select the Contents option.
Windows("DIVISION.XLS").Activate	Directs Excel to make the DIVISION workbook document the active window.
Range("B9:E9").Select	Specifies selection of the range of cells B9:E9 on the current worksheet. Since DIVISION is the active window, cells B9:E9 on the Worksheet Model worksheet are selected.
Selection.Copy	Specifies for Excel to copy the contents of the selection, B9:E9 to the clipboard.
Windows("BUDGET.XLS").Activate	Directs Excel to make the BUDGET workbook document the active window.
ActiveSheet.Paste Link:=True	Directs Excel to execute the Paste Special command on the Edit menu with the Paste Link option on the active worksheet using the current selection. In this case the links from the DIVISION workbook file are placed in cells B10:E10 of the Worksheet Model in the BUDGET workbook document.
Range("A1").Select	Specifies for Excel to make cell A1 the active cell.
End Sub	Marks the end of a macro.

Close the CONSOL workbook document.

Macros can be assigned to the Tools menu, a button on a worksheet, or as a button on a toolbar. For additional information, see the Microsoft Excel Visual Basic User's Guide.

Executing a Macro

A macro is executed by using the Macro command on the Tools menu. Suppose you want to execute the CONSOLIDATE macro you just completed.

Open	the CONSOL workbook file
Choose	Tools
Choose	Macro

The Macro dialog box appears.

| **Click** | on the CONSOLIDATE macro name in the Macro Name/Reference list box |
| **Click** | the Run command button |

The CONSOLIDATE macro is executed. Your screen should look like Figure 16-4.

Figure 16-4

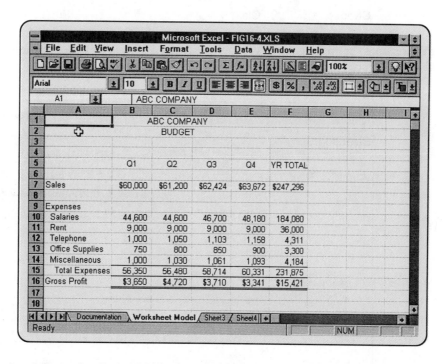

The total salary information in the DIVISION workbook document has been linked to the Salaries row in the BUDGET workbook document.

Close the BUDGET, DIVISION, and CONSOL workbook documents. Do not save any changes.

■ EDITING A MACRO

When you use the recording process to create a macro, Excel copies every task you accomplish. Therefore, mistakes as well as extra, unnecessary activities may be included in the macro.

In the example you completed in the last section, you had the macro open the DIVISION and BUDGET workbook files. Suppose that the files are always open prior to needing to use the macro for linking the cells in the DIVISION workbook to the cells in the BUDGET workbook.

Rather than create another macro, you can edit the existing macro. You need to remove the lines in the macro that open the BUDGET and DIVISION files.

To edit the CONSOLIDATE macro:

Open	the CONSOL workbook file
Select	the first two lines containing the steps for opening the DIVISION and BUDGET workbook files
Choose	Edit
Choose	Clear

The instructions for opening the DIVISION and BUDGET workbook files are no longer displayed. Your screen should look like Figure 16-5.

Figure 16-5

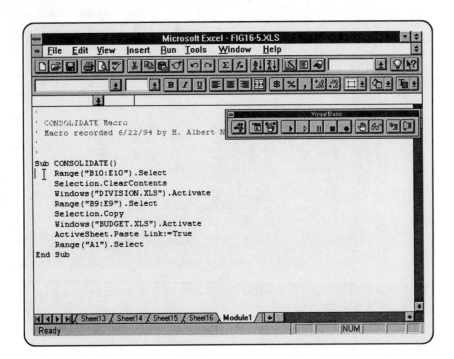

To illustrate the use of the new macro:

Open	the DIVISION workbook file
Open	the BUDGET workbook file

These two files and the file containing the modified macro are now open.

To execute the macro:

Choose	Tools
Choose	Macro
Click	the CONSOLIDATE macro name in the Macro Name/Reference list box
Click	the Run command button

The macro executes and the total salary cells in the DIVISION workbook are linked to the Salaries row in the BUDGET workbook. Your screen should look like Figure 16-6.

Figure 16-6

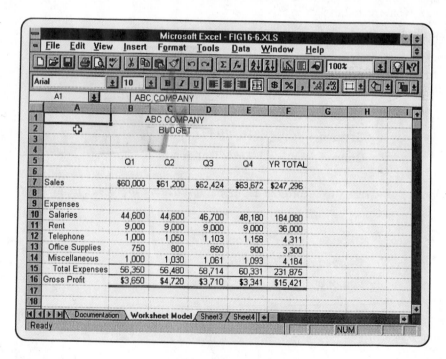

Close the BUDGET, DIVISION, and CONSOL workbook documents. Do not save any changes.

■ RECORDING ADDITIONAL STEPS INTO AN EXISTING MACRO

You can place additional steps or code into an existing macro. You can manually type the code into the macro or record the code using the Record Macro command on the Tools menu.

The basic steps are:

1. Move the insertion point to the location in the macro where you want to place the additional code.
2. Choose the Record Macro command from the Tools menu. Then choose Mark Position for Recording.
3. Switch to the worksheet from which you will record new activities.
4. Choose the Record Macro command from the Tools menu. Then choose Record at Mark.
5. Complete the activities you want to add to the macro.
6. Click the Stop Macro button. An alternative method is to choose the Record Macro command from the Tools menu. Then choose Stop Recording.

Suppose you want to include instructions for printing the BUDGET worksheet in the CONSOLIDATE macro you created earlier in this chapter.

To illustrate the process for including additional instructions in a macro:

Open	the CONSOL workbook file
Click	at the end of the last line in the macro (End Sub)
Choose	Tools
Choose	Record Macro
Choose	Mark Position for Recording

You are now ready to record the additional instructions to include in the macro:

Open	the BUDGET workbook file
Choose	Tools
Choose	Record Macro
Choose	Record at Mark

At this point, you are in Record mode. Notice that the word Recording appears in the status bar and the Stop Macro button appears again.

To record the instructions for printing the current worksheet in the BUDGET workbook:

Choose	File
Choose	Print
Click	the OK command button
Click	the Stop Macro button

The Worksheet Model in the BUDGET workbook is printed. Close the BUDGET workbook. Do not save any changes.

The CONSOLIDATE macro should appear. Your screen should look like Figure 16-7.

Figure 16-7

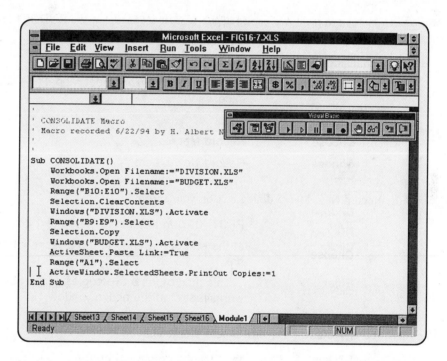

Notice the additional instruction that appears at the end of the macro for printing the active worksheet.

To execute the modified macro:

Choose	Tools
Choose	Macro
Click	the CONSOLIDATE macro name in the Macro Name/Reference list box
Click	the Run command button

The macro executes. After the appropriate linking of cells occurs between the DIVISION and BUDGET workbooks, the results shown in the Worksheet Model of the BUDGET workbook are printed.

Close the BUDGET, DIVISION, and CONSOL workbook documents. Do not save any changes.

■ SAVING A MACRO IN THE PERSONAL MACRO WORKBOOK

In some situations, you may want access to a macro anytime you are using a workbook. For example, you may want to have a macro that prints two copies of a worksheet in a workbook rather than one copy. You can place a macro that you always want to have available in the Personal Macro Workbook. The Personal Macro Workbook does not exist until you create a macro and place it in the Personal Macro Workbook.

You may save as many macros as you wish in the Personal Macro Workbook. Each macro is saved in a separate module.

Suppose you want to print two copies of the Worksheet Model in the BUDGET workbook. To create the macro:

Open	the BUDGET workbook file
Click	on cell A1 of the Worksheet Model (if necessary)
Choose	Tools
Choose	Record Macro
Choose	Record New Macro

With the Record New Macro dialog box on your screen:

Type	PRINTMAC in the Macro Name text box
Click	at the end of the entry in the Description text box
Enter	. This macro prints two copies of the selected worksheet(s) in the active window.

To place the macro in the Personal Macro Workbook:

Click	the Options command button
Click	the Personal Macro Workbook option button in the Store in box
Click	the OK command button

You are now ready to record the macro. To include the steps for printing a worksheet in the macro:

Choose	File
Choose	Print
Double-click	the Copies text box
Type	2
Click	the OK command button

When you finish the steps for printing the worksheet:

Click	the Stop Macro button

To view the Personal Macro Workbook:

Choose	Window
Choose	Unhide

The Unhide dialog box appears. Notice that PERSONAL.XLS appears in the Unhide Workbook list box. This is the Personal Macro Workbook.

To view the PERSONAL.XLS workbook:

Select	PERSONAL.XLS in the Unhide Workbook list box
Click	the OK command button

The PERSONAL workbook appears with the macro you created. Your screen should look like Figure 16-8.

Figure 16-8

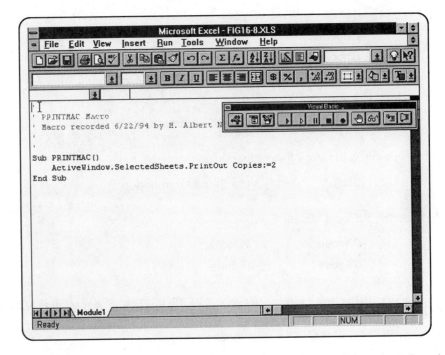

The single command in the PRINTMAC macro indicates that two copies of the selected worksheet in the active window are to be printed.

To hide the PERSONAL workbook document and save the macro:

> **Choose**   Window
>
> **Choose**   Hide

Close the BUDGET workbook document. Do not save any changes.

To illustrate the use of the PRINTMAC macro you saved in the PERSONAL workbook to print two copies of the BUDGET Worksheet Model:

> **Open**   the BUDGET workbook file
>
> **Choose**   Tools
>
> **Choose**   Macro

The Macro dialog box appears. Notice that the PERSONAL workbook name is listed with the macro name PRINTMAC in the Macro Name/Reference list box. If other macros are stored in the PERSONAL workbook, the names of the macros will also appear.

To run the macro:

Select	PERSONAL.XLS!PRINTMAC in the Macro Name/Reference list box
Click	the Run command button

Two copies of the BUDGET Worksheet Model are printed.

Close the BUDGET workbook document. Do not save any changes.

User Tip

When you exit Excel and have made changes to the Personal Macro Workbook, you will be asked whether or not to save the changes. Respond to the message dialog box as appropriate for the situation. In most situations, you will want to save the changes you have made.

■ REMOVING A MACRO FROM THE PERSONAL MACRO WORKBOOK

Sometimes you may need to remove a macro from the Personal Macro Workbook. Suppose you need to delete the PRINTMAC you created earlier in this chapter.

To view the PRINTMAC macro:

Make	sure you have a workbook document open
Choose	Window
Choose	Unhide
Select	PERSONAL workbook in the Unhide Workbook list box
Click	the OK command button

To delete the macro:

Select	the text in the macro
Choose	Edit
Choose	Clear

The macro is deleted from the Personal Macro Workbook.

To hide the Personal Macro Workbook:

Choose	Window
Choose	Hide

You can save a macro again to the Personal Macro Workbook at any time.

Close the workbook document.

■ CREATING A MACRO AND PLACING IT IN THE SAME WORKBOOK THAT USES THE MACRO

In some situations, you may only want to use a macro with a specific workbook. In this case, you can save the macro in a module within the workbook.

In Chapter 13, you sorted the list of employees in the ABCSAL workbook in alphabetical order within each division. Suppose you need to create a macro to sort the data in the desired order and save it in the ABCSAL workbook.

In this exercise, you will need to select the rows in the list to sort. It is a good idea to define a range name for the cells in the list before you create the macro. By using a range name, if you make changes in the size of the list by adding or deleting rows, the range name is updated. Then when you sort in a macro using the range name, the proper rows are included in the sort procedure.

To define a range name for ABCSAL:

Open	the ABCSAL workbook file
Select	cells A5:I13
Choose	Insert
Choose	Name
Choose	Define
Type	SORT_RANGE in the Names in Workbook text box
Click	the OK command button

Notice that the range name SORT_RANGE appears in the Name box.

Click	on cell A1
Save	the ABCSAL workbook to a file using the name ABCSORT

To create the macro:

Choose	Tools
Choose	Record Macro
Choose	Record New Macro
Enter	SORTMAC in the Macro Name text box
Click	at the end of the entry in the Description text box

Type	. This macro sorts the data in the ABCSORT workbook in alphabetical order within each division.
Click	the Options command button
Click	the This Workbook option in the Store in box
Click	the OK command button

You are now in Record mode. When you have finished recording the Excel commands, click the Stop Macro button.

Complete the following commands:

Click	the down arrow on the Name box
Select	SORT_RANGE
Choose	Data
Choose	Sort
Click	the down arrow on the Sort By box
Select	DIV
Click	the down arrow on the first Then By box
Select	LAST NAME
Click	the down arrow on the second Then By box
Select	FIRST NAME
Click	the OK command button
Click	on cell A1
Click	the Stop Macro button

The macro appears in Module1 to the right of Sheet16. After clicking on Module1, your screen should look like Figure 16-9.

Figure 16-9

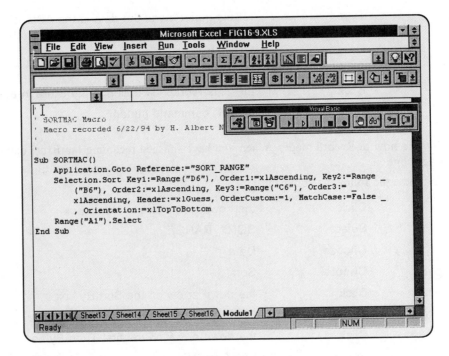

Save the ABCSORT workbook. Close the workbook document.

The Visual Basic instructions on your screen will sort the data in the ABCSORT workbook whenever you change the data.

■ USING A SHORTCUT KEY TO EXECUTE A MACRO

Excel allows you to assign a macro to a shortcut key. You can then use a combination of keys to execute the macro rather than select the macro name to use the macro.

The shortcut key can be a lowercase or uppercase letter. If you use a lowercase letter, you execute the macro by pressing down the CTRL key and then the letter. If the macro is assigned to a capital letter, the CTRL plus the SHIFT keys must be pressed down and then you press the letter.

As noted earlier, Excel has accelerator keys that are used to execute commands. For example, you can press the CTRL key and the letter C to execute the Copy command on the Edit menu. You should not assign a macro to the lowercase letter c. If you want to assign a macro to the letter c, make sure you use an uppercase C. The best rule to follow is to always assign a macro to a shortcut key that is a capital letter.

Suppose you want to assign the CONSOLIDATE macro to the uppercase letter K.

Open	the CONSOL workbook file
Choose	Tools
Choose	Macro
Select	the CONSOLIDATE macro name in the Macro Name/Reference list box
Click	the Options command button

The Macro Options dialog box appears. To assign the macro to a shortcut key:

Click	the Shortcut Key check box until an X appears
Click	the Shortcut Key text box
Type	an uppercase K
Click	the OK command button
Click	the Close command button

To execute the macro using the shortcut key method:

Press	Ctrl + Shift + K

The macro executes.

Close the BUDGET, DIVISION, and CONSOL workbook documents. Do not save any changes.

SUMMARY

Excel provides a method for creating a macro that lets you automatically repeat various commands available in the software. This capability allows you to save time when you complete repetitive processes. Excel uses the Visual Basic programming language to create macros. You can save a macro in a separate workbook, in the Personal Macro Workbook, or in the same workbook on which the macro will be used.

KEY CONCEPTS

Editing a macro
Location of a macro
Macro
Module
Personal Macro Workbook

Recording additional steps in macro
Stop Macro button
Tools Record Macro
Visual Basic
Visual Basic toolbar

EXERCISE 1

INSTRUCTIONS: Circle T if the statement is true and F if the statement is false.

T   F   1. You must take the name for a macro from a label already existing on a worksheet.

T   F   2. A macro is used to automate a repetitive procedure.

T   F   3. You can save a macro only on a separate workbook.

T   F   4. To execute the macro named ZEBRA, you must hold down the CTRL key and type the letter Z.

T   F   5. You can record a macro automatically as you use a workbook.

T   F   6. The Personal Macro Workbook lets you use a specific macro at anytime.

T   F   7. You can execute a macro by pressing the CTRL key and a specified shortcut key at the same time.

EXERCISE 2 -- Creating a Macro

INSTRUCTIONS: Open the DIVSALES workbook file that you created in Chapter 11. The file contains data on sales of mowers and edgers for the four divisions in ABC Company.

Write a macro that:

Inserts a new worksheet at the beginning of the workbook.

Creates a summary worksheet on the inserted worksheet that contains the total sales for each quarter of each division.

Computes the total annual sales for each division and the annual sales for the company.

Create a name and description for the macro of your own choice.

The macro should be placed in a module on a separate worksheet in the DIVSALES workbook.

Print the summary worksheet, the sales worksheets, and the worksheet on which the macro appears.

Save the DIVSALES workbook, including the macro worksheet, to a file using the name ABCMAC.

Close the ABCMAC workbook document.

EXERCISE 3 -- Creating a Print Macro

INSTRUCTIONS: Open the ABCMAC workbook file that you created in the previous exercise.

Create a macro that prints the summary worksheet and the division sales worksheets.

Create a name and description for the macro of your own choice.

Place the print macro in the Personal Macro Workbook.

Print the summary worksheet and the division sales worksheets using the macro.

Print the macro.

Save the ABCMAC workbook document to a file using the name ABCMACPR.

Close the ABCMACPR workbook document.

EXERCISE 4 -- Using a Macro to Sort Data

INSTRUCTIONS: Open the PERSON workbook file you created as an exercise in Chapter 13.

Write a macro that sorts the database in order by state, last name, and first name.

Create a name and description for the macro of your own choice.

Place the macro in a separate workbook. Assign the macro to a shortcut key. Use the shortcut key to execute the macro that sorts the database.

Create a macro that prints the sorted database. Place the macro in a separate workbook.

Print the sorted database and the worksheets containing the macros for sorting and printing the database.

Close the PERSON workbook document. Do not save any changes.

EXERCISE 5 -- Using Macros to Create and Print a Chart

INSTRUCTIONS: Open the PRACTICE workbook file you created as an exercise in Chapter 4.

Write a macro to create a column chart that includes the data for the Revenue, Profit Before Tax, and Profit After Tax variable for five years. Include appropriate chart title and legend information.

Create a macro that prints the column chart.

Create a name and description for the macro of your own choice.

Place the macros for creating and printing the chart in separate modules within the PRACTICE workbook.

Print the worksheets that contain the macros.

Close the PRACTICE workbook document. Do not save any changes.

INDEX

WORKSHEET FUNCTIONS
